The Reminiscences of
Captain Francis R. Kaine
U.S. Naval Reserve (Retired)

Interviewed by
Commander Etta-Belle Kitchen,
U.S. Navy (Retired)

U.S. Naval Institute
Annapolis, Maryland
Copyright ©1991

Preface

Few of the Naval Institute's oral history volumes are as specialized as this one. Captain Frank Kaine essentially made a career of service in the Navy's underwater demolition teams (UDTs) and training its sea-air-land (SEAL) teams. That it was a successful career is demonstrated by the fact that he was selected for the rank of captain as a Naval Reserve officer on active duty, a rare achievement.

As was the case for many young men of his generation, Kaine's career plans were dislocated by a call to wartime service. For Kaine it happened not once, but twice. He ended his college education in 1942 by enlisting in the Navy and soon was trained and commissioned as a Naval Reserve officer through the V-7 program. He was captivated by the sales pitch of Lieutenant Draper Kauffman and moved into the Navy's bomb disposal program.

Soon Kauffman was looking for men to form naval combat demolition units to eliminate beach obstacles expected to be encountered during amphibious landings in France. Kaine did well in his training and thus was in at the beginning of the special organization that came to be known as UDTs, and still later evolved into the SEALs. He never made it to France, however. His team was sent to the Seventh Amphibious Force in the Pacific and wound up participating in more than a dozen operations. Kaine's memoir provides fascinating recollections of work that involved a thorough knowledge of both swimming and explosives.

Once World War II ended, Kaine returned to civilian life and established himself. When the Korean War broke out, he was recalled to active duty and soon found himself back in UDT work that lasted throughout almost all of the 1950s. Since he was on the East Coast, he was not directly involved in the Korean War, but he had a lot to do with the growth of the UDT community and its achievement of permanent status in the Navy. That included public relations work, training with many other Navy elements, and the development of new equipment and techniques for diving and the use of explosives.

In the late 1950s, Kaine interrupted his UDT work for a "normal" tour of duty on the staff of the lively Rear Admiral Dan Gallery, Commandant of the Tenth Naval District in Puerto Rico, then returned to his work in the amphibious warfare/special operations world. He was involved in the

1960s in training hundreds of people for action in the Vietnam War--in counterinsurgency roles and for the clandestine special warfare missions of the newly established SEALs. Throughout the memoir, Captain Kaine displays a becoming sense of modesty--putting the emphasis on getting the job done rather than seeking credit.

Commander Etta-Belle Kitchen, USN (Ret.), did the interviews for this oral history. Ms. Linda O'Doughda of the Naval Institute oral history staff prepared the detailed index for the volume. I did some editing of the text and provided the footnotes. Captain Kaine also did some editing; he has reviewed and approved the final version. A copy of the original, unedited version of the transcript is on file at the Naval Institute.

                              Paul Stillwell
                              Director of Oral History
                              U.S. Naval Institute
                              August 1990

CAPTAIN FRANCIS RILEY KAINE, U.S. NAVAL RESERVE (RETIRED)

Personal Data

Born:	13 February 1920, Brattleboro, Vermont
Parents:	Dr. W. J. Kaine and Mary E. Murphy Kaine
Married:	22 May 1943 to Audrey Dyer
Children:	M. Christopher, born 4 June 1944
	Candace Bridget, born 6 June 1946, died 21 November 1946
	Carey Jeanne, born 4 January 1948
	Candace Therese, born 4 October 1950
	Claudia Dyer, born 18 November 1951
	Carole Melissa, born 30 June 1953
Education:	Loyola College, Montreal Canada, 1937-41, bachelor of arts
	University of Rochester, Rochester, New York, September 1941-March 1942, no degree

Dates of Rank

Ensign:	21 October 1942
Lieutenant (junior grade):	1 January 1944
Lieutenant:	1 May 1945
Lieutenant Commander:	1 January 1952
Commander:	1 July 1956
Captain:	1 August 1966

Decorations and Medals

Legion of Merit
Bronze Star Medal with Combat "V"
Naval Reserve Medal
Armed Forces Reserve Medal
Presidential Unit Citation (Underwater Demolition Team)
Navy Unit Citation
Pacific Ribbon with seven stars
World War II Victory Medal
Philippine Liberation with two stars
National Defense Service Ribbon
Philippine Commendation
Vietnam Service Medal
Vietnam Campaign Medal

Chronological Transcript of Service

March 1942:	Entered service
July 1942:	Active duty, V-7 program
October 1942:	Commissioned
April 1943-July 1943:	Bomb disposal school, Washington, D.C.
July 1943-November 1943:	Underwater demolition training, Fort Pierce, FL
November 1943-September 1945:	Naval Combat Demolition Unit Two
September 1945-January 1951:	Inactive duty
January 1951-October 1951:	Naval Beach Group Two, communications
October 1951-May 1952:	Underwater Demolition Team 4, executive officer
May 1952-June 1956:	Underwater Demolition Team 21, commanding officer
July 1956-June 1958:	Underwater Demolition Unit Two, commanding officer
September 1958-February 1962:	Headquarters, 10th Naval District, assistant chief of staff for personnel
March 1962-December 1964:	Beach Master Unit Two, commanding officer
December 1964-November 1966:	Naval Amphibious School, Little Creek, VA, special operations department head
November 1966-April 1970:	Commander Naval Special War Group Pacific, Coronado, CA
Retired:	1 May 1970

Civilian Employment

January 1946-December 1949:
   Sales Manager, C. E. Bradley Laboratories, Brattleboro, Vermont
January 1950-November 1950:
   Service and Sales Manager, Haus Buick Company, Brattleboro, Vermont
June 1970-July 1971:
   Marketing/Operations, Atlantic Research Corporation, Costa Mesa, California
July 1971-August 1974:
   Vice President for Operations, OMC Corporation, San Diego, California
January 1975-December 1979:
   Executive Director, Chamber of Commerce, Coronado, California
December 1980-May 1986:
   Manager, Bank of Coronado, Coronado, California

Authorization

The U.S. Naval Institute is hereby authorized to make available to libraries and other repositories of its choosing the transcripts of two oral history interviews concerning the life and career of Captain Francis R. Kaine. The two interviews were recorded on 7 and 8 November 1981 in collaboration with Commander Etta-Belle Kitchen, USN (Retired) for the U.S. Naval Institute.

Permission must be obtained from the undersigned, during his lifetime, in order to cite or quote from the transcripts of the interviews in any published work. The tape recordings of the interviews are and will remain the sole property of the U.S. Naval Institute. The copyright in both the oral and transcribed versions of the interviews shall also be the sole property of the U.S. Naval Institute.

Signed and sealed this 26th day of DEC. 1989

Captain Francis R. Kaine
U.S. Naval Reserve (Retired)

F. R. Kaine #1 - 1

Interview Number 1 with Captain Francis R. Kaine,
U.S. Naval Reserve (Retired)

Place: Captain Kaine's home, Coronado, California

Date: Saturday, 7 November 1981

Interviewer: Commander Etta-Belle Kitchen,
U.S. Navy (Retired)

Q: Good morning, Captain. It is very nice of you to give the Navy this time and this information. I'd like to begin at the beginning, and I know the year of your birth. But I think that for the record it should be on the tape as to where and when you were born and something of your parents, your youth, and start in that fashion.

Captain Kaine: I was born in 1920 on the 13th of February, which happened to be a Friday. My mother was Canadian; her maiden name was Murphy. My father was born and raised in Vermont. He was a medical doctor, primarily a surgeon and a gynecologist/obstetrician. We lived in a town called Brattleboro, Vermont. I had two brothers, one older and one younger. I was the middle man in a total family of five. We spent, I would say in retrospect, a very normal childhood for that time and that area. We were all very involved in athletics in school.

I got my secondary education in Montreal at Loyola College, which is where I met my wife who, although an American, was living at the time in Canada. Her father was a commercial artist who tripped back and forth between New

York and Montreal. That's how I happened to meet her. She was in Montreal at the time.

After I graduated from college, I was thinking of studying medicine, so I went to the University of Rochester in Rochester, New York, and did some graduate work. I got out of school in Montreal in 1941 and went to Rochester in September of 1941. Of course, Pearl Harbor happened in December of that year, and I went back to school in Rochester after December. However, I did quit in February, then signed up in the Navy in March 1942.*

Q: Do you remember Pearl Harbor?

Captain Kaine: I remember Pearl Harbor, yes. As a matter of fact, I was sitting in my room at school, and my room happened to be under the stadium. It was a room within the football stadium. There were a couple of us there. We were just glued to the radio that day. After I volunteered into the Navy, I went to Boston to sign up. Living in Brattleboro, there were no Navy representatives in the Vermont area at the time, and I was not called until, I think, July. I went to midshipman school in New York at Columbia University and was graduated from midshipman school in October 1942.**

---
*Kaine enlisted on 9 March 1942.
**Kaine was commissioned as an ensign on 21 October 1942 and began active duty on 26 October.

F. R. Kaine #1 - 3

Q: Before we go on to that, I have the impression that your graduate study was in zoology.

Captain Kaine: Zoology, that's right. I studied zoology and graduate English, literature, and stuff. I was planning to go to medical school, and I needed the zoology and also organic chemistry for medical school. Maybe the war was a relief from the zoology and organic chemistry; I don't know.

Q: When you say you signed up, what do you mean by that, exactly?

Captain Kaine: I signed up as an officer candidate in the V-7 program.* You were given an indefinite period of time before you'd be called, and I was called in time to finish in the Columbia class of October 1942. At that time at Columbia, I was in what they called John Jay Hall, which is a resident dormitory. They had two other dormitories running concurrently, Johnson and Furnald halls, and they also had the Prairie State, which was an old ship which

---

*V-7 was a World War II naval reserve officer training program through which volunteers with enough education--usually a bachelor's degree--were trained as line officers for surface ships.

they used as a barracks.* So they really had about three or four classes going simultaneously, with different graduating dates. They were all graduating about a month apart, and those were in the glory days of the "90-day wonders." They were coming out of Notre Dame and Northwestern universities also. They both had midshipman programs.

While we were in midshipman school, they had various military people coming to visit classes, recruiting for their specialty programs, and, of course, we knew very little about the Navy. We had only been in there "all day," I guess, and it was kind of intriguing the way these "pitchmen" would come along and try to sell their programs. I remember one of them was Bulkeley, trying to sell the PT program.** They also had a flight team that came in selling aviation, and--if I'm not mistaken--the aviation group would only take the top part of the graduates.

Then Lieutenant Kauffman had a recruiting pitch that he gave to all the midshipmen.*** He was quite intriguing and a very good salesman. One thing I was always impressed

---

*The former battleship Illinois (BB-7) was renamed the USS Prairie State (IX-15) on 23 January 1941. A house-like wooden structure was built over the hull to serve as a barracks for the men undergoing officer training.
**Lieutenant Commander John D. Bulkeley, USN, was awarded the Medal of Honor for his PT boat exploits during the early part of World War II. He evacuated General Douglas MacArthur in his boat from the Philippines to Australia.
***Lieutenant Draper L. Kauffman, USNR, was essentially the founder of the underwater demolition teams (UDT). He eventually became a rear admiral. His two-volume oral history is in the Naval Institute collection.

with--he personally interviewed everybody that he took into his program. He sat down and talked to them. Personally, I think he told them a bunch of lies, because he would inveigle you into this program by telling you how you could render bombs safe from absolutely safe distances by use of cords and lines and be well away from any danger. And we fell for it, because he had been there and was really impressive.

Q: What was his program called?

Captain Kaine: Bomb disposal. He was heading up a new program, only in existence probably at that time maybe a year at the most. He had been in mine and bomb disposal in England and came back to the States to set this bomb disposal program up.

Q: Had it had time to function up to the time he saw you?

Captain Kaine: As a matter of fact, he and another young gent named Adie DeWindt had worked on unexploded bombs in Pearl Harbor.*

Q: After December the seventh?

---
*Ensign Adrian L. DeWindt, USNR.

Captain Kaine: Yes, and as a matter of fact, Kauffman was awarded the Navy Cross for the work he did at Pearl Harbor.

Q: Did he actually go under and work on them himself?

Captain Kaine: Oh, yes. As a matter of fact, he was the only guy at a little earlier point in time in the United States who knew anything about it. He started by selecting a few people at a time and training them and built up the whole program from his personal knowledge and research.

Q: Was he a lieutenant when he interviewed you?

Captain Kaine: Yes, he was a lieutenant when I was interviewed. By the time I got down to his school, I think he had made lieutenant commander. In that era, a lieutenant or a lieutenant commander was like a god to us, because, boy, you came in from civilian life and got leaped on by chiefs and your own ensigns and jaygees at midshipman school.* We learned immediate and wholesome respect for rank. We kind of had a godlike worship for Kauffman, because after the blitz in England, he even rated campaign ribbons. At that time, of course, none of us had any experience at all, while he had been decorated by Great Britain and, I believe, was wearing a Navy Cross for work

---

*Jaygees--lieutenants (junior grade).

F. R. Kaine #1 - 7

he had done in Pearl Harbor, so we were quite impressed.

He had a great gift for choosing people and choosing people who were copacetic--that worked together but also people who would work on their own at the same time and could keep the program going while he was away. One of his great gifts was that he was a great and marvelous politician, and within the Navy he had enough savvy due to his upbringing as a Navy junior. His father was an admiral, and he had an uncle who at this time was a captain.* So he knew his way around the Navy, and--much to the advantage of his new organization--he could do a little wheeling and dealing and knew whom to talk to, when to bring his father in, and all this sort of thing. He had a current knowledge that was very valuable at the time, I do think, because the rest of us were all reserve officers, and he had only one regular officer working for him, and that was Means Johnston.** Means at the time was a jaygee, and everybody else was an ensign or new jaygee in the reserve.

Q: You were a jaygee when you left?

Captain Kaine: I was an ensign then.

---
*His father was Rear Admiral James L. Kauffman, USN, who eventually became a vice admiral. His uncle was Captain Frederick B. Kauffman, USN, half brother of James L. Kauffman.
**Lieutenant (junior grade) Means Johnston, Jr., USN. Johnston eventually became a four-star admiral.

F. R. Kaine #1 - 8

Q: You were an ensign when you came out of Columbia?

Captain Kaine: Yes. I was an ensign in bomb disposal, as were most of us. It just seemed we were ensigns forever.

Q: Anyway, he was a good enough salesman to sell you, I guess.

Captain Kaine: Well, he sold me--lock, stock, and barrel. There were times when I hated the idea that we might never get away from the D.C. area. With a war going on, we didn't want to miss it just because we happened to volunteer and went to bomb disposal school.

Q: It would be interesting to know what it was like.

Captain Kaine: Bomb disposal school at the time was growing, and it was a very difficult program. You could not graduate unless you made 4.0 on the final exam. The final exam took most people about eight hours to do. It was written, and it was also practical work. Kauffman and his staff had worked out a great program. I think it was eight weeks in duration, and you studied the bombs and fuzes and mines of various countries. If you started with

F. R. Kaine #1 - 9

the German bombs, mines, and fuzes, you'd go through that program, study that, and take an exam at the end of it. Then you'd study the Japanese and study whatever they had on Russian mines and fuzes, and you'd study American bombs, mines, and fuzes.

We also had practical work along with the program. About halfway through, they had about a two-week period where you did practical work and took an exam in it in a place called Stump Neck, which was down in Maryland. Stump Neck was a naval reservation, which I believe was owned by the powder factory in Indian Head, Maryland. On this reservation they used to do practical work on bombs and fuzes.

We would practice methods of rendering bombs safe and do trepanning, which is a method of cutting into the cases of the bombs. They'd also do practical demolition work and what we called shafting, which was a method of digging down to a bomb. You'd trace the hole of entry of the bomb and figure out its trajectory in the earth, and then you would dig a shaft down to where you estimated that bomb was. So this was the practical work area for the bomb disposal school in Stump Neck, Maryland.

Q: How did you shore up the hole?

Captain Kaine: It was pretty neat, because you shored up

the hole without using any metallic items at all. You just used boards and what they called stringers and wedges. You'd put the boards down by the side, you'd put the stringers in between, and you'd wedge one stringer up against the other and wedge the boards in back so that they were tight, and you'd have beautiful straight-line shafts.

Q: What's a stringer?

Captain Kaine: The boards in between the sides, along the sides. When you're digging a hole, if these are your walls, you'd have a board running across here and across here, and you'd butt these two together and wedge them at the corners.

Q: Would you use a hammer or a sledge hammer?

Captain Kaine: You used shovels, and we used mallets at that time.

Q: When you said no metal, I was wondering what you pounded with.

Captain Kaine: We used these big, heavy fiber mallets to pound the wedges in. These methods were all taught in classes as well, and these two weeks at Stump Neck were

F. R. Kaine #1 - 11

like a practical work exam. So at the end of . . .

Q: Wait a minute. You have me at the bottom of the hole. Then what did you do?

Captain Kaine: Then, depending on the type of bomb, there were very different procedures, but first you would have to identify it.

Q: Were they live?

Captain Kaine: No, but they would sometimes put caps in them so that if you did something wrong, they would go off. There would be a smack, nothing to hurt you.

Q: But scare you?

Captain Kaine: Oh, yes. It would scare the hell out of you. But depending on what you found down there, then you and your team determined your procedures and you would go through the procedures, and you'd be marked on whatever you did.

Q: This is somewhat off the subject, but English TV had a

whole series on bomb disposal.*

Captain Kaine: That's where Kauffman got his training, in England. In fact, their lives made it possible for that type of series; that's exactly what he did. He was one of the original British bomb and mine disposal people.

Q: Did you happen to see it?

Captain Kaine: I saw several episodes.

Q: Were they accurate?

Captain Kaine: Oh, yes. I don't know if you're aware of this, but the way they found out how to dispose of bombs and mines originally was by sending people out there with a microphone, and they would talk into the microphone: "I'm doing this" or "I'm doing that." If the bomb went off, they'd know the next time not to do that.

Q: That man would be killed.

Captain Kaine: That man would be killed. And so the next time, they go and instead of turning a doohickey to the

---

*The British television series, which was also shown on American public television in the early 1980s, was titled "Danger, UXB." UXB stands for unexploded bomb.

F. R. Kaine #1 - 13

right, they'd turn a doohickey to the left. If it didn't go off, they'd take another step.

Q: How could they get men to do that?

Captain Kaine: You can get men to do anything in the war, really. But that is basically how they first started building their intelligence and their methods and procedures.

Q: Was that called defusing the bomb? Was that the proper word?

Captain Kaine: Right. Defusing was sometimes possible in the process of rendering a bomb or mine safe. There were many terms used. One of the terms was UXB; that used to be a big term. It means unexploded bomb; that's really all it is. But the knowledge in that field was all empirical, and Kauffman was a real nut on the subject of having to pass with a 100% mark on the final exam. As a result, each succeeding class had a more difficult exam, because we were learning more every day.

Q: Had he actually done this work in England?

Captain Kaine: Oh, yes. As a matter of fact, he got back

F. R. Kaine #1 - 14

into the American Navy because he was blown up by a mine in England. About the only scar from the injury that I remember was a knot or bump on his head when I first met him, and he finally either had it removed or it disappeared. But when he was injured in England, he was in the British Navy, of course.* When he came home on recuperative leave back to the States, through negotiation or whatever, he stayed in the States and went back into the American Navy and became their bomb disposal head. So he had all kinds of practical experience and really is the true father of bomb disposal.

There was another man that did similar work in mine disposal, Admiral O. D. Waters.** He was kind of a running mate of Kauffman's. I think originally bomb and mine disposal started out one and the same, but they split very early. O. D. Waters took the mine side of it, and Kauffman stayed with the bomb side.

Q: How many bombs did you know how to defuse by the time you got out of school?

Captain Kaine: Supposedly all that you could run into.

---
*Later in the interview, Captain Kaine explains why Kauffman began the war with the Royal Navy and later moved back to the U.S. Navy.
**Lieutenant Odale D. Waters, Jr., USN, established the U.S. Navy's Mine Disposal School in June 1941. Waters, who retired as a rear admiral, has been interviewed as part of the Naval Institute's oral history program.

F. R. Kaine #1 - 15

Quite truthfully, our biggest problem was American ordnance.

Q: They were so good or so bad or technical?

Captain Kaine: It seemed that the design was overly protective to the releasers of the bomb. As a result, they built so many precautions into the bombs that a lot of them failed to function.

Q: I remember that was talked about in submarine torpedoes.

Captain Kaine: Same thing, same type of thing. I believe what caused it was the first bombs that they used to drop from airplanes were maybe unsafe, and some were detonated prematurely. But then there was a big period of overcompensation so that many of our bombs and projectiles--especially projectiles, I believe--and torpedoes became horribly unreliable and ineffective. One example of that involved the French battleship Jean Bart, and they used it as coastal artillery in North Africa because they couldn't use it as a warship.* If I'm not

---

*Even though not complete, the Jean Bart was at Casablanca when Allied forces invaded North Africa on 8 November 1942. She fired both her 15-inch main battery and her antiaircraft guns before being put out of action by 16-inch projectiles from the USS Massachusetts (BB-59).

mistaken, two of our ships fired on it, and not all of the projectiles went off on impact. We later had a bomb disposal team go over there to examine them and find out what was wrong.

Q: Did you go?

Captain Kaine: No, I didn't. I think a guy named Tom Boardman went; he was later editor of the Cleveland Plain Dealer.* So we had a lot of problems with American ordnance. The Japanese ordnance was pretty simple, pretty direct, and pretty effective. Theirs usually went off. They didn't have many duds, because they were very simple fuzes, and they usually worked. The Germans were primarily electrical fuzing; they did a lot of electrical fuzing. They did a lot of double fuzing and triple fuzing, and theirs was pretty effective. But the least effective ordnance was the American, for a period, until we got everything organized.

Stump Neck was one area where we worked on some of these problems of disposal and tried to find out what methods were effective and why. They also had teams in bomb disposal that did experimentation with the Bureau of Ordnance at that time. They had civilian ordnance specialists that would come down there and work on these

---
*Ensign Thomas L. Boardman, USNR.

F. R. Kaine #1 - 17

problems. I remember one of the major problems of the time was to be able to neutralize the fuzing in German ordnance, and all these people working came up with one of the fine developments at the time for rendering electrical fuzes safe, and it was to freeze them. They developed a method of freezing the fuze with CO_2 to render it inoperable so they could remove the fuze.

Q: So it would be safe to work with?

Captain Kaine: So it would be safe to work with. It was a very interesting time, because we had come from the more primitive, if you will, ordnance to more sophisticated, with built-in safety, to the point where things didn't work! And then we were eliminating and starting again to make them work, and simultaneously we worked on the enemy's ordnance. Based on what we were learning on our own and learning about the enemy stuff, the ordnance field made quantum advances.

Q: How did they get this enemy ordnance?

Captain Kaine: Well, that was another thing. Kauffman set up a really good intelligence system in that he had everybody write reports on everything captured and get them back as soon as they had anything to report. He had people in the field and on ships. I think every ship, cruiser and above, had a billet for bomb disposal officer.

He had people in harbor control units; he had people in what they called at the time Acorn and Lion units, which were a composite organization like Seabees.* They dealt with harbor management and everything to do with a waterfront, and they'd go in and take over a port as it was taken. They'd come in and be the management people. He had people in all those places. And these guys, while there, were going in and ridding the beaches and the areas of all our ordnance and all enemy ordnance and writing this stuff up as fast as they could and sending it on to him or his staff.

A lot of the time, they even sent some of the live ordnance in. If some of these things were known at the time, my God, it would have been terrible. And Kauffman did raise hell about it, but the young, eager Americans were ingenious and voilà, live ordnance in D.C.

Q: What did they do, fly them back?

Captain Kaine: Oh, yes. Flown back on airplanes and carried on vessels and tell them they were boxes of shoes or anything. They had all kinds of stuff coming in, and

---

*Seabees (CBs) was a nickname for the Navy's construction battalions that specialized in building a wide variety of things in forward areas.

F. R. Kaine #1 - 19

this was going into--of all places--Washington, D.C. The school at this time was at American University. We'd receive this ordnance in back of American University, and as soon as we'd see it, we'd take it down to Stump Neck and get it out of the area. Most of the equipment shipped in was small: fuzes, detonators, etc.

Q: I should think. That is a story all its own, isn't it?

Captain Kaine: It was amazing, some of the things people would send in.

Q: Do you want to expand on that? I don't know of any other place where it might be told.

Captain Kaine: We'd get things like live fuzes. I won't point to any carriers, because I don't know of any specific people that carried them back, but they got back.

Q: By carriers do you mean people?

Captain Kaine: People. We'd have grenades, various types of grenades.

Q: Live?

Captain Kaine: Live grenades would come in, oh, nose fuzes, side fuzes, tail fuzes. We used to have a lot of whatever was new in the field shipped in rear bases, and shortly thereafter there would be a piece of it back in bomb disposal school. Nobody was ever very anxious to say how it got there, but it always arrived. And it was invaluable for intelligence and for developing procedures. The people--again I say, Admiral Kauffman's astuteness in picking people with ingenuity, inventiveness, and nerve. A lot of--not brashness, but the ability to know within reason what they could get away with, pretty much legally, and always done with proper motivation in an attempt to get answers.

Q: How did they get from American University to Stump Neck?

Captain Kaine: We used to go down in trucks. As a matter of fact, after I was in bomb disposal and graduated, I was picked to stay on the staff, and my job was to teach explosives and the shafting and disposal work. We had a big truck, a six-by-six truck, and it was covered.

Q: Was it marked?

Captain Kaine: No, just a U.S. Navy truck. We did have a

bomb buggy at American University, a big gray and red thing not used much, as I recall, but it had special heavy metal compartments on it and all kinds of tools, and we used to use it on occasion. One occasion I remember they sent a group down to Boise.* She came back and was all shot up and had a lot of live ordnance in it, and I believe they took it into Philadelphia. They sent the bomb buggy down to defuse the Boise, and they took a lot of ordnance out of her. They got a lot of intelligence out of that trip, because they pulled unexploded shells out of it.

Another one was the Marblehead. That came back all beat up, and they took a lot of ordnance out of that.** I heard about this from an acquaintance who was aboard the Marblehead and later discharged.

Q: That would have been enemy ordnance?

Captain Kaine: Enemy ordnance. But to get back to Stump Neck, we used to go there every second week. I used to take a class to Stump Neck, and we'd be there for approximately five days. We'd take a class of Marines. The Marines' classes were usually mixed, enlisted and

---
*The light cruiser Boise (CL-47) was damaged by Japanese gunfire in the Battle of Cape Esperance, near Guadalcanal, the night of 11-12 October 1942. She was subsequently repaired at the Philadelphia Navy Yard.
**The light cruiser Marblehead (CL-12) was hit by Japanese bombs off Java in the Dutch East Indies in January 1942. She finally reached the New York Navy Yard in May.

F. R. Kaine #1 - 22

officers. We'd take a class of maybe officers and then a class of maybe officers and enlisted, depending on how they came in, really.

Q: Were they also selected the same way as you had been?

Captain Kaine: Yes, everybody was handpicked by Kauffman.

Q: Enlisted, officers?

Captain Kaine: Everyone, the whole works.

Q: How many are we talking about?

Captain Kaine: Well, when I went, the classes were limited to 20 men. And I was in class 14, so there had been 280 up till October, say, of that year, 1942. We used to start a class every two weeks: Marine, Navy, Marine, Navy. And every once in a while we'd start an army class. We were glad to take an army class in, because the Army, at that time, was not into bomb disposal formally. They later started a big bomb disposal school at Aberdeen, Maryland.

We'd go down to Stump Neck and spend a week. We had a barracks where the people all stayed, and we'd work with ordnance and teach them various methods of extracting fuzes. We had some great tools that were designed at the time by previous students. One of them was called the Eigell wrench, designed by a young man that was in the bomb disposal program.* His name was obviously Eigell.

Q: It might be one of his claims to fame.

Captain Kaine: Some of these tools were unique. The only one I mention for an example is the Eigell, because it was unusual. Once you got your problem and located your bomb and dug your shaft down to it, you could rig up an A-frame over the hole and run ropes up over the pulleys and down to the bomb. You would attach this Eigell tool to the fuze-- the nose fuze, say--then tighten it on with a set screw. It was rigged with a spring, and really all it was was a ratchet, but it had two blocks that acted as a hammer, and they were counterpoised. When you pulled on the rope, you separated them, and the spring would bring them together, and it would hammer and have a loosening effect on the fuze, just like if you're pulling on a wrench. You could lead your ropes well back from the bomb and shaft hole and operate the wrench quite safely. If in an actual case the bomb exploded, no one got killed.

Q: That was an incredible discovery.

---
*The inventor was Boatswain's Mate Robert W. Eigell, USN, who had been involved with Lieutenant Kauffman in the ordnance disposal at Pearl Harbor. Eigell later became an officer and retired as a commander.

Captain Kaine: Oh, I think it was fantastic, yes. These guys really had some great, great ideas.

Q: This is when you were teaching?

Captain Kaine: Yes. Actually, this tool was developed before I got there. This guy Eigell had been in one of the first classes. And this tool is why I say Kauffman with his sales pitch in midshipman school used to say, "Oh, it's a perfectly safe occupation, because you get way back there and pull these lines." It would take a nose fuze out eventually. And when it fell, you could always tell from the way it worked how loose it was. You'd just go down and bring it up.

Q: How did you get down?

Captain Kaine: By ladder.

Q: How deep would the shafts be?

Captain Kaine: They could vary. We ran kind of fun experiments on how far we could shaft one down, just for no purpose. We got them down to 90 feet. Some were 20 or 30 feet.

Q: Oh, I would think the amount of wood and the safety of the shaft would be . . .

Captain Kaine: We ran this one down very far just for that purpose, to see about the safety, to see if it loosened up. We left it in the ground for a long time, and it was as safe as this house, because all we'd do is go around in a few days and tighten up the wedges and tighten the whole thing, and it was strong. What we did as an experiment, we had every class dig a little bit on this one particular shaft, so we kept it there for a number of classes, and it got down to somewhere around 90 feet. It was perfectly safe.

Q: I'd think the wood . . .

Captain Kaine: The shrinkage? That's why we had to tighten the wedges.

Q: No, I mean the length of the siding that you'd put around, it would be hard to get wood.

Captain Kaine: As you go down, you start with, say, ten two-by-sixes, and you'd put these in, and you'd wedge them

F. R. Kaine #1 - 26

so that you had four sides wedged against the hole. You'd slide those down, and as you dug farther, you'd drive those down. Then put more behind them and drive those down, so the first ones you put at the top were way down at the bottom.

Q: I see. You didn't have to get a 90-foot timber.

Captain Kaine: No, and then you'd slide those down, and you'd wedge farther down. Actually, the first boards you put in were the ones that traveled the farthest.

Q: That I understand. And then the ladders would be increasingly . . .

Captain Kaine: We used to hang ladders from frame to frame. I call them trusses--they were really frames, I guess, that went around, and we'd just hang a ladder from one frame to another and climb on down. The whole program was ingenious: as I say, an empirical development of many, many people that died and many, many people that worked on these things.

Q: Did you have casualties in any of your classes?

Captain Kaine: Not in any of our classes. We had some

F. R. Kaine #1 - 27

people hurt later on as they went overseas. I was trying to think. I don't remember very many casualties in bomb disposal once it got to the States. I truthfully don't know the British casualty numbers, but they were tremendous when it first started out. I can remember one lad that got eye damage taking a fuze apart, and we thought that was terrible, so I'm sure we didn't have a lot of casualties. This lad lost the sight out of one eye, but I don't remember any Americans that I can think of offhand being the victims of disposal accidents. Now there may have been some.

Q: That's remarkable, isn't it?

Captain Kaine: Yes. There may have been some after I left. I was there maybe a year before I went into the UDT. But while there on the staff, we had a great group. I thought it was a great program, because he didn't limit the staff, keep it permanently. He kept changing the staff and kept moving people in, and he kept exposing operators to staff work so that later on he could bring them back, and they would be acquainted with what the staff was doing. I think it was a very cleverly managed operation, because he felt secure in picking his staff. But he also felt secure that if he wasn't there, somebody else could pick the staff and know that he had good staff people there to do the

F. R. Kaine #1 - 28

work.

Q: Did you see a great deal of him during this?

Captain Kaine: Oh, God, yes.

Q: He was there all the time?

Captain Kaine: Now he did go on a lot of trips. He went on recruiting trips and whatnot, but he was there a lot of the time. We lived in a thing like a Quonset hut, kind of a nice Quonset hut, and the back end of it was made up into two bedrooms. Kauffman had a little suite down there at the end.

Q: Is this in Stump Neck or in Washington?

Captain Kaine: This is on Massachusetts and Nebraska avenues, at American University. The front end of it had a T put onto the Quonset hut, a wider one than in the back, and this was a lounge and a bar at times--a good, fun place. I had a buddy that I met in bomb disposal; his name was Lloyd Anderson, and we were together from then on.*
We went to UDT together, as a matter of fact. He was, and still is, a wonderful person. He was a good athlete; he

---
*Ensign Lloyd George Anderson, USNR.

was co-captain, along with Jackie Robinson, of the UCLA basketball team.* Andy was inherently religious, humorous, and a great leader. I could not have had a better partner.

Andy and I had a room right at the head of the Quonset hut going back toward Kauffman's area, just off the lounge. Kauffman would invite his father down for a visit. God, I'll never forget it. His father would be down there in the suite with Draper, and you'd hear these slippers padding up at the hallway at 4:00 o'clock in the morning. We had gotten used to the cold and damp in Washington, but his father hadn't. We would hear the admiral say, "Goddamn ensigns. It wasn't like this in the old days." He would be turning up the thermostat near our room because he was cold. We had more laughs over that, because every time the admiral came to visit, it seemed like it was cold, and he'd be mumbling all the way up the hall to turn the thermostat. We had some good times in that group. We had a particularly good group.

Q: Well, that selection in the early days was probably the key--the way the selections were made.

Captain Kaine: After looking at it for a number of years,

---

*Jack Roosevelt Robinson was a versatile athlete who played for the University of California at Los Angeles before entering the Army in World War II. In 1947 Robinson became the first black player in major league baseball.

F. R. Kaine #1 - 30

I think it surely was, because I can't think of any real losers in the whole bunch. Those that stayed in had a successful career, and those who opted out had a successful career outside. I think it was a tremendous tribute to Kauffman, the people he picked. I didn't always think so greatly of Kauffman at that time, because at that time I thought that we weren't going to get away from him. It wasn't true, really, but we just didn't know. We used to discuss it a lot, because here we were.

I probably should interject this: another thing they were recruiting for when I was in midshipman school was the amphibious force. And that was one place we all knew we didn't want to be, because they talked about going to war in boats, and all we could visualize was rowboats. And we thought, "Oh, the hell with that." So no matter what our druthers were, we felt we were better off with Kauffman, but we were always devising ways to get away from him. We had visions of spending the whole war in Washington as teachers, and that wasn't such a great idea at the time. I don't want to get ahead of this thing, but that's how we got into the UDT, finally.

Q: I want to ask if there were any other people. You spoke of Anderson as one of your friends that went with you. Were there other people whose names you want to note?

Captain Kaine: When we went to UDT ultimately, Kauffman picked from his people at bomb disposal and from other places too. He wanted some key people to go with them that he knew and had worked with. Ultimately, he picked Anderson, a lad named Bert Hawks, Neil King, Larry Heideman, and Frank Hund, who was another one from bomb disposal.* And then he also picked some from mine disposal, I guess based on the recommendations of Lieutenant Waters. Two of them that I recall the names of particularly are Culver and Vetter.** The third was a lieutenant named Jacobs, and there was another one from mine disposal, and I just don't recall his name.*** That was the core group of UDT officers from mine and bomb disposal. Then he picked officers also from the Seabee outfits to start the first UDT. So, quite truthfully, he was the only one who knew what the hell he was doing. We had no idea what this new organization was going to be.

Q: I want you to explain it in some detail. Before we go to that, were there any other comments that you want to make about American University and Stump Neck, both the

---

*Ensign Albert Hawks, USNR; Ensign Myles Cornelius King, USNR; Ensign Lawrence L. L. Heideman, USNR; Ensign Frank C. Hund, USNR.
**Ensign William Culver, USNR; Ensign Alvin E. Vetter, USNR.
***Lieutenant Charles Jacobs, USNR.

training and the instructing?

Captain Kaine: The training and the instructing were super in this program, and they kind of had to be, because if you didn't pass the final exam, you couldn't stay in the program.

Q: You couldn't go back and take it over again?

Captain Kaine: No, you were washed out. Kauffman's thought behind that was, "If you can't get 100% in this program, you don't need to be down working on a bomb."

Q: Good sense.

Captain Kaine: Yes.

Q: Was there any attrition?

Captain Kaine: Oh, yes, heavy attrition. I would hesitate to give you a number, but I would say upwards of 30%. And one thing you've got to consider is there really wasn't a lot of physical attrition involved in bomb disposal training, because it was mostly a classroom and thinking thing. The only physical aspect of this was to dig a ditch or a dig a shaft or maybe handle a board or something. So

it wasn't physical on a level comparable to UDT or SEAL.*
So all the attrition in this program was scholastic.

Q: That's what I was wondering; it was on a written exam.

Captain Kaine: Written.

Q: He was probably saving their lives.

Captain Kaine: Oh, definitely. In retrospect, again, I can see where that was a keynote of Kauffman's training programs all the way through, because you'll see after we get into the UDT thing that it was his prime effort there, too.

Q: I saw a picture of him, and I was curious to know--was he a tall man? He appeared to be a tall, slender man.

Captain Kaine: Very slender guy, not too tall--just under six feet. Heavy, heavy glasses, very thick glasses. He just had lousy vision. As a matter of fact, that's why he ended up in the British Navy, really.

---

*SEAL--the acronym stands for Sea-Air-Land. SEAL teams are the Navy's special warfare forces; they go ashore, whereas UDTs, which have since been incorporated into the SEAL organization, did beach reconnaissance and clearance prior to amphibious assaults.

F. R. Kaine #1 - 34

Q: That's interesting, I think.

Captain Kaine: This is an aside, and he may have covered this in his own oral history; I don't know. But when he got out of the Naval Academy, they wouldn't commission him.* That was in the days of the Depression, and there was a shortage of money and everything else. Kauffman had this eye problem, so they wouldn't give him a commission. He went to work for one of the ship lines and sailed for a while.** When war broke out, he went to work with an ambulance corps serving the French Army. He drove an ambulance and got captured by the Germans. Somebody got him out and got him into Britain, and then he joined the British Navy because he was there and it was handy, I guess, with a war going on.

When he came back after being injured was when he got into the American Navy, and he came in as a reserve. That was one of his big sayings at the time, "By God, they made me a reserve. I'm going to get nothing but reserves into this outfit. We're going to make it a good reserve outfit." And he did.

Q: Was that true? Were all of his people reserves?

---
*Draper Kauffman was graduated from the Naval Academy in the class of 1933.
**Kauffman was employed by United States Lines prior to World War II.

F. R. Kaine #1 - 35

Captain Kaine: Oh, yes, everybody was a reserve then.

Q: I would imagine at that time in the war you would have to be.

Captain Kaine: We were all reserves, so Kauffman and this Means Johnston that I mentioned before were the only regular Navy people that we knew for a year or two, and even Kauffman was officially a reserve. It was a great time of bantering and teasing about reserves and all this stuff.

Q: Some of it, regrettably, was not in good humor.

Captain Kaine: No, it wasn't. A lot of it was bad, but in reality the reserves--due to their mass, their numbers, and their political clout--were the only thing that got pay raises for the regulars. You can look at every pay raise that has been since, and it's reserve clout. Whenever a big war comes on or you get involved in something where there are enough numbers . . .

Q: Well, reserves were the Navy in those days.

Captain Kaine: Absolutely.

F. R. Kaine #1 - 36

I can't think of any further items that might be of interest other than that the history of bomb disposal speaks for itself, because from the humble beginnings it had with one man, it grew and grew and became the tremendous organization that EOD is now.

Q: How many people do you venture went through that school? Do you have any idea?

Captain Kaine: I have no idea. It must be thousands, though, because as time went on, the EOD school became the EOD university for more or less all the forces--foreign forces and everything else. They trained, I guess, oh, thousands and thousands of people.

Q: Where did it move from American University?

Captain Kaine: Eventually, it went to Indian Head and stayed at Indian Head. Schaible was head of EOD back there for four or five years.*

Q: I suppose we should say what EOD is.

Captain Kaine: Explosive ordnance disposal. It's a

---
*Commander David L. Schaible, USN, was commanding officer of the explosive ordnance disposal school from April 1973 to September 1977.

combination of bomb and mine disposal and nuclear weaponry, and it's a tremendous program now. I don't know the duration of the classes or the training, but in those days it was, I'll say, an eight-week program. Now it's probably, I would think, maybe 30 weeks or something like that. You'd have to check that number.

Q: I would say that what I'm interested in is your experience. If we're through with that, then I'd love to have you give me some background on UDT--the man who planned it and actually explain it.

Captain Kaine: Sure. Admiral Kauffman was the one who came up with the concept of UDT.

Q: Which is?

Captain Kaine: Underwater demolition team. Actually, he didn't call it that; that is a term that's grown since about mid-World War II. He called them naval combat demolition units, NCDU. And the reason that he started working on this was that he knew the beaches were reinforced and had obstacles on them in France and that they were being made impenetrable to boats and landing forces.

The more he thought about this and the more he thought

F. R. Kaine #1 - 38

about how the war was going and where it would have to go ultimately, he thought, by God, maybe he could do something about it. And in as simple and direct a fashion as that, he started his politicizing and using daddy and uncle and everybody else. He was knocking on doors and generating interest and telling the people that had the power to know through the good graces of whoever he could use; it didn't matter who it was. If he could use you, he would.

He generated enough interest so that in 1943 he was able to pull out of bomb disposal--not fully, because he always kept a foot in bomb disposal. But he was able to set up a deal where he and his so-called staff would move to Fort Pierce, Florida, for what he alone knew. None of us knew exactly what was going on. There were people in Washington who did know what he was doing, but most of the people who went with him just knew that this had something to do with the second front in Europe. The second front was the big buzzword at the time, so they knew that this operation would have ultimately a lot of excitement and would be a way to get off the staff in Washington. So he asked for volunteers, and some he didn't ask to volunteer; he just said they were going with him.

Q: And you were . . .

Captain Kaine: I was one of the non-volunteers, but really

I volunteered, because I figured it would be a way to get out the door. This buddy of mine, Andy, was a "non-volunteer volunteer," too. I'll put it this way: realizing fully that the Navy is not that democratic, we said to Kauffman, "We'll go with you if you'll give us a first assignment." He said okay, so we went down there, knowing that we didn't even know what it was, really. But he said, "Yes," so we said, "Yes."

Well, now there's a lot of stuff that went on that I didn't know about, but this was all between Kauffman and BuOrd, the planners and whatnot.* That was at a level that we weren't interested in at the time. To get something like this off the ground nowadays, I think it would just be almost impossible for one man to do it. But at that time, the Navy, although growing like mad and having a war on, was willing to listen to this guy who was running around saying he knew about this and he could do this and could do that. Literally, truthfully, he didn't know what he could do at that point in time or what he could do about a second front or whether he could even bring about the training to do something about these obstacles.

Q: You mean the obstacles on the beach?

---
*BuOrd--Bureau of Ordnance.

F. R. Kaine #1 - 40

Captain Kaine: The beaches in France, yes.

Q: Oh, in France.

Captain Kaine: Yes, that's what this was designed for.

Q: Oh, I was thinking of the Pacific, but he actually was talking about France.

Captain Kaine: This UDT thing was all designed specifically to get into France. It had nothing to do with the Pacific at first; that was an afterthought.

Q: That's very interesting.

Captain Kaine: Yes, a lot of people have misconceptions about this.

Q: That's certainly true for me.

Captain Kaine: But he got enough clout together to sell this program and to get a group of us moved down there and to get a ticket for something like 500 men from Seabee units for this program. He also somehow or another got a couple of British commandos over here. He borrowed some

F. R. Kaine #1 - 41

Army rangers, and there was an organization in Florida at the time called Navy Scouts and Raiders, which had been formed just before this. He found out where they were, and he decided that's where he should be, down there in Florida, for the training. So we actually set up just more or less across the street from the scouts' camp.

Q: Was that part of the Navy?

Captain Kaine: That was part of the Navy. You may have heard of a guy named Phil Bucklew.* That was his pigeon down there at that time. They were another very interesting group, as a matter of fact. So we got to Florida, I think, around the first of June in 1943, and there were ten of us. Kauffman was off on one of his trips somewhere, and we went down there. I think there was one jaygee, and the rest of us were ensigns at the time.

We reported in to a Captain Gulbranson, who was the skipper of this base in Fort Pierce.** He said, "Oh, good, you're the new organization, and your place is out such and such on the island." So we went out to this place, and there was nothing--like in the middle of the Gobi Desert. It was just a big, big sandpile, nothing there at all. We were there a few minutes, and some truck

---
*Lieutenant (junior grade) Phil H. Bucklew, USNR. Bucklew eventually retired as a captain and is the subject of a Naval Institute oral history.
**Captain Clarence Gulbranson, USN.

F. R. Kaine #1 - 42

came out and dumped a bunch of tents, and that was our home.

Q: Was it an island?

Captain Kaine: Well, it was in Fort Pierce, Florida. Yes, it was across the causeway on a little island. Scouts and raiders were down the street, and they were living in tents. And there was some kind of a boat unit up the street, and they were living in tents.

Q: All of you on this island?

Captain Kaine: Yes. So a bunch of us got together and put up a couple of tents, and then they came down and dumped a bunch of cots. I guess the scouts and raiders had a place to eat, and we started eating there. A few days later, Kauffman showed up. He had been off on a recruiting trip and recruited all these Seabees, I guess.

Oh, we had some fiascoes down there. None of us knew a heck of a lot about living in sand in a place where it rained cats and dogs. Also, you'd get wind gusts down there, and some of them set up their tents in a gully to keep out of the wind, and then it rained, and they got flooded out. We went from bad to worse, and finally we got

F. R. Kaine #1 - 43

it all together. We just no sooner got set up in tents down there--these eight or ten officers, including two from the Seabees--and in came 500 enlisted men. They appeared on the scene with no place to live or anything else, so in came the tents, and we went through the whole thing all over again.

We finally set up a whole area and got everybody in there when Kauffman showed up on the scene, and he had with him a fellow named Bill Flynn.* He was more or less Kauffman's administrative aide, overseer of training, and whatever else you want to call him. He was an older man, older than the rest of us; I think he was maybe a lieutenant commander. He brought in a couple of other guys, including a naval reserve officer named Bill Collins who was a demolition expert with one of the big explosives companies.**

Q: So we're at tent city?

Captain Kaine: Yes.

Q: What did they call it? It surely had a name.

Captain Kaine: No, I don't recall that they ever did have a name for it. We called it the Naval Combat Demolition
---
*Lieutenant William Flynn, USNR.
**Lieutenant William Collins, USNR.

F. R. Kaine #1 - 44

Unit Training Area, and that's about it. Once we got all this organized, we started bringing all these specialists like Collins that I told you about from the explosives company and the British commandos and the army raiders.

Q: And you said mine people.

Captain Kaine: And we had people from mine disposal who reported in and bomb disposal and the Seabees, and that was the nucleus of the whole mishmash. The way this training was set up, those people who had a specialty and were in the program would teach their specialty as well as take the rest of the training. Now, to illustrate what I mean, I had a modicum of demolition expertise from teaching in bomb disposal, and I had expertise in swimming, because I had done a lot of swimming as a youngster. I had done some diving with a bicycle pump and an air hose and an old bucket and stuff like this in a lake, so I had been exposed to the water. So I taught swimming and explosives. Another guy might teach reconnaissance techniques. We would teach bomb disposal and whatnot to those who had not had it yet--not a complete course but an exposure to it so it could be of help in the event it was needed.

Then they brought in these sadists, as we used to call them: the rangers and commandos. They were teaching knife fighting, disarming sentries, garroting, whatever--anything

F. R. Kaine #1 - 45

you want to teach. And this is where the program got its start in the manly arts, say. I think the program, as we finally had it organized, was eight to ten weeks long. It became extremely physical. They built obstacle courses. They'd work you night and day, and they had this thing called "hell week." This was introduced by a combination of the commando and the ranger training people.

Quite frankly, the idea of this hell week, which was one of the first weeks, was to get rid of all the people that would not make it. It was designed primarily as a time and expense saver, because they figured they could screen out the obvious people that would not make it physically. That's where the term "hell week" was born. Hell week is a famous thing in UDT. It's been looked upon--depending on who you are and where you're looking from--as bad or good for years. Anyway, this was designed in the first week of the program, and if you survived hell week, then you went on with the training, which was eight or nine weeks.

Q: I would think it of interest to describe hell week.

Captain Kaine: Well, in those days hell week was comprised . . .

Q: And did this become part of every training?

F. R. Kaine #1 - 46

Captain Kaine: Absolutely. And it's still with it today.

Q: Then I definitely think it's worthwhile to describe it.

Captain Kaine: It was five days of, as they said, hell. One of the things that made it almost totally intolerable down there was everything was done in the sand and in the Florida heat and the Florida water, which was full of jellyfish, Portuguese men-of-war, and whatnot. In those days, you didn't have the equipment that you have now. You didn't have the uniforms that you have now, and you didn't have the improved footgear and whatnot.

One of the things that made hell week almost totally unbearable was you were in groups of six, one officer and five enlisted men, and you never went anywhere without your rubber boat. Your rubber boat in those days weighed 400-some pounds, so if somebody wanted to go somewhere, the whole crew went, and you carried it on your heads or on your shoulders. If you ever put it on your shoulders, it would always tear your shoulders up from the sand. They kept you wet most of the day, and in those days you used to wear green coveralls with single belt and legs that could button. We used to wear what they called sand shoes; they were low-cut rough suede shoes with composition soles. The idea of hell week was to keep you up as many hours as you possibly could in a day; give you physical training every time you turned around; keep you with the boat; feed you; expose you to this guerrilla training, knife fighting, survival, etc.

Q: All the training you had had?

Captain Kaine: Yes. Just for one whole week they kept you going, and I would guess probably 20 out of 24 hours a day. And during the 20 hours you were wet, chafed with sand, cold, just completely miserable--with the idea being you would keep your boat crew together, keep your crew going, try to keep your spirits up, and try to keep your entity right there.

I think they felt they were in a kind of luxurious position in that they had 500 Seabees to work with. Truthfully, we had a lot of trouble with enlisted people who were not in good condition. At that time, there was a recruiting program going on for UDT, and it was a kind of spooky program, because this whole thing was classified. I forgot to mention that--this whole operation was classified.

Q: From the beginning?

Captain Kaine: From the beginning, from the beginning.

F. R. Kaine #1 - 48

You couldn't tell your wife where you were going. You could tell her you were going to Florida, but you couldn't tell her what you were going to do. When we were sent to Florida, I had just been married. I was married the 22nd of May 1943; Kauffman was married the first of May. He put out an edict no wives would go to Florida. We went down there. This did not contribute to the happiness of the group, because there were a few of them married. So I left Audrey in Washington. Peggy, Draper's wife, was in Washington. A couple more wives were in Washington.

Now, Kauffman, as I've told you, was a wheeler-dealer. But he also had an idea how rotten this training was going to be. We really didn't. But we also knew he wasn't a great athlete and everything, and he had the big thing he was going to take this training and all this stuff. And we said, "Hell, if he can take it, anybody can take it, so we'll make it." So we weren't worried about that. Well, as those things go, he did or did not take it as he felt that day, and he thought this no-wives thing was a macho thing and all this stuff. And his big thing was, if anybody was moaning or groaning about it, he'd say, "Well, my wife's not here." And this was the way he operated. He always made himself an example. And he would do anything anybody else would do. He was a fearless, fearless man.

Q: Of course, that is the ideal leader, isn't it?

F. R. Kaine #1 - 49

Captain Kaine: Yes, he was, he was. But we, while not having all his characteristics, had been chosen on what he valued in life. So he got what he picked, and that meant a bunch of sharp kids that weren't above putting it over on him, too, if they could.

Q: How old was he at this time, by the way? Was this his first marriage?

Captain Kaine: This was his only marriage, yes. You know, I don't know how old he was there. This was in 1943.*

Q: I wondered if he was maybe not much past the age of the people in the class.

Captain Kaine: He wasn't much. He was maybe five or six years older than the rest of us. Now this was another admirable thing, you know. He was a swinging guy when he could manipulate the people in the Bureau of Naval Personnel who were "God" then. I mean, they had big names there, but he could get to them, and he could get things out of them you wouldn't believe.

Anyway, on this wife deal, nobody's was coming down. Well, one of the wives was pregnant, and the first thing

---
*Draper Kauffman was born 4 August 1911. In May 1943, he was 31 years old.

you know, she appeared on the scene, and we'd hide her out. We had a place. And Audrey heard about it, and she wanted to come down, and so we snuck her down, and we got a place with this pregnant girl whose name was Hund, married to Frank Hund. And we shared an apartment, and we were hiding these girls from Kauffman. Finally, his wife got wind of it, and she appeared on the scene. From then on, wives got in. But we used to do some awful things.

Q: Were you able to stay with your wives?

Captain Kaine: Oh, about one night a week. But they were on the scene, and we would sneak off the island in the afternoon for a while and see them or go to dinner with them or maybe sneak into a movie or something when we were supposed to be doing something else.

Q: It made a happier situation.

Captain Kaine: Oh, yes, it made a fun thing, and it made it more challenging, because we were sneaking around on Kauffman. But we used to do some dreadful things; I don't know if this is the kind of stuff you're interested in.

Q: I think what you think is interesting is interesting.

F. R. Kaine #1 - 51

Captain Kaine: Kauffman couldn't see from here to that tape recorder without glasses. I mean, he had the original Coke bottle things. We used to steal his glasses and break them.

Q: That was a rotten thing to do.

Captain Kaine: Oh, it was terrible, but this was when we were sneaking the wives down there, and we could walk down the street with our wives, and he wouldn't know who we were. We did that many times. We'd see him coming down the street, and he loped. He never walked; he just went 90 miles an hour. We'd see him coming and just look in a store window, and he'd go right on by us and never, never see us.

To get back to hell week, it was a designed combination between the commandos and the rangers, and the ranger program basically was designed from the commando program. The British commando program was the first of these programs in World War II, really. So between the two of them, they designed this program and designed the hell week as the first part of the training. And it was designed, really, more as a motivational thing than a screening thing, but it was also a screening thing to get rid of the ones that they knew could not make it. It was motivational in that they put prime emphasis on keeping a

F. R. Kaine #1 - 52

group together and helping your buddy. It was a buddy program; everything was buddy-buddy. And if a guy got lagging behind, two or three would go back and haul him up.

Q: Did you stay with the same group all the time?

Captain Kaine: Yes, you stayed with your same group all the time. There was an exception to that in that I had an extremely strong group going through training. Another boat lost a guy through an injury, and because mine was so strong, they took my leading PO and put him in the other boat.* But that was the only time that I recall changing a crew. It was the only one of the starting crews that made it through training that changed people. It was a change for the good, because it helped the other crew out, and it didn't hurt mine that much, really. Our crews got through, but we had a lot of attrition. We had a lot of people from the Seabee units, and at that time they also had people coming in from other places. The Seabees were the best of the lot, of the enlisted men.

A lot of the people that came in were from Argentia, Newfoundland, and you probably remember this, because at one time in the Navy when someone wasn't a good performer, he would be sent to a station that was off the beaten track--Argentia or someplace like that. Well, the only way

---
*PO--petty officer.

F. R. Kaine #1 - 53

that a lot of these people could get away from places like that was to volunteer for something like this new training that we were starting. So we had a lot of these guys in there. Although some of them had bad reputations and were supposedly bad people, a lot of them performed very well in this type of work and had the motivation to make it through.

With a pool of people like this, the program got off to a pretty good start, although our attrition was high due to hell week, per se, and also due to the fact that a lot of these people coming in were not in any kind of physical condition. A lot of them were not capable and had no ability in the water. Many of them were claustrophobic.

See, at this time in the program, we did not have the knowledge or the ability to screen any of these things out, whereas now they can. In those days, if people volunteered, they'd go, and that was it. So a lot of our attrition, high as it was, might possibly have been lessened through psychiatric tests or more careful screening at sources, which they do nowadays. We had nothing but to take the raw material and put them through training. This we did, and we did it with pretty good success, I think. The first class that went through, we all made a choice of what fleet we would go to.

Q: Did you tell me how many were in a class and how long

F. R. Kaine #1 - 54

it was?

Captain Kaine: In the first class there were ten officers and 50 men, because that was what made up the crews. That was true for the next class and the next class and the next class. The only reason there was one officer and five men per unit was the size boat we used. That became the integral unit. You remember I said we didn't know what it was all about or where we were going or what we were going to do or anything. Well, as the people reported down there and the training started to unfold, we found out that this was a classified unit. The operations we were going to were classified, where we were going was classified, and what we were going to do was classified. But we also found out that none of the techniques that we were going to use on whatever we were going to use them on were developed yet, either.

Q: Even at the school, you mean?

Captain Kaine: No, no, this was a feel your way. As they got designs of all the obstacles on the beaches in France, they got a Seabee unit, and they came down there, and they built these obstacles. And we would go out and demolish these obstacles as fast as they would build them and train and train and train how to get rid of them, how most

F. R. Kaine #1 - 55

effectively to blow them. Where you'd blow them on the land, we'd blow them in the water.

Q: Can you describe the obstacles?

Captain Kaine: Yes, they were things that they called horn scullies. Each one was a block of concrete with two pieces of railroad track sticking out the sides. They were probably four and a half feet long coming out of those, and the cube would sit immersed in water. These four prongs of steel would stick out, and they'd hang the boats up. They also had jetted rails that they'd just put a block of concrete down and jet rails down and sharpen the ends for impaling boats. They had something they called some kind of a hell's gate or something, which was scaffolding put up in the water. It was just a huge barricade to prevent anything coming in to the beach. They strung barbed wire in the water, and they used anti-boat mines which really was a development of the old land mine.

Q: Were they live?

Captain Kaine: Well, in some of the training, yes, but not at the beginning.

They had what they called cribs, which were nothing but big, big blocks of concrete that they'd put out there to block areas of beaches. These Seabees would make these obstacles and put them up, and we'd set up fields, and they'd become part of the training equipment. Like, you'd train so much, and you'd teach so much, and then maybe at the end of one week your unit would go out to sea, and you'd try to sneak in and reconnoiter this obstacle field that was designated as your problem for that time.

Q: This is not something that you were teaching; this is you doing this. You're taking this training.

Captain Kaine: That's right, because I would teach the explosives and how to do the demolition work, but then I'd have to take my crew out and do it. Frank Hund was head of demolition training. He knew my demolition background from working for him at bomb disposal school, so I worked here too.

Q: You were head of your crew?

Captain Kaine: I was head of my crew, yes. So you'd go in, and this was part of your training program. This is when we found out what we were supposed to do, when we got into this program. And then we had to go along and find the most effective way to do this.

F. R. Kaine #1 - 57

Q: All of this was on-the-job training, so to speak; there was no schoolwork?

Captain Kaine: There was schoolwork. There was demolition formula work: how much explosive to use for so much concrete and all this stuff. It came in the form of a regular handbook that the Seabees had developed over a number of months or years. Yes, we got into a lot of schoolwork along with this, because there was also channeling--how to blow channels in water, coral.

Q: We are talking about training courses such as channeling.

Captain Kaine: Oh, yes, and they taught you how to make channels in the sand as well, how to remove damaged piers, docks, trees that may be in the way. It was a full course in, if you'll permit the term, constructive demolition, really.

Q: That's fine with me.

Captain Kaine: The idea behind all of the training was to make a path to the beach so that people could get in and so you could get ships in. At this time, the main emphasis was in getting people into France. We really hadn't thought of the Pacific yet, and the reason we were doing blasting in coral was because it was there and it was good training.

Q: I don't mean to interrupt, but I am interested in weapons that you carried, uniforms or clothing that you wore.

Captain Kaine: Okay. The uniform that we wore for all this stuff was a green coverall that I think came from the Army.

Q: You spoke of that during hell week, but that was what you wore.

Captain Kaine: That's what we wore all the time we were doing anything.

Q: Even if you were in the water?

Captain Kaine: Even if you were in the water, especially around coral, because the coral was so abrasive, and everybody suffered from coral poisoning or abrasions or contusions.

Q: They became infected, didn't they?

F. R. Kaine #1 - 59

Captain Kaine: That's right. They infected very badly. You were always getting bumped or hit in the surf or something, you know.

Q: So you weren't wearing swimsuits at that time?

Captain Kaine: No, we weren't wearing swimsuits.

Q: Which is the picture of frogmen, wearing swimsuits.

Captain Kaine: Yes, and that's kind of a big misconception of the early people, because truthfully they did more walking and labor than they ever did swimming. Now we did have fins, and we did have face masks, and after a while, once we got started, we did get into breathing equipment. But when we first started, there was a lot of skin diving and a lot of holding your breath, and a lot of just plain hard work. And it's reasonable, too, because most of the work we were doing was right in close to the shore. It was in the surf line, where you're not your own person, because the surf is so much stronger than you, and you have to hang onto everything. You have to develop the best method to put your explosive onto these obstacles where it won't get washed off or where it will do the most damage. So there was a lot of development time going into the training as well.

Q: You mean developing of weapons?

Captain Kaine: Yes, demolition systems type thing.

Q: How much equipment would a man have to carry?

Captain Kaine: The only thing developed at the time was what they called a Bangalore torpedo, and that had been developed by the Italians. This was primarily a land use weapon, and it was used by the American Army, too, for clearing barbed wire and brush and everything out ahead of troops when they were going in to some place. It was a system of steel pipes about three feet long and loaded about two pounds per foot with explosives. It had metal clips, and you put a rounded nose cone on the first one, and you could slide it out and clip another one on and slide it out, clip another one on, slide it out, and shove it out to maybe 50 to 100 feet ahead of you. Then you get down in a ditch and fire it off and clean out all the foliage and barbed wire and minefields, whatever was in the area. It would counter-detonate any other explosives. So this was one piece of demolition equipment that was available.

Q: That you carried?

Captain Kaine: That we stocked down there at the time, and we used that for cleaning out jungle stuff around Florida just as practice. And then we'd bundle these things and try using them on obstacles, and we could use them for clearing barbed wire. Then they developed packs of other explosives, tetratol, and these packs had straps on them so that you could hang them over the horns of one of these scullies and maybe hang one front and back and have it detonate simultaneously and completely wipe out the block. These people were working on developments as we were going through training.

Q: It was the beginning of a program with equipment and clothing and ordnance at the same time.

Captain Kaine: Everybody was working on everything. I remember one of the big original arguments was what kind of weapons will these guys have: "We'll get them this rifle and that rifle and all this stuff." Well, when you're swimming in to the beach, what good is a rifle? Where are you going to put it? So ultimately it ended up that everybody was issued a .45, and it was strapped on a belt. Well, then you had to find out how to waterproof it, because they were no good to you if you got on the beach and they were soaking wet and the bullets were wet and everything else. So you had to find out a way of waterproofing all this equipment. Ultimately, we did away with it, and the only thing that was really handy was a knife. So we had a knife on a belt and cap crimpers and things you would use fixing demolitions.

Q: But you actually had nothing to individually protect yourself?

Captain Kaine: No. When it came right down to it, some of them carried a .45, if they wanted to, in a waterproof bag, but it was a nuisance. Anyway, the . . .

Q: Did we finish? I know I'm interrupting, but you were speaking of the coveralls.

Captain Kaine: Yes, we actually wore coveralls, and we wore boots, too. We were issued fins, and if you were working in the water or if you were on swims or anything-- now if you were on a mile swim, you wore swim trunks. But if you were on a practice demolition where you were going to swim into a demolition area and do demolitions, you wore your green coveralls and boots. We always wore boots, really, in the water; because of the coral you were cutting your feet up all the time. In trying to gain entry to a

F. R. Kaine #1 - 63

beach, you're more of a worker or a walker than you are a swimmer, because you are working from one obstacle to another, and you're wiring and you're hooking this in and that in. Demolition work off a beachhead is just a lot of hard, hard work and long hours. So we were learning this, too, along with everything else.

There was on the horizon a big vision of swimming with an air supply for 45 minutes or an hour or, ideally, three hours. I remember the ideal thing at the time was to be able to be underwater for three hours. Why three hours, nobody knew; they just pulled it out of the air somewhere. Do you know that they are just barely getting to the point where they can be under the water for three hours right now? I mean, this was 38 years ago. But that was the ideal number.

At the time that we were going through all this training, somewhere or other Kauffman got word of a Jack Brown unit, which was a self-contained underwater breathing apparatus. And that is where you get that term "scuba."

Q: I didn't know it was an acronym. I just had heard of scuba so much.

Captain Kaine: He found this thing called a Jack Brown, and it was an oxygen breathing device, and it's what they call a rebreathing device. It had a canister in front that would filter your exhalation, filter out the CO_2, and recirculate it with the addition of oxygen from time to time. It had no demand valve on it; it was a hand-controlled thing, very rudimentary. It was decided by all these brains that were developing this program that this was going to be our equipment. One reason for that was that in rebreathing equipment, everything goes through this recycling program, and there are no bubbles to trace along the water. Also contributing to this fact was that it was the only thing where you could be a free diver. The aqualung was not developed, and the only other way you could dive on air was if you were attached to something.

So this became our unit, and we were told it was the greatest thing in the world, that it was in production and we would have it before we went overseas and all this stuff. So we were all excited about this and thought this was going to be great, because once you get that, you don't have to keep going down and coming up to get air and going down and coming up to get air. Well, the ultimate to that was that we got two units, so that everybody got to look at it, and a couple of us got to try it, and everybody went overseas without having it. But that's a little bit ahead of the story. This was another piece of equipment that was not developed specifically but was taken from the diving unit and brought into UDT and adapted for our use.

The people were so hot to develop ways of blowing

these obstacles that they developed a lot of things. They were working on limpet mines that would attach magnetically to things. When we were playing in the sand, blowing up sand to see how we could move it or whether we couldn't move it, somebody came up with the idea of filling a fire hose up with explosives and tried that. As a result of that, they developed a demolition hose which was 25 feet long, loaded two pounds per foot, and made of kind of semi-hard rubber or rubber-coated hosing with boosters in each end so you could cap. They had a little cap well in there, and they developed this explosive hose as a result of just playing down there. This later, in the Pacific, proved to be the greatest thing going, because all you did was work in coral and sand. But this was one of the developments of this early group that was going through.

They were just starting to work with plastic explosives then. The plastic was an explosive with a higher brisance and a little more powerful than any that we had.* It was like one and a quarter times as powerful as TNT. We also had TNT blocks, but that was a standard thing. And this plastic was a mixture of what they called torpex; it was a basic torpedo-type explosive and was an RDX with aluminum powder that gave it a little more oomph.UDT)** They started to plasticize it, and it came out in little blocks, almost like a Bit-O-Honey candy bar.

---
*Brisance is the shattering effect or crushing effect of a specific explosive.
**RDX is a white crystalline solid used with other explosives, oils, or waxes. It is considered the most powerfully brisant of military explosives.

This was a great explosive but not for work in the surf at the time, because you had to mold and mold and mold the little bars before you could get anything. That was really not great for this surf-type work.

So the explosive hose, Bangalore torpedo, and tetratol packs were the three prime explosives that we used on any obstacle works. Those seemed to be the main explosives we had for the whole of World War II. Plastic did develop, and they packaged it better, and the tetratol developed a little more so that we could take it out of the packs and string it out in blocks. It was connected with primer cord so that you get a simultaneous detonation of, say, six or eight blocks. So those were what we had to deal with obstacles. Being limited to that type of explosives, then we had to adapt the use of those explosives to the obstacles, and that was primarily the demolition side of the training done there. We knew what the obstacles were in France, so we primarily worked on those obstacles and ignored the sand and the coral, because we weren't interested in the Pacific at that time, truthfully.

As we progressed in training, Kauffman's field of employment progressed also. Just about this time, they had made a couple of landings in the Pacific, and he had somehow or another got a commitment not only to Europe but to the Third, Fifth, and Seventh fleets in the Pacific. We just went on with the training. It really had no impact on those of us who had extracted a promise from him that we would go with the first group to go out. As it turned out, to show how ignorant we really were, when we got towards the end of training, he said, "All right. You guys who are going, you can pick your fleet." And we really didn't even know what he meant.

Q: You didn't know what fleet was where?

Captain Kaine: No, we couldn't care less. So Andy said to me, "Well, what's your lucky number?"

I said, "Seven."

He said, "Well, okay, mine is, too." So we picked the Seventh Fleet. A couple of them picked the Third Fleet and the Fifth Fleet, and I forget how many numbers he gave us. Primarily he wanted people to go to Europe, and he had selected a number of them. See, we had ten units finished.

Q: How long was the course?

Captain Kaine: I think ten weeks totally. Eight weeks of the real training.

Q: Hell week?

Captain Kaine: Hell week was the first week and designed specifically that way to eliminate wasted time.

Now, as an aside here, hell week since that time has

been everywhere from first week to as far back as fifth or seventh week, I think. I know it's been as far as fourth week in an effort to retain more people.

Q: To get some orientation before they went into battle.

Captain Kaine: You know, this whole program, up until there appeared a need for it in Vietnam, has been a continuous struggle to keep alive. Korea helped it a little bit. But any of these little programs, when there isn't a screaming need for them, they get rid of. They just blow them right out. This is a little bit ahead, but I was talking about it specifically to tie it to training and how hell week moves back and forth, depending on who's in BuPers, how humanitarian he is, or how much money he has for whatever.* Hell week would go back and forth, trying to scrounge as many bodies out of UDT training as you could, because the attrition in UDT is about 60%. It has been for years. It's kind of funny how we would dance with this guy, whoever was heading BuPers, and move it whenever we went and always end up with the same attrition.

Q: Is that so? That is really interesting, isn't it? I would have thought having it the first week, the attrition would have been much higher than in later weeks.

---

*BuPers--Bureau of Naval Personnel.

F. R. Kaine #1 - 69

Captain Kaine: Really, the earlier it is, the more money it saves the Navy. I give great credit to these old trainers in World War II--these rangers and commandos--because they're the ones who really set this training up, and they knew what they were doing. I think probably the best evidence of what they knew is the fact that the program did survive, and it is almost the same now as it was then. The basic training is still the same. The basic thought behind the training is the same, and the people are pretty much the same.

Q: I want to talk about that a little later down the route, too. So you said the Seventh Fleet.

Captain Kaine: We said the Seventh Fleet, and we had no idea where it was; we didn't know what it was or anything else. When we found out, we were quite shocked, because the Seventh Fleet at that time was right off New Guinea.

Q: Before we get out into the Pacific, how many went to Europe?

Captain Kaine: Let me see. Four units out of the first ten went to Europe. Andy and I went to the Seventh Fleet, and two went to the Third Fleet, and two went to the Fifth Fleet. It was Fifth Fleet when Spruance had it, and it was

Third Fleet when Halsey had it.*

Q: But the attrition in Europe, I understand from my reading, was enormously high.

Captain Kaine: Yes. Omaha Beach was bad.**

Q: Did any of your classmates go to Europe?

Captain Kaine: Yes, a couple of them were killed in Europe, and a lot of the enlisted people were killed. I forget the numbers now.

Q: Luck runs with you, perhaps. You said the Seventh Fleet.

Captain Kaine: Oh, well, I hope so. Truthfully, I'm glad I went to that side of the war. It's warmer, and those Japanese are lousy shots.

We were rapidly on our way out there, and it was a good choice as far as we were concerned, because we got a lot of experience out of it.

Q: What was the state of the war in the Pacific when you

---

*Admiral Raymond A. Spruance, USN, commanded the Fifth Fleet; Admiral William F. Halsey, Jr., USN, commanded the Third Fleet. They were two command groups that alternated; the mix of ships stayed essentially the same.
**Omaha was the code name for one of the landing beaches in the American sector when the Allies invaded Normandy on 6 June 1944.

F. R. Kaine #1 - 71

went out? How many landings had occurred?

Captain Kaine: We were on our way overseas when Tarawa occurred.* We left San Francisco, I believe, on November the 19th. At the time we didn't really know what our mission would be.

Q: You mean even when you went out, you didn't know what to do?

Captain Kaine: Well, we knew what we could do, and we knew what we were going to do in France, but we didn't know if they had any of this out there or anything. We had never heard of any obstacles in the Pacific. We had no idea when they were going to land.

Q: Well, tell me more. I think that's awfully interesting. You went out by ship, I see.

Captain Kaine: Yes, as a matter of fact, we were on one of the first Liberty ships that sailed by itself, unescorted.** This was one of the new Liberties that

---

*U.S. Marines made the initial amphibious assault on Tarawa Atoll in the Gilbert Islands on 20 November 1943.
**The Liberty was a standardized 10,000-ton cargo ship designed for quick construction in large numbers during World War II.

Kaiser built.* We left out of Port Hueneme, where we picked up all our equipment supposedly.** This was another flair that Kauffman had. He was a great believer in identity, and I think that's why he got a lot of his stuff done. He decided that all our equipment would be painted red, white, and blue. So we went to pick up our equipment, and, God, all these red, white, and blue boxes were out there on the pier, and they were all ours.

We loaded all that stuff, and we had arbitrarily decided that everybody would take 50 tons of explosives with them and X numbers of these Jack Brown diving units; I forget what the number was. And you must remember we had never seen those things again. We just saw them one day, and a couple of us tried them on and dove in them and never saw them again. We had a lot of this explosive rubber hose with us.

Q: Were there enough of the Jack Browns on board when you picked them up?

Captain Kaine: Yes, one for each.

Q: Oh, he had gotten them by then.

---

*Industrialist Henry J. Kaiser got into mass-production shipbuilding as part of the war effort.
**Port Hueneme, California, was a base for West Coast mobile construction battalions.

F. R. Kaine #1 - 73

Captain Kaine: Yes, they were all shipped out to us.

When we landed in Australia, some Marine colonel was there and just couldn't wait to see us, because so many of his people had been killed getting into Tarawa. As a matter of fact, he brought a mine right up to the ship that they had pulled out of there and wanted to know what it was and where it came from and everything else and what you could do about it. He was terribly distraught, as a matter of fact, and justifiably so. He had just flown out of Tarawa because he had heard we were coming out there. He wanted to know what we could do about things like this in the future. So we had a big discussion with him and told him what we thought.

Q: Were you in charge?

Captain Kaine: Yes, I was the senior guy, a jaygee. Andy was junior to me by three numbers or something, one of those things. So we were the first two who went to the Seventh Fleet, and this was in Brisbane on our way to reporting in. We went to Townsville, and the Seventh Fleet amphibious force wasn't there. We finally worked our way up to Milne Bay in New Guinea, and that's where we finally reported in.

F. R. Kaine #1 - 74

Q: Now where did you meet the Marine?

Captain Kaine: In Brisbane. And he had just had word that there was one of these kooky units coming out.

Q: Were you able to help him?

Captain Kaine: We were in a way. We told him to get ahold of some bomb disposal people. The Navy had bomb disposal people there, and they could just go out and remove these things. So as long as a boat didn't hit them or something didn't hit them, they were not dangerous. They could stay there for years. He went back relatively happy about how to remove them, because their problem was they didn't know what to do with them.

They're still in the water. They're still all over the water all over there.

What had happened at Tarawa is these boats went in there, and a lot of them blew up. The people, of course, were killed or machine-gunned or blown up by mines, and they had terrible casualties. Then, what the guys in the Japanese Army did, they came out and manned their boats and their machine guns when they were hung up on these reefs and were just shooting them down as they came in. The Japanese just went out to the boats and took over the machine guns and things.

It was a terrible slaughter, and that's one of the best examples of what you can do with obstacles off a beach, if you use them wisely. They used them very wisely by putting these mines in there, because that just creates havoc and panic and everything else with the big explosions. The boats sink, and the people are screaming, and more boats are coming in on top of them, and you just get a whole big mishmash of nothing but confusion, fires, and everything right off the beach. The Japanese are sitting back there just making mincemeat out of everyone.

Q: It sounds absolutely horrible.

Captain Kaine: It is, terribly.

Q: To say the least.

Captain Kaine: So that's what the people in Europe were headed for, to clean this mess out. And if I may switch back to Europe right here, these people did. When they were sent into Europe to clean the beaches, there was some real cross-up in the pre-bombardment group. I don't know what the story was, but they were supposed to wipe out these German gun positions, and for whatever reason they weren't wiped out. So when the UDT people went in, these German 88s just blew the heck out of them. Fortunately, enough people got in to blow paths through the obstacles so they could get troops in there. I'll say, and maybe we can correct it later, about 40% were casualties.

Q: I had heard that figure.

Captain Kaine: Somewhere around there. As a matter of fact, several of my good friends were in there, and they said it was just terrible, just unbelievable. And what happened to help them out, a lot of them got ashore and could go back out and work their way back through and help out getting boats in. That was the biggest casualty I believe we ever had.

Q: In Normandy?

Captain Kaine: Yes.

Q: That's my understanding. But you didn't know that, which is good.

Captain Kaine: So we went on and reported in to this Seventh Amphibious Force. Admiral Barbey was the Seventh Amphibious Force Commander, and Admiral Thomas C. Kinkaid was Seventh Fleet Commander.* We were just little pipsqueaks in a whole big pattern out there. We didn't have any big daddy with us or anything like that anymore, so we reported in, and they turned us over to a Marine colonel named Brown. He had a little place on the beach in a place called Dowa Dowa in New Guinea.

I have never to this day figured out why he was there or what he was, but he had this little camp at Dowa Dowa. In the camp he had a beach jumper unit, and he had a few of the scouts and raiders which I mentioned before as being at Fort Pierce. They had this little settlement there, down at the end of nowhere on Milne Bay. All he reminded me of was the caricature you have in your mind of the British colonel in India. He used to smoke a pipe and walk around like he was King Tut, and he had a little dog that followed him everywhere he went.

Q: Oh, that's funny.

Captain Kaine: And, I thought, "Jeez, this is a funny war," and I said, "God, I don't know what the hell we're doing with this guy."

Q: He was a U.S. Marine?

---

*Rear Admiral Daniel E. Barbey, USN; Vice Admiral Thomas C. Kinkaid, USN. For details on the work of this force, see Barbey's book <u>MacArthur's Amphibious Navy</u> (Annapolis: U.S. Naval Institute, 1969).

Captain Kaine: U.S. Marine Colonel--Colonel M. G. Brown. And to this day I have never totally figured out what he was doing there.

Q: Maybe he was one of the people they didn't know what to do with.

Captain Kaine: Yes, and he really didn't like us, and he didn't like this mishmash of people he had there, and he was more or less just there to see that these damn reserves remembered they were in the military and did things right-- or something, I guess. But, anyway, we were there, and after we reported in to the amphibious force, they said, "Well, what can you do?"

We told them in a few minutes what we thought we could do, and they said, "Swell," and then they took me and introduced me to some Army colonel. I don't remember who he was. But the next day I got a message through the Marine colonel that So-and-so wanted to see me over in the flagship. So I went over to the flagship, and someone there said, "Well, Kaine, I want you to give a little talk on your capabilities to a group tomorrow morning."

So I said, "Fine," and I went over there, and they had just a whole damn division of people sitting around. It was a big, big army base, and, as it turned out, they were

F. R. Kaine #1 - 79

elements of the 32nd Division, which was out there at the time. They would spend most of their time working up and down New Guinea and the Philippines and Borneo. Instead of talking to a small group like I thought, maybe 30 or 40 people or something like that, God, there must have been 1,000 people or so, all sitting around. So we had to get up and expound on what we thought we could do. I guess we were convincing, because from then on, every landing they had, they had some of our units in it.

Now, in the meantime, another class was going through in Florida, and we were getting more people in. We got, I guess, two more units shortly. It just so happened that one of the officers had been with me in bomb disposal, and the fourth one was a Seabee officer. Then we got two more units, which gave us a total of six, I think, out there in the Seventh Fleet area. Now these are six six-man units.

Q: Thirty-six people.

Captain Kaine: Thirty-six people. The other areas were building up at the same time. The Fifth Fleet and Third Fleet were working their way up after Guadalcanal, the Marianas, and whatnot. We were working up New Guinea, Philippines, Borneo, and they were going up the other way. As the war progressed a little, the first landing we went

F. R. Kaine #1 - 80

on was the Admiralty Islands. We went in there, and we didn't go in ahead of time. This was a landing that was really a reconnaissance in force and turned into a pretty good-size fight.* I forget the number of people they put in this reconnaissance group, not expecting to have a big brouhaha in there.

They ran into a bunch of Imperial Japanese Marines, so then they had to reinforce and bring people in and really drive these people out. Well, when it came time to do some reinforcing, they found out that, hell, they couldn't get in to reinforce except on the backside of the island. They landed originally on Lorengau Beach. Over on the back of this island was Hyane Harbor, but they found out it was landlocked by subsurface coral reefs. It had a neat entrance that came up to the shore on both sides, and it was maybe half a mile across. But in the middle was a submerged reef that was only about 20 feet under the surface, and they wanted to send in APA-type reinforcement ships that drew 26, 28, 30 feet.** So they sent us a dispatch and said, "Get on the first ship going up there and do something about it." And I mean, this is the type of orders you got in those days, too.

---

*This reconnaissance landing took place on 29 February 1944.
**APA was the Navy designation for attack transport, a merchant-type ship equipped for amphibious warfare by being outfitted with troop berthing compartments and a group of landing craft that could be lowered by davits.

F. R. Kaine #1 - 81

Q: Did they come to you, or who did the orders go to?

Captain Kaine: They just sent this message to the colonel, so we got on an LST and loaded explosives all night.* And, you know, people hate you when you bring explosives on board a ship. They just don't like you. We had to load it out on the open sea, and it was a mess.

Q: You mean the LST was out on the open sea and you had to take the ammunition there?

Captain Kaine: Yes, the ship was under way, and they stopped it to come pick us up, and we had to take a lighter out there and mule-haul this stuff by hand up there. We did it with just ten people, because the other officer, Andy, was off on another meeting somewhere, so we had to go without him. So we got it all on there, and when we got up there, they gave us an LCM, which is a lighter boat, to work from.

They were having this big fight in there, and we could not find anybody who knew what they wanted done, and we were not aware of what they wanted done at the time. We were just told to get up there, and we were to report to

---
*LST--landing ship tanks, a landing craft capable of oceangoing voyages, it had bow doors and a ramp that opened directly onto landing beaches.

Joe Blow, whoever he was, and he wasn't to be found anywhere. I think he was the beachmaster, but I'm not certain of that. So we went around looking for this name we had to find and eventually found him.

Captain Kaine: Where were you? You weren't ashore?

Captain Kaine: Yes, we went ashore. They were fighting in the center of the island. They had taken some of the troops from one side and brought them around to the back side and were putting a pincer on the Japanese.

So we finally found this guy, and he said, "We have to blow this reef out of here. You guys said you can do this. You've got to do it, because we've got reinforcements coming in tomorrow morning or the next morning."

So we said, "Good, no problem." We didn't know whether we could do it or not.

Q: But you weren't going to say, "No," I bet.

Captain Kaine: No, not at that point. So we went out there, and we looked at this reef, and it was thick as this room.

Q: That's what, about 12 feet?

F. R. Kaine #1 - 83

Captain Kaine: Yes, 12 feet thick, and they wanted it down 40 feet, I think, because they were hoping eventually to bring maybe a tanker in. So we looked at it, and fortunately we had loaded a lot of Bangalore torpedoes. The Bangalore torpedoes came in boxes--three feet, six inches long and flat. So we had a lot of this stuff, and we loaded this in, and we went out and looked at it, and we swam around this thing, and it was just loaded with fish. God, unbelievable--a lot of shark and a lot of huge fish.

Q: And what were you wearing, swimming trunks?

Captain Kaine: We were wearing green coveralls, because it was all live coral.

Q: That's good.

Captain Kaine: We went down there and looked at this thing and said it looked pretty feasible. So instead of taking the Bangalore torpedo out of the boxes and using it individually, we took it in boxes and hooked the boxes together, maybe two or three feet apart, with rope. We ran prima cord, and we cut a hole on the top of each box, and we'd prime two or three of these pipes in there, which was the Bangalore torpedo. We ran the priming cord from box to box, and we'd take these things and feed them off the end of the ramp of the LST and lay them right over this reef. When we got through, we had like a blanket hanging down over the reef, across the top and down on both sides. Of course, we had never done anything like this before.

Q: You had never seen coral that size in Florida, had you?

Captain Kaine: No, and we had no idea what the hell this was going to do. We had worked all of one day until pitch black and then got up early in the morning. About noon we figured we had enough explosives running to fire one shot and see what we'd get, then figure out how much more we needed.

Q: And you were underwater?

Captain Kaine: Well, yes, we were working underwater, under 20 feet of water. And we said, "Well, we'll give it a shot and see what it does. And then we can figure out if we can do a whole lot more." They had just upped the date, and the guy was coming in the next morning. So we went back and said, "Well, let's fire." Well, we fired it.

Q: How did you explode it?

Captain Kaine: We ran an electric wire out, and we got in

F. R. Kaine #1 - 85

the boat and backed the boat way, way off and fired it with a hellbox.

Q: With a what?

Captain Kaine: What they call a hellbox. It's an initiator, a small electric generator. We fired that rascal, and we had put in, I think, 47 tons of explosive. When that went off, the slap on the bottom of the boat would almost fracture your feet, it was such a thud, a rap. Of course, when you fire a big explosion like that, everything looks like it's in slow motion at first, and everything starts coming up--water and everything. We saw fish flying and coral flying and everything flying. When that thing went off, I knew that it was a good thing.

We had dropped those things down on the sides of this reef, probably two or three down on each side. So we had maybe 14 feet down each side, and of the 14 feet, there was nine feet of it that was explosives, and we'd spaced them three or four feet apart. When we went in to measure this thing, we had dived down so far you couldn't believe it. We finally measured it with lead lines and swimmers, and we had taken it down to 47 feet, and we had a breach in the thing about 70 or 80 feet across. We had to go in to see if there were any unexploded explosives in there and whatnot or any big pieces of coral that would be in the way. By the time we got through examining it, we looked out and there was a ship coming in.

Q: Oh, that's unbelievable.

Captain Kaine: Everything just fell into place like that.

Q: You see, part of that was you were perfectly trained for it. It didn't just happen.

Captain Kaine: Well, yes, we were trained, but a lot of it is luck, too.

Q: I told you you were lucky.

Captain Kaine: We were working with a bunch of Australians, and they had a coastal survey ship. I forget what was the name of it, but they came in and did soundings for us and got actual depths and everything else for us. So it was fine, and that ship steamed in there as big as life the next day. And that was our first operation. So we felt good.

Q: But didn't the people out there think you did a super job?

Captain Kaine: Oh, yes, great. One of the sidelights of this thing--it was later written up, I think, in _Time_ magazine or one of the magazines.

We killed so many fish that it was unbelievable, but one of the fish we killed was a big, big jewfish. I don't know if you're familiar with them, but they have a massive head. This thing was 11 feet long, and it weighed 780 pounds. We had it out there, and we couldn't get it in the boat, it was so big.

One of the groups that were brought in there on the first day of this reconnaissance was a Seabee group, the 40th Seabee Battalion. And nobody to this day knows why they were brought in there, but they were there anyway, and we went in and talked to them and asked them if they had a wrecker truck. They said yes, so they put it in the boat, and we took the wrecker truck out there, and we put a line on this fish and hauled it in. We took it in to the Seabees, and they fed the whole battalion off of one fish--unbelievable, unbelievable.

We watched them butcher it, and they had four filets off that thing almost eight feet long, and then they cut them up into steaks--just unbelievable. We had a lot of good fish as a result of those shots. We were in there for three or four days, I guess, and then they took us back down to Dowa Dowa, and we were based there.

F. R. Kaine #1 - 88

Q: May I read this comment that I have from you which indicates that you directed 36 UDT operations and participated in 12?

Captain Kaine: That's right. What we did in the Seventh Amphibious Force was a little different from the rest of the Pacific in that our individual five-man, one-officer units maintained their identity as such. We didn't combine into one larger unit. The other fleets found that they could be more effective as a large unit and combined into units of ten officers and 50 men at first. Then they went to 13 officers and so many more men and made a single operating team out of that group rather than staying as individual units.

The people that we worked for, the Seventh Amphibious Force, thought that they'd have more coverage and better mileage out of our units by keeping them as separate entities and operating two at a time for each beach or each colored beach, whatever it was. What we didn't realize was that we were getting a heck of a lot more work than the rest of the UDT or combat demolition units. But we were getting an awful lot more experience, and we were brought in on all the planning for every operation.

Q: I wanted to ask about that. Who decided who would go in and where and how? Can you give me a stand on maybe one?

Captain Kaine: Sure. From the unit standpoint, we tried to take turns. Within the amphibious force, various units took various landings. Like if LST Group So-and-so was going to make this next landing, we would put one of our units with it, and we'd get to identify with various landing groups, either from the point of view of division--whether it was the 32nd Division or the 41st Division or whatever--whether it was an LST unit we were attached to or not. We were assigned ultimately to either an LCI, which was a landing craft infantry, or an APD, which was an old, cut-down four-stack destroyer turned into a high-speed transport, or whatever they decided to put us on. That even included, later on, YMSs, an LST, and PT boats.*

We kept a parity between the units as to the number of landings. One of the things that we worried about out there was with people getting injured or people getting nervous disorders, hypertensive, and whatnot, because we could see we weren't going to get home. They were out there, they were going to get the war done with, and were going to keep the same team and operate us as a team, and we were going to win the war. So with that in mind, what we did try to do was be as equitable as we could within ourselves by alternating landings. We didn't know it at

---

*YMS--motor minesweeper; PT--motor torpedo boat.

the time we were doing it that there would be 35 or 36 landings.

We had no idea how many there were going to be, but we did know that we could say, "You take this one, we'll take the next one, and so on." With six units, that would give you like one in three. Sometimes they ran two at once; in one instance they had a three-headed landing at the same time, so all three of us got to go on that one. They'd have planning conferences, and we'd go to them. They'd tell us what information they had, which was usually lousy. Most of the sailing charts out there were accurate within a mile, which is . . .

Q: It's a long way to swim.

Captain Kaine: That's right. Many of the markings were not true at all. So, as a result, they determined on a system that we would go in ahead of the landing and do a reconnaissance on the main beaches. In this way, we would operate with what they called then in the fleet the pre-bombardment group. This was a group that would go up and soften up the area beforehand, and we'd ride a ship in that group and go in and do reconnaissance of the beaches, primarily to see if there were any obstacles.

Q: Describe that, please.

Captain Kaine: In a pre-bombardment group we'd usually ride an APD. We'd go up, and as the pre-bombardment group was working over the beaches, we'd get a time slot in there when we could approach the beach on the APD. We'd be off-loaded onto an LCPR, taking a rubber boat with us.* The LCPR would go in as far as they thought it was feasible, and then we'd paddle in in a rubber boat. We'd take the boat in either until we started getting fire or we thought it best to leave it somewhere. We'd anchor it and swim in the rest of the way. Well, when we started our swimming or if we started getting fire, the destroyers behind us would start laying 5-inch fire close over our heads, right at the beaches.

Q: That was scary, too, wasn't it?

Captain Kaine: Well, it felt good.

Q: Really?

Captain Kaine: We always felt great when the destroyers were firing over us, because nobody ever bothered us. We used to get a lot of enemy fire--rifle fire, mortar fire, and whatnot when we were swimming in. But we always felt

---
*LCPR was a landing craft designed for reconnaissance work.

F. R. Kaine #1 - 92

safe in the water. You're not very visible in the water, and we always thought that a lot of it was just accidental; maybe they'd see a head or something.

Q: Were you swimming underneath the water?

Captain Kaine: No, swimming on the surface.

Q: Right on the surface.

Captain Kaine: And in daylight, usually--well, whenever it got daylight, 8:00 o'clock and sometimes out there, 9:00. And many a time we'd hear reports that the Japanese had repelled another invasion, and it was just a bunch of our swimmers going in and out.

Q: Oh, really?

Captain Kaine: So we would go in and recon the beaches. We swam in, and we had a fixed plan. We usually tried to do it by holding a line. Each of us had a slate, and we'd take soundings as we were going in. You end up so you can draw a regular profile of the beach and tell how much beach they've got, whether it's sand or rock, coral, or whatnot. Most of the beaches out there were coral. We'd tell them whether or not it needed any demolition work. If it needed demolition work, then we would come back and go in maybe the next day and do the demolition work.

Q: And there were only five of you doing this tremendous . . .

Captain Kaine: Well, 12 of us on a beach, yes. Don't let anybody ever tell you it wasn't work; it was work. It was hard, hard work, but we didn't know any better, so it was fine with us.

Q: Did you feel now that at least you were fighting a war?

Captain Kaine: Oh, yes. We had a definite part of that war, and we left some marks on it.

Q: You were saying you were so scared you wouldn't get away.

Captain Kaine: Yes, we thought, "God, they must have forgot us out here or something." But we had a lot of good opportunities. We had a lot of slack time, too, you know, because you just can't run an invasion every day of the week. You mention 12 landings; well, the 12 landings were over a two-year period. And in between times, we had equipment to take care of, and we used to get updates on techniques sometimes from Kauffman. We didn't get a lot out there.

Q: Did he come out there very often?

Captain Kaine: I don't think he ever came out to see us.

Q: Oh, he didn't?

Captain Kaine: No. Finally he went down and he took over a team in CinCPac, and he became a CO of one of the big teams.* He made two or three landings maybe.

Q: In Saipan?

Captain Kaine: Saipan and a couple of others. As a matter of fact, he saved a kid's life in there. One of the boys got left on a beach, and when they mustered back on the ship, he was missing. And old Kauffman got in what we called a flying mattress then--it was a little tiny rubber boat with an electric outboard motor--and went in and got him.

Q: Daytime? Broad daylight?

---

*CinCPac--Commander in Chief Pacific.

Captain Kaine: Broad daylight, and the kid swam something like 19 miles trying to survive. He had even tried to drown himself and everything else and couldn't, because he thought they had moved out and left him. And Kauffman found him. And how he found one kid--my God, I know times when I couldn't even find a ship, and he found this one boy right out there.

Q: There's a story that they tell about him, as you know, and I'm curious as to whether it's in his biography. You read when on Saipan he surfaced with his goggles and swimming trunks, and one of the Marines said, "Good God, the tourists are here before we even have the beach secured." You know that story, I'm sure.

Captain Kaine: Yes, I've heard that story. I don't know if it's authentic or not.

I do know one story that was told as fact about Kauffman. He was swimming out from a beach one time, and you know when you go in to a beach and do a reconnaissance, then you've got to swim back out to where the boat line is, usually where the boats can safely pick you up. A lot of these beaches were hot beaches, a lot of fire. He was swimming out with a face mask, and he used to squint a lot when he didn't wear his glasses. He couldn't see, and he was swimming along. He had big, big teeth, and supposedly one of the frogmen swimming off the beach looked over and thought this was a Japanese swimmer. We used to get reports of Japanese counter-swimmers a lot during the war. I never saw one, but we used to get these reports. I guess this kid thought it was a Japanese swimmer after him, and he almost killed Kauffman right there, swimming in the water.

Q: What did he do?

Captain Kaine: Oh, he grabbed him around the neck, and he finally convinced him who it was. He took the face mask off, and he recognized him, but for a few minutes it was pretty touch and go.

Q: It's a remarkable story.

You were on 12 operations. I was wondering if you might take one. I'm sure some were different. They weren't all the same; is that correct?

Captain Kaine: No, they were all different. Every one of them was different.

Q: I'd love to have as much detail of one at least or of each one, and I'd like you to list what the 12 were.

Captain Kaine: Okay, I've got a list of them somewhere. The landings in themselves varied tremendously. The biggest landing, of course, was the Philippines, the Leyte landing. In that instance, the teams from SoPac and ours worked in conjunction on all the beaches all over the place.* We went in there on D minus four to do reconnaissance, and the beaches were perfect. There were no obstacles or anything like that, and there were beautiful soft sand coral beaches. So there was no demolition work to do.

Some of the beaches in other places--there was a beach in Noemfoor Island in the Dutch Schouten Islands, which are up off the northern tip of New Guinea. We had a landing at Biak before landing at Noemfoor, another island.** These were coral reef beaches, and after doing reconnaissance we found no obstacles, but we also found that they wanted to directly off-load LSTs on these beaches. In order to do that, we would have to blow out some of the reefs and make what we called sets. It's like a dock the LST could drive into, putting her bow on a soft spot in the reef. Now, those beaches were a lot of work, because you had to blow coral again, and we had to use the demolition-type rubber hose. What you do is try to blow enough of the reef out so that the LST could drive its nose right up in there and

---
*SoPac--South Pacific.
**The landing at Biak was 27 May 1944, and the landing at Noemfoor was on 2 July 1944.

drop its ramp on dry land or at least walkable water.

One or two landings we ran into--not obstacles, but there were buried boat mines. The Japanese boat mine was a hemispherical explosive charge with two horns sticking up from the circular side. These were soft lead acid-type horns, and a boat hitting them would cause the acid to melt the wire, and the detonator would go off, blowing the boat up.

Q: How would you find them?

Captain Kaine: Very carefully and swimming. You had to swim to do this, swim and walk, because they were always just out in the surf where a boat has to land. We did one beach where we had to pull out something like 59 of those things.

Q: How many men were involved?

Captain Kaine: Ten of us. And we'd just look and look and look, and the ironic part of that one was that the first boat blew up after we had taken out 59 mines.

Q: Oh, dear.

Captain Kaine: But it blew up in another area where we had

not been. But you're never sure you're all clear.

Q: I would imagine.

Captain Kaine: It's a difficult thing, and the thing that certifies some beaches is the pressure from people that you've got to get in. You've got to do this and got to do that, and you do the best you can.

Q: Well, what would you do with these mines then when you found them?

Captain Kaine: Well, just pile them up somewhere or detonate them.

Q: You would detonate them?

Captain Kaine: Yes, get rid of them.

Q: Of course, then the Japanese know you're there.

Captain Kaine: Well, usually when you're clearing the mines out, it's just before our troops are landing, so we get them out to one side and let the troops land.

Q: Oh, I see, and at that point no . . .

Captain Kaine: It makes no difference.

To give you an idea of another type problem that we ran into, one of the landings that we made in Borneo, they put in X number of LSTs. I think it was five or six LSTs, and they landed in a mudflat. And they did this without proper knowledge. This was primarily an Aussie landing. It was a landing where the only Americans involved were the ships and American crews, and I think the Seabees were in there, plus the UDT. We got involved after the fact on this, because the part of the reconnaissance that we did was in another area, not where they landed these LSTs. The reason we got involved with these LSTs was that they had a neap tide, which is a massive tide. They went in on the highest tide, and when the tide went out, the LSTs were high and dry in the mudflats. They had no way out. The next highest tide, I think, was something like nine days.

Q: Oh, goodness.

Captain Kaine: So they sat there six or nine days. They sat there, and they had one mortar that was firing against them. And whoever was spotting for the mortar had the spacing right for the shots, but he had the wrong line of fire. He was dropping mortars every 60 yards or whatever, but about a half mile away from the LSTs. And he did this every three or four hours for the first two or three days and never hit anybody or anything at all, but he just kept it up, kept it up.

We went in and we helped, and we had none of our own explosives. We had to use an Australian explosive, which basically was nitro starch which we were familiar with through reading but had never used. What we did was set charges away from the sides of the ships and up by the bows of the ships, and then used PT boats to make waves. We got another ship to take the stern anchors of these LSTs out as far as they could, and the PT boats would come in under their anchor cables and create large waves in back of them, and we'd fire the shots and had a tug out there pulling on the LSTs, and finally they got them off. But they were high and dry for a number of days.

Q: But that was a creative operation.

Captain Kaine: Just to break the suction.

Q: That's remarkable.

Captain Kaine: So you can see that every landing is different. You did get different problems, and at the same time we did a lot of diving, along with everything else. Because if there are small outfits around in a war, there's

F. R. Kaine #1 - 102

always somebody that has something for them to do that nobody else can do. These demolition units got to be that type of thing.

We had one landing where they were off-loading military vehicles, and they lost an anti-tank vehicle. The cable broke, and it dropped over the side of the ship. It hit the pier and pushed the ship out and fell down underneath the ship. Immediately they came after the UDT people to go down and dive and look for this vehicle. You get involved with a lot of funny things.

Q: Now you did that? You were there? You did the diving?

Captain Kaine: Yes. We didn't know where we could hook onto this thing, and there wasn't another vehicle around. So this army guy says, "Come on. We'll find one." So we went back into the hinterland, and he found a bunch of these vehicles that were just leaving to get involved in an anti-tank battle way up in back of the beach area at Cebu in the Philippines.* We were up there, and we had to stop one of them on the way into the battle to find out where the lifting eyes were so we could hook our lines to the vehicle. So you get involved in a lot of different areas.

---
*The amphibious landing at Cebu was on 26 March 1945.

F. R. Kaine #1 - 103

Q: No one is the same?

Captain Kaine: Nothing is the same. Cebu is a good case in point. We went in, and we did a reconnaissance in there, and we found out that where they were landing was fine, but our bombing and our ships firing had partially destroyed the pier. It was a beautiful big pier with a lot of steel piling on the face of it. It should have been straight up and down like a wall, and it was all jagged and torn. So we went in and did a lot of demolition work in there, blowing this steel off.

Q: Were you being observed?

Captain Kaine: No, not really at that time. We had an interesting experience. We were in there one day doing this work on the pier for the landing, and a young lady came down the pier dressed in a brown-and-white dress and had brown-and-white spectator pumps on. She was a nice-looking little Spanish-type girl. She came running down the pier and came to where we had our LCI that was lying off there. She said, "I have to see the captain of that ship." So we took her up, and he was a young JG, and she couldn't get over that, because she was brought up in the Philippines, where captains were four-stripers. She thought this was great, but what she was there for was that she was afraid her brother was being killed.

Her brother was working with the Filipino guerrillas in the Philippines, and she wanted somebody to go look for her brother. We ultimately took her to intelligence, and, yes, her brother was in danger and, yes, they got him out. They sent somebody in after him with another group of Filipinos and got him out. So she came back to the ship afterwards and was just crazy mad about this JG, that he was captain of this ship. She just couldn't thank him enough and all this. See, you run into funny moments.

In the same place, we were working one day, and we were in there at Easter time. We landed a few days before Good Friday. We were sitting there, and we'd finished work for the day, and this big, tall man came down in white robes, and it was a Catholic priest from Tipperary, Ireland--brogue and all. He was one of the missionaries down there and wanted to know if there were any Catholics on board the ship. He said, "It's Easter time, and I'm here to hear confessions, and I'll come and say Mass and everything else."

So we went in, and we all started talking to him, and brought him into our little wardroom there. We gave him some juice, like tomato juice or pineapple juice or something, and he'd never seen any canned juices. We kept him there for dinner, and we asked him where he lived. He said, "We have a monastery up in the hills."

I said, "How did you get down here?" Because there was fighting going on, 300 or 400 yards inland.

And he said, "It was a bit exciting, but we got through all right."

So we said, "Well, can we do anything for you?"

And he said, "Well, you might give me a lift."

So there was an army jeep on the pier, and we got ahold of the guy who had it, and he said, "Sure, go ahead and take it." And we gave this guy a ride back to his monastery.

Q: When you say "we," do you mean you?

Captain Kaine: Yes, and Andy. We drove up, and, my God, he was right in the midst of the war in this formerly beautiful big monastery. Firing was going on all over the place while we were going up the road. When we drove up to this old shell-shocked monastery, he was in there with about five or six monks and brothers. They had 19, I think, when they started out, and 13 of them had been killed. The guerrillas would not fight without a priest along with them. One of these priests would go along with them, and the Japanese had been killing them off all during the war. The community was terribly upset, because they had a convent nearby, and all the nuns had disappeared. The Japanese had hauled them all out of there.

So we took him up there and told him, "We've got to get back."

And he said, "Wait, I've got a gift I want to give you." And he went out and started digging in the yard.

And I thought, "What the hell is this guy? He must be a little loony." Anyway, he started digging, and he dug up a bottle of Irish whiskey. When the Japanese had come in, the monastery hid all their goods, stuff like silver, whiskey, etc., in the yard.

Q: All their valuables.

Captain Kaine: Yes. And so he gave us a bottle of whiskey, and we went back to the ship. And he came down on Easter Sunday and said mass on the pier for anybody that wanted to go.

Q: I believe you're a Catholic.

Captain Kaine: Yes.

Q: And I was going to ask how that affected you, with the war. Were you able to pursue it?

Captain Kaine: Not very much, no. We didn't have that many chaplains available to the amphibious forces, as I

F. R. Kaine #1 - 107

recall. I don't remember many chaplains. I remember one terrific chaplain, a chaplain Pyle.* He was a Presbyterian, I believe, and he was with us for a while, but I don't remember a lot of chaplains during World War II.

Q: Did that distress you, to not be able to . . .

Captain Kaine: No, not in the least. What could you do about it?

Q: I want to continue on with some of your other operations.

Captain Kaine: Okay.

Q: I thought that I could ask you to give me in detail a typical operation of UDT, and I'm finding that is not possible since each one was of its own and completely unique. Am I accurate? Is that correct?

Captain Kaine: That's right. There was no set procedure or standardization of any of the operations that we went on, for the simple reason that we were operating in small units. We were an entity that was so small; they put us on

---
*Lieutenant John W. Pyle, CHC, USNR.

every kind of ship going, and we would change the amount of equipment that we would take, even the number of people that we would take, depending on what we were going to do.

Oftentimes, that decision was made for us by higher-ups in the amphibious force that we knew nothing about. Whether they were qualified to do that or not, we still had to do the work ultimately. One of the examples is an operation that we went on with dispatch orders that said nothing more than streamline our units and report to YMSs and perform our function at the destination without interfering with the minesweepers' sweeping capability. And with no more instruction than that, we were sent on the job and ultimately had to do it. While the sweeps were doing their sweeping, we would just be off and do our reconnaissance work. Then we'd report back.

Q: So the minesweepers were doing that function, and you were doing the reconnaissance.

Captain Kaine: That's right.

Q: Where was this?

Captain Kaine: This was off the coast of New Guinea at Hollandia, Tanahmerah Bay, and Aitape in New Guinea.*

---
*The amphibious landing at Hollandia, New Guinea, was on 22 April 1944.

And at other times we operated, as I've said, from APDs, LCIs, and an LST. So the standardization of UDT operations did not come about until well into World War II. Truthfully, it has been more standardized since World War II than it was during World War II. It's only since the teams have become in the numerical size of 80 to 100 men and 13 or 14 officers that they set up a standardized routine for reconnaissance and demolition. And still with demolition, there's no fixed pattern. It depends on what you run into and the type of work you have to do.

Q: But you were the first teams out there, and you were doing the first of this nature that had ever been done anyplace; is that right?

Captain Kaine: That's right, yes, and all of it, in truth, was a matter of feel or sense or whatever. The higher-ups in the chain of command really didn't know the extent of our capabilities nor our limitations.

Q: Were you ever sent to do something that you thought you couldn't do?

Captain Kaine: No, no, never.

Q: Did they leave it up to you pretty much?

Captain Kaine: Always. If you went to a briefing, they'd brief you on what they knew. And they didn't know much, truthfully. By today's standards there wasn't a lot of knowledge of really what to expect, the number of troops, obstacles, what kind of currents, or anything like that.

Q: You said the charts were pretty poor.

Captain Kaine: Oh, they were terrible. And we had the grace of God and a lot of luck and some awfully good people to work with. I mean, that's the best thing. The amphibious forces in the Seventh Fleet were just tremendous. They were so busy and making so many landings and did so much practicing in Australia, even before they undertook the war part of it, that they were really good, and they cover so much territory, and the strategy was excellent.

MacArthur was a tremendous strategist, and as he permitted the war to develop out there after he started back, he just saved a lot of American lives by isolating pockets of Japanese and just starving them out.* They didn't have to fight them.

---

*General of the Army Douglas MacArthur, USA, Commander Southwest Pacific Force.

F. R. Kaine #1 - 111

Q: So you were an admirer of his strategy?

Captain Kaine: Oh, a big admirer, a big admirer of MacArthur.

Q: That's interesting.

Captain Kaine: I wasn't always. I had, I think, originally had the built-in prejudice that you heard in the papers about "Dug-out Doug."*

Q: And "I will return."**

Captain Kaine: Yes, and running from the Philippines and taking a mattress instead of General Wainwright and all that stuff.*** But once you get out there, you find a lot of it was non-truth, and he was a brilliant warrior.

Q: You are referred to in some places as MacArthur's frogmen. You know that phrase, of course.

---
*This nickname was derived to ridicule MacArthur for issuing communiques from the rear areas rather than being where the action was.
**This statement, made when MacArthur was forced to evacuate the Philippines in early 1942, was his commitment to return and liberate the islands, which he did in 1944.
***Lieutenant General Jonathan Wainwright, USA, was left behind on Corregidor to surrender to the Japanese. He was a prisoner for much of the war.

Captain Kaine: Well, we were MacArthur's frogmen, I guess, because we were the only ones there, and he really was a theater commander out there, definitely. And we were on the beach when he came into the Philippines, the second time.*

Q: Did you see him striding ashore?

Captain Kaine: I sure did.

Q: Did you feel it as a dramatic moment?

Captain Kaine: Oh, yes, we thought it was great, really, because you heard a lot about it, you know.

Q: Had seen pictures?

Captain Kaine: Saw pictures of it. We used to listen to Tokyo Rose and all the people saying they'd never come back and they'd never get there.** And then you'd hear an

---

*The amphibious assault on the island of Leyte was on 20 October 1944. General MacArthur walked ashore through the surf to celebrate his return.
**"Tokyo Rose" was a nickname attributed to Iva Ikuko Toguri D'Aquino, an American citizen born of Japanese parents. Her English-language radio broadcasts from Japan during World War II were intended to demoralize U.S. fighting men who heard them. In fact, many servicemen found them amusing because of the greatly exaggerated claims of American losses.

F. R. Kaine #1 - 113

American broadcast where MacArthur reiterated that he would return, and he finally did.

Q: I have a feeling that you never were frightened out there.

Captain Kaine: Oh, we were frightened. Fear is something that worries everybody when they go to war. But I think what you fear is the unknown. I think once it happens, you get over that feeling, because you have a much better idea what to expect. What I'm thinking of specifically is the first time we were bombed or attacked, I was scared to death. But I looked around, and I wasn't reacting any differently from anybody else, and I was doing what I was supposed to do. So I felt immediately, "It's not really that bad." The incident was a bombing, and I could look up and see the bombs and see that they weren't going to hit us.

Q: Where did this happen?

Captain Kaine: It was one of the ships, off Leyte maybe. So then I felt, "Well, it's not so bad, and I'm not shaking nearly as much as that guy or that guy." So then it gets to be a matter of experience after that. You know what to look for, and you don't really worry that much about it.

F. R. Kaine #1 - 114

Everybody's in the same boat.

Q: So then I was going to ask the next question, and I guess I know the answer: if you ever thought, "I can't go through this anymore."

Captain Kaine: No, I never got to that point, no. I did get to the point where I'd say, "I am sick of this stuff and would love to be home every day." But we never got to the point, I think, where we couldn't go on or didn't want to go on. We almost looked at each operation as another step closer to home; that was the way you had to look at it. Now we had some individuals in the units that things got to be too much for them, but they were temporary things. They built things up. Maybe something would happen at home, and all these landings and everything would be too much for those guys. But a little rest or a little leave or something, and they'd come back.

Q: You were fortunate enough to be with your same five through the war?

Captain Kaine: Yes.

Q: Through the whole war?

F. R. Kaine #1 - 115

Captain Kaine: Yes, didn't lose any.

Q: To have that close-knit feeling must have meant a great deal.

Captain Kaine: Oh, yes, because everybody knew everybody else so well, and you lived with them. You're on a little, tiny ship.

Q: We are going to continue on with the UDT operations in the Pacific. You have named some of them. I think it would be interesting if you could list the 12 names so we will know the operations on which you actually participated.

Captain Kaine: All right. The first one was in the Admiralty Islands, which is a group of islands off the coast of New Guinea.

The next one was a triple-header. We landed at Aitape and Tanahmerah Bay and Hollandia.

The next two we participated in were the Dutch Schouten Islands, one in Biak and one at Noemfoor, and along about the same time we had another one at Halmahera.*

The next landing we went on was at Leyte Gulf, which

---
*The invasion of Morotai in the Halmaheras was on 15 September 1944.

was MacArthur's major re-entrance to the Philippines.

We were on one after that in the Philippines at Mindoro and followed in order by Lingayen Gulf and Palawan.*

The next two were in Borneo, one at Sarawak, one at Brunei Bay.**

I think that's 12, if I'm not mistaken.

Q: You've mentioned the Admiralties and the Dutch Schouten Islands and Leyte Gulf. Are there any specific interesting items that you would like to discuss about any of these others? You have indicated the difference between each one of them. But you might have some recollection of one of these if you'd like to.

Captain Kaine: Well, there are many different aspects or maybe incidents that might be of interest. In the Leyte landing, for instance, we had early reconnaissance. We went into Leyte, I think, on October the 16th, and the landing was the 20th. We did a reconnaissance around some of the offshore islands off of Leyte Harbor, and afterwards we did a lot of booby trap work, getting rid of booby traps and unexploded rockets and whatnot and cleaning up after

---

*The island of Mindoro was invaded by U.S. forces on 15 December 1944. The Lingayen Gulf landings began on 9 January 1945. The landing date for Palawan was 28 February 1945.
**The invasion of Brunei Bay was on 10 June 1945.

the landing, which is one of the first times we got into that in a wholesale manner.

Mindoro, the next landing that we made in the Philippines, was a very quick and dirty landing as far as we were concerned. We had nothing to do on the beaches, but in going in there, we got hit on the ship by a kamikaze. And while we were lying at anchor, we got rammed by one of our own ships at night and had to steam back at about three knots and get repaired, because we were afraid the ship would break up. The APA that went through our stern cut one shaft and went just about to the mid-line of the ship and then backed out. We lost only one man, however. He happened to be standing right where the ship was hit and went over the side, and we never did see him.

Lingayen was unusual; we went in there with the pre-bombardment group at something like D minus 16. As I recall, we were riding an APD, and I forget how many ships were in the group, but out of the group there were about 20 of them that were hit with kamikazes on their way up there. As a matter of fact, on this trip the Ommaney Bay was sunk, and we picked up survivors.* One of our destroyers went back and sank it, because it was burned.** As we were steaming away, the Ommaney Bay broke in the middle and sank

---

*USS Ommaney Bay (CVE-79), an escort aircraft carrier, was sunk in the Sulu Sea south of Mindoro on 4 January 1945. She lost 93 men--killed and missing--and had 65 wounded.
**The destroyer that sank the escort carrier with one of her torpedoes was the USS Burns (DD-588).

from the middle down. The last sight I remember was that of the bow or the stern going down, and you could still see an airplane on the ship. So there were different interesting things that occurred on these.

We had another interesting occurrence while we were going up to Borneo. When we were steaming by one of the islands, we saw a bunch of people on a raft from a distance. When we put our glasses on them, they looked like their heads were shaved or very white. We thought, "Gee, there's a bunch of survivors from one of our ships." As we got closer, it was obvious that they were Japanese, and they were paddling on a raft and yelling to come closer and come closer. This was after we had been out there for almost two years, I guess, and you become wary and savvy of things that happen out there and things that you learn either through experience or by conversation or something.

We had a young skipper that was driving this LCI. We told him, "Well, we wouldn't get too close to that thing. See what they want, but stay clear of it. And if they want anything, make them swim over to us." So he kind of ignored us and got a little closer than we wanted to. As he did, why, a couple of the men got up and started throwing Japanese hand grenades. We backed down immediately, and he opened fire with the bow 40-millimeter and hit the raft with the first burst. The whole thing

F. R. Kaine #1 - 119

went up in a huge geyser. It was loaded with depth charges. So in reality what they were trying to do was just get close to a ship; then they would attack and detonate their own depth charges. It was one of the first suicide rafts.

Q: I had not ever heard there were such things.

Captain Kaine: Well, they weren't an official weapon, but they would try anything like that. They were very dedicated.

Q: Were there any other incidents that you know of besides that?

Captain Kaine: They had suicide boats. These were little fast boats, and we actually picked one up somewhere; I don't recall where. But they were kind of light boats, and they had a load of powder in the nose of the boat and an impact fuze so that they'd just drive right into the side of the ship and try to blow it up. An interesting part of them was that a lot of them had Chevrolet engines in them. The ones we had seen were powered by Chevrolet engines.

Q: Well, what happened to these grenades? Did they hit? Did they miss?

Captain Kaine: No, they didn't come anywhere near us. They didn't come close at all.

Q: If they hadn't thrown those, though, your skipper would have . . .

Captain Kaine: Would have kept easing in and would have been too close. But we had had some sort of incidents similar to that, so that we were a little bit leery of that. But I can't remember what that incident was.

The Japanese were clever in ways like that. They would make an outlandish scheme pay off sometimes. They were given to patience at times. Like, they'd let our troops go by them and wait until they were behind them and attack them from the rear, oftentimes, which led to total confusion. Because then they'd have help from the front, too, and attack from the back and, God, you just never knew what was going on.

Q: Were you ever involved with any of those?

Captain Kaine: Not to any extent. We were caught on a beach one night, and, as a matter of fact, this was in the Admiralties, too. We were in there trying to get the rest of our explosives off the beach that we had not used. For a while we had been sleeping in foxholes on the beach, and every night the Japanese would infiltrate. What they would do was crawl up on the beaches and roll into a foxhole with somebody and detonate a hand grenade to kill themselves and kill whoever was in the foxhole.

Q: Where were they coming from?

Captain Kaine: Another island. There was a little island.

Q: They'd swim.

Captain Kaine: Yes, they'd swim; it was just a spit, a little bit away. These guys would infiltrate. So, being totally ignorant, we decided the best place for us to sleep was between two machine gun posts on the perimeter. Had we known what we know now, we would have been as far away from them as possible, because what they were actually trying to get were the machine gun nests and everything else. Plus the fact that at night in a tropical island where people are infiltrating and the machine gunners are as new as anybody, they were very nervous. We got into these slit trenches at night or foxholes, and those machine guns would go all night long. You'd never get any sleep--shadows, possible infiltrators, birds, dogs, everything.

Q: Anything that moved?

Captain Kaine: Anything that moved got shot. But to get back to the night we were on the boat and were back trying to get our explosives and move out of the Admiralties, we decided that rather than go back to the damn foxhole, that we'd sleep that night on the LCM, on the boat. So we just slept inside the well deck, and that night the machine guns kept going. These were not the machine guns on our boat but the machine gun on the boat beside us and the machine gun on the boat down a little farther. We were so tired from being up all the other nights that they didn't bother us. It got so that it fit right into our pattern and we'd hear them, but so what?

Well, the next morning we got out there, and there were something like 28 dead Japanese in front of the boat. They had actually put on a fairly big movement to come over and capture these boats. Again, ignorance was bliss, because we did not know about it, and we could not have cared less. But the two boats next to us were really alert and had killed something like 28 Japanese.

Q: You can't say that you haven't had a lot of close calls.

Captain Kaine: Well, yes, but there was always some kind

F. R. Kaine #1 - 123

of humor. There's a levity to living in an atmosphere like that.

Q: Did you laugh that next morning when you saw that?

Captain Kaine: No, not then, but later we did.

Q: Afterwards in thinking about it.

Captain Kaine: Yes, when you think about it. And also sometimes things like that maybe build up a false confidence, because you figure well, you've been that close that time. Maybe nothing's going to happen.

Another time we were in the Philippines when my buddy Andy and I did something out of sheer boredom and a desire to get off the ship. We saw a little island that was, oh, I'll say, a mile or two miles away. And we said, "Well, let's go over, and we'll take some pictures or something." So we got in the boat, and we had a little outboard motor on it.

Q: These were your own landing boats?

Captain Kaine: Yes, rubber boats. But the two of us went over. We dragged the boat on the beach, and we started walking around. With that, two Japanese airplanes came in and started strafing. We were there to take pictures, and as we dove, the next thing we knew we were both lying behind logs and Andy said, "You get any pictures?"

I said, "No, I didn't get any pictures."

And with that, two P-38s from our Army Air Forces base came and engaged these two Jap Zeros and put on the best dogfight you ever saw and shot down both Zeros. By that time, Andy had the camera, and I said, "Did you get any pictures?"

And he said, "Hell, no, I didn't get any pictures."

We were just goggle-eyed, watching this thing, so we never did get any pictures of that. But there are a lot of incidents that happen that lend a certain, I guess, levity or confidence or something to the situation you're in.

You can get into some pretty terrible situations--or things that look more terrible than they are sometimes. To give you an example, one time when we were out there in New Guinea, they had a new ship come out there called an LCS(L).* It was a type of miniature gunboat. It had a rapid-fire 3-inch gun on it. It was a takeoff on an LCI, which was a landing craft infantry, but 135 feet long by maybe 35 feet wide. It was supposed to be a hot-rock little ship. And all these craft we're talking about, their maximum speed was maybe ten knots. They were not going to burn up the world.

---

*LCS(L)--landing craft, support (large), a 123-ton vessel.

I think they sent three or five of them out, and the first thing that we knew, they were there, and they were supposed to be great ships. One of them was beached, because it had been hit by gunfire or a mine--I don't remember which. In order to save the ship, the captain beached it on an island that wasn't ours. So they wanted somebody to go and look at this thing and see if it was possible to get it off. We had been working pretty hard and a couple of our kids had been hurt slightly, so Andy and I said we'd go and do it. So we went and took a boat over. It dropped us off, and we swam into this thing and decided that . . .

Q: This is daylight?

Captain Kaine: Yes, daylight. He'd take the port side of the ship, and I'd take the starboard side, and we'd look it over and see how badly it was hurt. Well, when you're doing things like that, you get so wrapped up in your work that you completely forget everything else. I'll never forget it--we were going along examining this hull and evidently making the same rate of speed. When I got up to the bow, there was Andy looking around it, and it scared me to death, because I thought it was an enemy. He thought the same thing, and we both turned tail and started swimming the other way. I got about ten feet and turned

Q: Did he have goggles on?

Captain Kaine: Yes, he had a face mask on and everything else. And you just get so wrapped up in what you're doing that you look up and see a face, and it startles you.

Q: Of course.

Captain Kaine: We were ten feet back of the boat before we realized that it was each other. So those things happened.

Q: What about the boat?

Captain Kaine: Oh, yes, they got the ship off. I forget exactly what happened. But it was a good thing that they got it off, because it had a lot of classified documents in it that they had not taken with them.

When you were involved in this stuff, extraneous things happened that had nothing to do with the war, typhoons and the like. We had a case where we were on an LCI and got caught in a typhoon in the little waterway between the islands of Leyte and Samar. We were out in the anchorage, and the wind was so strong that we at times were backing down two-thirds and still going forward. And our big problem was that it was blowing up towards Samar. Leyte was ours, but Samar was not. We dropped the stern anchor, hoping that would hold, but it didn't, and the upshot of this thing was that we beached on Samar. We were doing all we could not to beach, but we beached.

Q: Tail-end first?

Captain Kaine: No, bow first--perfect landing, just a perfect landing. But we had no control over her whatsoever. The impulse of the skipper of this was to abandon ship. Well, he was new in the area, and--to give him his due--it was a horrible situation. We had a lot of explosives on there; we had a lot of people on there, extra people because of the demolition work. And he had classified material, and the island was not ours. So his first thought was to get all the classified documents and burn them and abandon ship.

Fortunately he was a man you could talk to, and we said, "Well, that's great, but where are you going to go?" The water was coming over the stern of the ship. At that point the waves were probably ten feet over the stern at times and sometimes going right over the conn. I said, "What are you going to do with these people?"

He said they'd go ashore.

I said, "The place is enemy held. It's not ours. What better could you be? You've got a bow 40 looking right down anybody's throat that's up there; you've got

F. R. Kaine #1 - 128

.50s here; you've got 20s up here. You're better off here than anyplace."*

He got to thinking about that and said, "I guess you're right." So if you get a chance to think, it's great. If you don't get a chance to think, some people panic.

Q: Well, you had had some experience, and he listened.

Captain Kaine: Well, we'd been there longer. Yes, he could listen.

Q: So tell me what happened.

Captain Kaine: So we stayed on there, and nobody bothered us. Nobody was going to come out in that weather, I don't care who it was. We backed off just like we beached there on purpose; it was just a perfect situation.

Q: I'll bet he was grateful to you, plus all the other people aboard.

Captain Kaine: Well, yes, it was just a good, good thing. And there were several other ships that night that didn't

---

*The numbers refer to a 40-millimeter antiaircraft gun; .50-caliber machine guns; and 20-millimeter antiaircraft guns.

get beached that hit each other and rammed each other. There were all kinds of bumps and gouges, so we really were very fortunate. We had a nice, tight berth with a stern anchor out and the bow on the beach.

Q: I tell you, you're lucky.

This was an example of your skill as a naval officer, not just a demolitions specialist. How did you spend your time on board ship in between UDT operations?

Captain Kaine: We usually stood watches. When anchored in an area subject to air attack, Andy I would often take all the night watches. Our enlisted men worked in their ratings to augment ship's company. A couple of them were good bakers, and the ships let them bake goodies for the crew at night.

We got along great with ship's company, and there really was no differentiation, except that the COs didn't like having our explosives on board.

I kind of got off the subject there.

Q: Well, we were going on our way to Borneo. I read someplace that Borneo was a perfect example of the use of UDT.

Captain Kaine: I don't know where that would be, unless it

F. R. Kaine #1 - 130

was at Balikpapan. That was one of the landings. I think we made three landings at Borneo. I wasn't in Balikpapan; one of the other units was. But in Sarawak we had very little to do other than get those LSTs off the beach that I told you about before. Borneo, to me, was the end of the world. God, that was terrible. That was the only place-- after being out there for two years, we all got terrible sunburns in Borneo, and the water coming out of the rivers was terrible. Oh, it was a mess. I thought it was a horrible place.

Q: But you did do some UDT work.

Captain Kaine: At Brunei Bay, and I can't remember what we did at Sarawak, if we got into anything that was interesting, other than reconnaissance work.

Q: Did you do any operations at night?

Captain Kaine: No. We had no reason to, and you have to be awfully lucky for night operations. We were not equipped; of course, you know at that time we didn't have radar, and we had no reason to operate at night, really. By operating in daylight you sometimes increase the hazard to the individual, but you also tremendously increase the probability of doing the job, so you were far better off in

F. R. Kaine #1 - 131

daylight operations. That may sound like a silly statement, but it's a true statement.

I think that any type reconnaissance or search or anything to do with water--you know, it gets awfully black down there. Light diffuses rapidly, especially if there's any particulation; it just dies very fast, and I think that to get positive results, you really have to work in the daytime. I know of no operations that went at night as far as underwater surveys or demolition work. I can't think of any anywhere.

Now I can see where you might do some sabotage work or stuff like that at night, but out and out demolition work, I see no reason for it, especially if you have an ocean to swim in. You've got lateral protection from waves, and the incompressibility of water also helps the swimmer. We did experiments, and I hope I'm right in saying that we used to be able to catch a .32-caliber bullet by hand under about two or three feet of water. It just tumbles and falls after so many feet of water. The same is true at a different distance for a .50 caliber. So there's a lot of protection in water.

If you've ever been on a beach trying to see something in the ocean, it's awfully hard, awfully hard. And when you swim, say, ten people off 1,000 yards of beach, and you spread them out, why, they're pretty hard to see, especially when you've got the up-and-down motion of the waves. So I think there's probably no reason to do reconnaissance work without the help of daylight.

Q: Now you also did planning on many other operations that you didn't participate in. Any comments that you should make about that?

Captain Kaine: No, other than that we more or less participated as a group in all the planning. We all went planning a thing, and I went to all of them. They gave me a task group number because I was senior by all of a day, or something like that. But all the planning was pretty much the same, and all the planning was, I thought, terrific, because the people there left it up to you and would be frank. They would say, "Well, you're going to do this work, and this is where we're going to do it, and tell me what you need to do." And you would tell them, and the only caveat they ever gave you was, "Just make sure you're right."

Q: Then go ahead.

Captain Kaine: Who can tell whether you're right or wrong in that kind of business? We were trained well enough to think we were right, and we always did think we were right.

F. R. Kaine #1 - 133

Q: Experience shows that you were.

Captain Kaine: Yes, well, not that that may be a good premise to go on, but it's a good premise when you were trained to the best of anybody's knowledge. Who knew any more about it than we did?

Q: That's right.

Captain Kaine: We got the best training we could from England and from the U.S. Army Rangers.

Q: So you would not necessarily go on all of them, but you were in on all of the planning.

Captain Kaine: Oh, no, no. I didn't go on all of them, God, no.

Q: Because it would have been way too many.

Captain Kaine: Another thing they used to think about out there was probability. One thing that we all shied away from like poison was that you never volunteered to take another guy's mission. You tried never to be a substitute for a person. Now, the difference is the volunteer would take this thing, and the other one would be forced into taking it. We tried to shy away from those things, because in everything that we watched, it seemed that everybody that got killed was volunteering to take someone else's place. Like wearing a black sock and a white sock, that was a little bit of a superstition type thing that you get into out there. I mean, if your turn came up, that's fine. But if it didn't come up and somebody wanted you to do something, you'd shy away from it like mad.

Q: Were there any casualties in the two years?

Captain Kaine: We didn't have a single casualty.

Q: Isn't that incredible?

Captain Kaine: No, didn't have any casualties. We had a couple of kids get hurt some. We had one kid that got gored by a fish. I don't know the names of fish, but there's a fish that looks like a good-size mackerel or one of that type. It's kind of a purple and yellow color, with a dorsal fin and a spine that comes up in front of the dorsal fin. We got into a school of these one time, and one of them gouged one of our kids, and he almost lost his leg. It immediately set an infection, and that was bad.

My buddy Andy went blind from coral poisoning.

F. R. Kaine #1 - 135

Q: For how long?

Captain Kaine: I guess about two weeks, something like that.

Q: It must have been a frightening experience.

Captain Kaine: Oh, terrible, terrible. There are a lot of supposedly bad things under the water, but we never ran into very many of them. We did run into the great white sharks off Australia and New Guinea and the Great Barrier Reef and up through that area. I don't mean to apologize for the great white shark; they'll eat anything. They'll eat each other and everything else. But for some reason, if you're working down there, they don't seem to bother you. I don't know why. We've had them swim over us many times.

Q: What were you doing?

Captain Kaine: Working on trying to blow up a reef or setting explosives or stuff like that. You're down there, and you know the sun is shining beautifully out there, and the shadow just goes over you very slowly. You notice everything underwater, and you're very alert underwater--I think possibly because it is not your medium, and there are a lot of things that can hurt you accidentally under there, too. There are little bitty fish out there called stone fish, no bigger than that and very deadly.

Q: About the size of a clam?

Captain Kaine: Yes, and very deadly, poisonous. Speaking of clams, there are giant clams out there that are quite big. You've seen them with a corrugated mouth.

Q: They make sinks out of them.

Captain Kaine: Yes, and they just close on you, even though they're not mad at you or anything.

Q: Did you ever see any of those?

Captain Kaine: Oh, yes, we saw all that stuff. Sure. The moray eels have a terrible reputation, but they are as scared of you as you are of them. They don't necessarily have anything against you; they just get frightened, and they grab and hold you. They have their tail locked inside a little cave, and they just hold you, and either you kill them or you drown, one or the other.

Q: When you were doing this, you always kept a knife with

F. R. Kaine #1 - 137

you, didn't you?

Captain Kaine: Yes, you always had knives and always had a buddy who swam along. But we never had any horribly bad experiences with anything like that.

Q: It's interesting when you say if you were working--I wonder if there's some instinct in that animal.

Captain Kaine: He knows you belong there, even though you don't look it, I guess.

Q: Yes, but that you're not there to hurt him. Is that possible?

Captain Kaine: I think it's quite possible, yes. Well, all the ones you hear about, you kind of explain it with everything under the sun, I guess. We've seen whales, blackfish, all kinds of eels.

Q: The greatest variety of fish is in the waters in that area, isn't it?

Captain Kaine: Oh, I believe so, yes. It's fantastic. It's probably the most fascinating area to be underwater.

Q: Did you see beautiful things?

Captain Kaine: Oh, gorgeous, absolutely gorgeous things. It got so great out there that we took a couple of our rubber boats and put glass bottoms in them and just would go cruising in the rubber boats and watch the sights. The color was unbelievable, absolutely. The fish are gorgeous colors, and the coral is all different colors, all different sizes, all different shapes, different names. They had brain coral, fan coral, stag coral, this coral, that coral; it's just exquisite beauty under there.

Q: So you saw the beautiful and the harmful.

Captain Kaine: Yes, and out there coral is live. Most of your coral in the Caribbean and down in the other areas is dying or dead. Out there it's all alive and growing, and it's far more colorful. The fish are so prolific and the distances you can see in the clear areas are just unbelievable. I mean, you can dive and see 80-100 feet with no sweat at all. It's just beautiful.

Q: Down?

Captain Kaine: Sure.

F. R. Kaine #1 - 139

Q: How could you do that?

Captain Kaine: It's just clear.

Q: It's that clear? I thought water below a certain level was dark.

Captain Kaine: Well, it gets darker as you go down, but a lot of the Pacific areas and the Mediterranean and some of the Caribbean areas, you can see 80 feet with no sweat. Beautiful. It's just clear, clear blue-green.

Q: Now how do you evaluate that whole experience in the Pacific with UDT? You are rapidly coming to the end of your tour out there, aren't you, when you are in Borneo?

Captain Kaine: When we get to Borneo, we've had it. I think it was a tremendous experience, and I think it did an awful lot of good. I think they accomplished a lot. I know all the commanders thought they did a lot, and we did a lot to ease the burden of getting people ashore. We did a lot of recovery work like the time I was telling you about, the anti-tank weapon.

I think the UDT made a big enough reputation with theater commanders in the various theaters they operated in that later on they were saved when there were threats of

F. R. Kaine #1 - 140

possibly doing away with them or cutting down. The good impressions stuck in enough people's minds that had a little horsepower so that they helped save them. Because immediately after any war, they start cutting back, and the first units to go are the little units, the specialty units. The fact that they did survive, I think, was due to other reasons, too, but there wasn't a bad mark against them in World War II. Anything they took on, they did.

Q: They were in Sicily as well as Normandy, am I correct, on the Atlantic side?

Captain Kaine: They were in Normandy. No, I don't think Sicily. I think Normandy was the only place that they used them.

Q: Is that so? How many UDT personnel were there at the end of World War II? Do you have any idea?

Captain Kaine: I'll give you a figure, and I think it's pretty close. I think there were 27 teams finally, in 1945.

Q: Times five?

Captain Kaine: No, now these were 80 men to a team. We

F. R. Kaine #1 - 141

got home in 1945, and we were the only units that were five-men units. Everybody else was a team.

Q: Oh, I see.

Captain Kaine: And I think one of the last team numbers was 27. I think that's the team Doug Fane got.* He was in team 27 or 25 or something like that.

Q: I had a figure of about 3,500 in both major theaters at the end of World War II. Would that be reasonable?

Captain Kaine: Probably close to it, close enough for government work. Because 27 teams--now that would be 12 officers and, say, 80 to 100 men. That's 2,700, and 13 times 27 would be another 200, so that's around 3,000 men.

Q: I like your phrase "close enough for government work." I hadn't heard that for a long time. So are we back to Borneo now?

Captain Kaine: Well, we're just about wrapped up. Borneo was the last place we went.

Q: And did you know ahead of time that that was going to

------
*Lieutenant Francis Douglas Fane, USNR.

be your last?

Captain Kaine: Oh, heavens, no. We got ordered back for cold-weather training. We had been in the Southwest Pacific for nearly two years, and we had orders to go to Seattle or someplace in the Northwest for cold-water training and underwater demolition. We were to have 30 days' leave en route. That's how we got back home.

Q: Where were you when you got your orders?

Captain Kaine: We were just back from Borneo. We were in the Philippines. Leyte had been secured then, and the fleet was basing out of Leyte. We got orders to a ship, and we got all ready to go, and one of our kids came down with malaria. His name was John Wilhide; I'll never forget him--a little kid.* He was from some small town in North Carolina. When we got our orders to go home, they took him and put him in a hospital on Samar. We were leaving from Samar, and none of these kids would go home without him.

Q: Did that include you?

Captain Kaine: Oh, God, we just spent two years together, from Florida on, and he was my boy; he was my troop. So we

_____
*Gunner's Mate Second Class John N. Wilhide, USNR.

didn't know what to do, but we knew we had to be on the ship by something like 7:00 or 8:00 o'clock at night. So we decided that we'd go over and say goodbye to Johnny, and when we'd go to walk out, we'd walk Johnny out with us. We'd bring some clothes, and they wouldn't know he was a patient, because they had him in a bed. The poor kid was so ill he couldn't have cared less whether he lived, died, or anything.

So we went over and snagged him out of the hospital and carried him up and put him into the sick bay on the ship. I thought, "Boy, I'll never get home now," because that doctor was so mad at me. The CO of the ship was going to throw us all in irons.*

Q: When did they discover him, before or after you sailed?

Captain Kaine: Just as we were leaving. We had dropped all the lines, and we were going, and we didn't turn him in until we got under way. They were mad; we had broken every Navy regulation we could.

Q: So it was their duty to be mad.

Captain Kaine: Yes, and he went up to the sick bay and got well in about five days, so we never heard any more about

---
*CO--commanding officer.

it.

Q: He was well by the time you docked?

Captain Kaine: Yes. I think what happened was he had just forgotten to take his atrabine, which was a quinine derivative that turned you yellow. It was terrible, terrible stuff. In the excitement of going home, or something, he had just forgotten to take his atrabine.

I can't remember how the hell we got home. We got into Hawaii on this troop transport, maybe an APA or something or a _President_ ship--I can't remember. Then I think we caught a destroyer out of Hawaii, and I think we caught a plane out of San Francisco to the East Coast. I think we had to lie; I can't remember what we did, but we did something terrible to get home, too. You couldn't get on an airplane at that time because everything was overcrowded.

Q: The war was over actually at this time?

Captain Kaine: No, the war wasn't over. It must have been in May of 1945. We finally got ourselves onto an airplane.

Q: I want to know how you did that.

F. R. Kaine #1 - 145

Captain Kaine: It was a matter of something like I walked up to the lady that was handling the seating. We had to tell them our name and rank and organization, and when she saw the organization that Andy and I were in, she said, "Oh, I have a brother in such and such a place."

And Andy said, "Oh, we know him. He's in the Philippines. We remember him. As a matter of fact, we had a drink with him last . . ."

"Oh, you did? Oh, you poor boys." And we went right onto the airplane.

Q: All six of you?

Captain Kaine: Yes, the whole bunch of us. She let us right on the airplane, and there were people all over the place trying to get seats. But this girl was so impressed that we knew this guy--I can't remember whether it was a husband or a brother. But it was probably the greatest thing that ever happened to us, because then we got home; we had 30 days' leave.

Q: Where was home?

Captain Kaine: Actually, the home I left from was in Vermont. I think Audrey met me in New York, and we went to my home in Vermont for a few days or something like that,

F. R. Kaine #1 - 146

and then we went to Montreal to visit her folks.

Q: Where did she stay during the time you were gone?

Captain Kaine: She stayed for a while with my folks and for a while with hers. And while I was gone, I had a son born. I think he was 16 months old when I came home.

We went to Canada, and we went on a picnic. While we were at the picnic, V-E Day was announced.* Our first thought was, "Oh, boy, we'll get out of the Navy now." But, no, we were still going to go fight the Japanese somewhere. So we still had orders to go back to Fort Pierce and from there to the state of Washington and cold-weather training. But after the leave was over, there was talk of possible lessening of the fighting in Japan and everything else. To make a long story short, we never did get to the Northwest for cold-water training. We got to Fort Pierce, and we stayed there for a little bit.

Q: The six of you still lived together?

Captain Kaine: Still there together, yes. I think all of them got out of the service about the same time. Well, there were a lot of enticements to stay in. They'd promote you to the next rank and all this stuff. But I opted to

---
*V-E Day--victory in Europe.

F. R. Kaine #1 - 147

get out, and they sent me up to Newport, Rhode Island, while they processed me to get out. I'll never forget--I was there for two or three weeks, and I got sick as a dog.

When I went in there, they said, "What can you do? What have you been doing all during the war?"

"I can blow down anything you want."

And they said, "Oh, you've been working underwater. Okay, well, we'll put you in charge of the swimming pool." So I was officer in charge of the swimming pool for about two weeks. And I got the flu, and I suppose coming back from a couple of years in the tropics and going up there, it was as cold and damp and miserable as a place can get in the fall. So I went to bed for about two or three weeks. Then I got out in December.* My leave carried me to January.

Q: I was going to ask you why you got out of the Navy, but now I don't need to.

Captain Kaine: Well, I didn't ever think I was in a career. And yet I had no other career that I really laid on. I had been in premed and studied a year of zoology and chemistry with a view of going forward in medicine, but by this time I had gotten sick of that. I think you did what you had to do, and it was time to get out and get on with

―――――――――
*Kaine reported to Newport on 20 October 1945 and was released from active duty on 10 December.

your life; maybe that was the sort of thing. So I got out. And we went back and lived in Vermont with my folks for a while.

Q: Your parents were still living?

Captain Kaine: Yes. We lived there for a few months, and then I went to work for a company there, Bradley Laboratories, which was a paint and lacquer company. I went in there on the GI Bill, sort of learn-a-trade type thing.* I forget what the salary was; they paid me maybe $50.00 a week plus the GI Bill. There were so many people getting out, and there were so few jobs at that time, that I was fortunate to even get anything, I guess. I had a couple of interviews in New York with advertising firms, to get into advertising or maybe copywriting or something like that. But I really didn't know what the hell I wanted to do. I don't think anybody did when they got out--or very few.

Q: Were there any vacancies for explosives experts?

Captain Kaine: None, none.

---

*The GI Bill of Rights, officially the Servicemen's Readjustment Act of 1944, was signed into law on 22 June 1944. It provided support for the education of all veterans with six or more months of honorable service after 16 September 1940.

Q: What could you say when they asked you what you did in the war?

Captain Kaine: See, this was still classified. You could say you were in a naval combat demolition unit, but you just couldn't willy-nilly tell them what was going on. I don't know when it was declassified, or if it was. I know nobody knew what it was. I mean, they looked at you like you were a stupid idiot when you told them.

Q: And it was referred to as the Navy's secret weapon.

Captain Kaine: Right, yes, yes. So, anyway, I went to work for this firm, and while there on this so-called training program, one of the salesmen quit, so I said, "Hey, I'll be your salesman." So I got a job as a salesman.

Q: You were still only 26 years old.

Captain Kaine: Yes, and I worked as a salesman with them and got to be sales manager and really kind of made too much money for the company. It was a family company, and I ended up making more than the vice president, who was the

F. R. Kaine #1 - 150

son of the firm's owner. I had a few lucky breaks, but I worked, though. I traveled 65,000 miles a year by car selling paints, lacquers, and synthetics. They had one speciality which was a lacquer they sold to pencil manufacturers. It was a very expensive and very specialized paint, and they were pretty good at it. I was doing well, but then they were getting worried about this salary I was getting. They had me on salary and commission, and I opted to go straight commission. The difference was tremendous, because you got a bigger commission when you paid your own expenses. But the money you pulled down was a lot better. So then they started cutting down my territory.

Q: Where did you go from them?

Captain Kaine: I worked for them from 1946 through 1949. It got untenable. They kept cutting the territory down and cutting the territory down, so I switched over and went to work for a car agency there in town with the idea of going to General Motors. I was offered a job by General Motors, but they said before they confirmed it, I had to clarify my status in the reserves. So I wrote in and told the Navy that I was thinking of going with this firm, and was there any chance of being called back on active duty? This was late 1950, and they said, "None whatsoever. We're not

F. R. Kaine #1 - 151

recalling any UDT people."

Q: Because Korea had already started then.*

Captain Kaine: Yes, yes. And I think this was September or October. Lo and behold, then I got a set of orders. I just ticked that computer, I think.

Q: You shouldn't have mentioned it.

Captain Kaine: So I got orders, and I came back in January 1951, and I was ordered to a naval beach group, which to me was a new command. It had been put together at the time to be kind of a grandfather for UDT, beachmasters, the Seabees, and boat unit. This was like an administrative headquarters for the smaller units.

Q: Where?

Captain Kaine: They had one on each coast, one in Coronado and one at Little Creek. I was assigned to the beach group at Little Creek as the communicator, as a matter of fact. Unfortunately, I didn't know a radio from a tape recorder. But I had a good friend in there who was a yeoman, and we

---

*The Korean War began on 26 June 1950, and many Naval Reservists were recalled to active duty in the following months.

F. R. Kaine #1 - 152

designed and schemed and wrote a letter to BuPers. It said that at the present time UDT was in sore need of experienced officers, and I had probably more experience than any of them on active duty, and what was I doing as a communicator in a beach group?

We had a commanding officer of the beach group who had an idiosyncrasy that he let all his paper work go until 4:30 in the afternoon, and then just signed everything off. So this yeoman slipped that in his pile with the proper endorsement on it, and he just signed it right off. Inside of about a month, I was transferred back to UDT, still at Little Creek.

Q: On the same base?

Captain Kaine: Yes, but he almost blew his mind when he found out about it.

Q: Did he ever know how it went through?

Captain Kaine: No, never did, never did. And I went as XO of UDT Four, and I was there for about two months, and I became CO of UDT Two.* At that time the UDT on the West Coast were heavily engaged in the operations of Korea. And while I was not privy to a lot of the action over there,

---
*XO--executive officer.

having not been there, I know that they took part in the amphibious landings at Inchon, and they did surveys and were doing a lot of work in the harbor and removing the reefs and were working off APDs at the time.

When the U.S. forces went into retreat, they helped blow up the harbor and all the facilities at Hungnam. They were used to some extent in blowing up railroad lines, one of the first places that they used them as a land force rather than purely a water force. They took and made up raiding parties of, I believe, UDT Five and Three and sent them inland. They blew up the railroad lines, and they blew up a couple of the railroad tunnels.

Q: How would they get there?

Captain Kaine: Hoof it, just walking in. They were not that far inland. They were right off the coast.

Q: Would they have their faces covered with camouflage?

Captain Kaine: Well, they used dark grease and stuff like that. It's the first time that UDT were used as a raider outfit and accomplished the missions of blowing them up. They blew up some bridges and dams, power lines, and they also used them in their regular mode of swimming-- destroying fish nets to have some effect on the economy of the fishermen on the coast.

At that time they had two UDTs on the East Coast and three on the West Coast. One, Three, and Five were the teams that were involved totally in Korea. And on the East Coast we had Team Two and Team Four. Just prior to this, the UDTs had become kind of lost souls as far as the Navy was concerned, because they had cut back prior to Korea from 27 teams at the end of World War II down to basically one team on the East Coast and one team on the West Coast.

Q: I had a count from someplace of about 500 during the Korean War.

Captain Kaine: That's about right. And at this time we're talking about now, during the Korean War, there were 500 men. They had five 100-man teams and had grown to a fairly firm position. This, again, was very typical of the survival problem in small units in the military, because right after World War II they went down to one team on each coast. Many of them became manned with people who were trained but inexperienced. When some of the experienced people started coming back in for Korea, the upshot of it was that they started fighting and using every possible employment to enhance the overview of the UDTs and their value to the Navy--to try and make sure that after the Korean War they weren't wiped out totally.

F. R. Kaine #1 - 155

This really became an all-day job, as much as fighting World War II or Korea, because depending on who was in the catbird seat in Washington, a lot of the thinking from the higher brass was that UDTs were a cocky, arrogant, brash group. There was some thinking from the people who worked with the UDTs in World War II and Korea that they were good at what they did and had a good reputation. So we had a real factional fight, whether UDT survived or whether it didn't survive. So we used to use every ploy that we could to enhance their picture.

It was really the first time we got involved in community relations, per se, or anything like that. We used to volunteer for lifeguard duties, volunteer to teach Red Cross instructors diving. By this time we had aqualungs, a standard piece of equipment, and the world was going crazy over diving and scuba gear and whatnot. So we would take our instructors and put them on loan to the Red Cross and on loan to firemen and on loan to anybody who would take them so we would get some good press.

The successful operation of the West Coast teams in Korea and the good press we were getting on the East Coast as community relations helped so that we kept our two teams on the East Coast and kept three teams occupied on the Korean front. When Korea closed down, instead of losing all the UDTs again, the West Coast went down to two teams, and the East Coast stayed at two teams. Then the West

Coast got involved with big community relations projects and making movies. They made a couple of movies; one of them was *Frogman*. And they assisted in the making of several others, such as *Away All Boats*, just looking to improve the image.

Q: Did UDT personnel have an aversion to being called frogmen?

Captain Kaine: At one time they didn't like the name, and I can't for the life of me remember what caused that, except that the original British counterparts of UDTs were called frogmen. And whether it was that they didn't want to be associated with the British name, I have no idea. Yet there was a lot of animosity towards the word "frogman."

Q: What did they want to be called?

Captain Kaine: Just underwater demolition people. Some of it was silly; they may have thought the term frogman was degrading. I don't know, but frogman it became, and it became very popular, especially after the movie came out, *The Frogman*.

Q: It became a romantic group.

F. R. Kaine #1 - 157

Captain Kaine: That's right. So from then on, we had a constant fight over training. It was not an out-and-out fight, but it was a matter of survival and a matter of philosophies, really, within the Navy as to whether the UDT survived or not. We took the offensive, and we added to the capabilities. We tried to add tremendously to the capabilities: we borrowed broken-down Italian midget submarines; we got a British midget submarine; and we trained the people in the operation of these things. We got interest rallied enough to try and develop our own midget submarines for use by UDT.

Q: What happened to that?

Captain Kaine: They're still going; they still have them. We didn't get them for a long, long time, though. But everything was a constant scrap and hassle.

Q: That's kind of tiring, isn't it, exhausting?

Captain Kaine: Oh, it's terrible, terrible. Everything that we could possibly dream up as an added capability, we would add on. I think in the early 1950s we just went out of our way, especially in the way of good press. Body hunts--any time anybody was lost; any time anybody was thought drowned, we'd send people in and scout lakes or rivers. We had several incidents there in St. Thomas, where we used to do training. Several people were lost, and we were fortunate enough to find them unharmed, and that led to good publicity.

F. R. Kaine #2 - 159

Interview Number 2 with Captain Francis R. Kaine,
U.S. Naval Reserve (Retired)

Place: Coronado, California

Date: Sunday, 8 November 1981

Interviewer: Commander Etta-Belle Kitchen,
U.S. Navy (Retired)

Q: We were talking yesterday about your first duty assignment after you went back on active duty. If you'll continue on.

Captain Kaine: Okay. When I first came back on active duty, I went, as I told you before, to the beach group and managed to get to UDT Four as executive officer. The commanding officer of UDT Four at the time was Dave Saunders, who had been with me in bomb disposal for a short time while I was there and had gotten into UDT late during the war after a tour of duty on a carrier.*

When I reported to UDT as XO, we found out that I had an awful lot more experience than any of the officers there. Most of them, if they had been in World War II, had just been in on the tag end of it and had not been deployed. In the interim, after the close-down of World War II, the underwater demolition teams had really come on hard times in that they weren't a supportable entity in peacetime. They had dwindled down, and the training had deteriorated to a certain extent. Although it was
_____
*Lieutenant Commander David G. Saunders, USNR.

basically the same, it was not carried out with the same gusto, and the people that were supplying the money weren't as financially interested in training frogmen for peacetime.

Q: What had happened to Draper Kauffman in the meantime?

Captain Kaine: Draper had gone on to bigger and better things. He had gone into the regular Navy and went to sea. He had become skipper of a destroyer first, and after staff duty in Washington he became skipper of the Helena; then he went back to Washington and carried on his career from there.*

Q: You probably missed him, with the zest and the gusto that this outfit had had originally.

Captain Kaine: That's right. Dave Saunders and I decided that what we would try to do was weed out what deadwood we had accumulated, where possible, and give these guys more reason for living than they had. So that's why I say we put a big emphasis on PR and deployments; we looked for deployments for these people. We found them. We had, of course, the Korean War, which added a lot of gusto to it

---

*The details of Admiral Kauffman's post-World War II service are covered in his own oral history.

F. R. Kaine #2 - 161

and helped the training phase of it and everything else. But that was really a West Coast war as the Navy visualized it from a UDT point of view, so that East Coast UDT were not really allowed to participate in that.

It's kind of hard to believe now, but at that time—other than a couple of personnel transfers—nobody from the East Coast UDTs got to get into the Korean War. As a result of that, we had to look to other places to deploy our people. So we got involved in things like cold-water training, which was a point that was brought up at the end of World War II. They knew we were qualified in warm water, but they were very interested, so we kind of resurrected that thing.

At the same time, the DEW Line radar sites and protective umbrella were becoming big things.* Through the good graces of some of our admirals, we were able to convince the necessary people that they needed UDTs up on that. The Antarctic trips were going on, and we convinced them that they needed UDTs up on that. They actually did, and they had a lot of good experimentation for diving equipment and whatnot. So the UDT people went down on those Antarctic trips, and we deployed them to the Arctic, and we had a continuing commitment to the Mediterranean.

---

*DEW—distant early warning. A number of radar sites were constructed in the Arctic to provide advance notice of Soviet bombers approaching the United States.

Q: What would they actually do in the Arctic and Antarctic?

Captain Kaine: They were testing equipment. They did diving, checking the type of ice and current flows. They salvaged equipment that became mired in the water and stuff like that.

Q: That could have been very dangerous because of the temperature of the water, I would think.

Captain Kaine: Absolutely, absolutely. And when we got into these things, we had to kind of parallel them with experimentation on how to keep these people warm and also how to keep the equipment from freezing.

The aqualung had just become a Navy piece of equipment in 1949, and we didn't know all the things we should know about that in cold water. So we found an old refrigeration plant on the naval amphibious base, and we got the experimental diving unit and some people from the Bureau of Medicine interested. We had a big tank put in there that we could refrigerate down to about 28-30 degrees. And we got some people from an experimental unit in Rhode Island that was under the cognizance of BuShips; it was a naval research unit, really.* They put together these tests

---

*BuShips--Bureau of Ships.

for our people as to how to keep warm in the water and to extend time in cold water. In 28-degree water, with the equipment that we had, you had about one or two minutes that you were effective. As part of this experimentation, they'd put people in the water, and they'd study where the greatest heat loss was.

Q: In your body?

Captain Kaine: In a swimmer, yes. They found out it was right through the top of his head. They rigged up a thing that looked like an old scouring pad, but it was brass-colored. They hooked wires up to it and rigged it to a little battery so that it just kept warm and kept that right on the fellow's head while he was in the water. Through a series of experiments, that equipment increased his time in the water ultimately up to about 45 minutes in the same degree water.

Q: That's incredible, isn't it?

Captain Kaine: Yes. They found out that they had to build special enclosures for the wrists, the ankles, and around the neck, because those are places where you immediately become numb in the water if you don't have proper circulation. So what they did was build big O-rings with

F. R. Kaine #2 - 164

rubber bands, and they'd detach the gloves from the rubber suits that we would wear and then put them on with this O-ring so you had no pressure on the feet, ankles, or neck. That's why most of today's rubber suits have detached feet and hands. You put them on if you need them, and you don't put them on if you don't need them.

Q: Did you go on any of these?

Captain Kaine: We went on most of the things. I didn't go to the Antarctic. They'd never let any of the COs go there, because it was a six-month detachment away from the place. But we made trips to the Arctic; we made trips to the Mediterranean; and we spent a lot of time in the Caribbean with the training units.

Q: I'm not sure if you're aware that you very rarely use the word "I." You very rarely say, "I did this." You say "we."

Captain Kaine: I don't know where it comes from, other than maybe the fact that I'd been part of a team for so long that I think of it as "we" all the time, because we never operated singularly. Now that you mention it, almost everything that I did, we did, because wherever you operated in UDT or any of the units out there, you were

F. R. Kaine #2 - 165

always operating with someone. You and your exec are usually far closer than most COs and execs, because you've been operating the same field, and it's just a way of operation, I guess, and you learn to talk that way.

Q: I think it's worth commenting on.

Captain Kaine: I had never thought about that before you mentioned it.

Q: If you want to carry it a step further, I suspect that that is also a good ploy for personnel relations. I doubt if you ever had any personnel problems, did you?

Captain Kaine: Other than behavioral things, we very rarely had personnel problems. That was one of our big drawing cards, I think--that everybody in UDT more or less got along. We had a few bad apples along the way, of course; everybody does. But primarily our discipline problems were very, very low. We had extremely low accident rates; we had no absenteeism at all in the military. As a matter of fact, we used to laugh when people were complaining of absenteeism and people going over the hill. I don't think we ever had anybody go over the hill that I can recall.

F. R. Kaine #2 - 166

Q: It's almost a joint venture, of course. Being few was one advantage.

Captain Kaine: That's right. Small-unit operations are great that way, because if your screening system is any good, you end up with good people. Of course, we had the best screening system in the world.

Q: That's very interesting, and now we'll go on. Could you identify when you were speaking of UDT Unit Two and 21?

Captain Kaine: We were stationed at Little Creek, and I was XO of Team Four for a few months, and then I went over as CO of UDT Two, which later became UDT 21.* I forget what year it was; it was later on.

Q: And you had spoken of meeting your commitments in the Arctic and Antarctic, and then you were approaching the Mediterranean, I believe.

Captain Kaine: We also had a constant deployment in the Mediterranean for the amphibious forces. At that time they used to deploy for, I believe, six months at a time, and they rotated. At one time we sent a whole team, I guess,

---

*Kaine was executive officer of UDT Four from October 1951 to May 1952 and commanding officer of UDT Two/UDT 21 from May 1952 to June 1958.

to the Mediterranean. Then, as we built our commitments to other things, we cut that back to a partial unit so we could supply the others. In other words, we had commitments in the Arctic, Antarctic, Mediterranean, and Caribbean simultaneously. Plus we had training commitments every year; we used to take a cadre of people through the underwater phase of the training.

The way our training worked, all our new people went through the underwater demolition team training program at the U.S. Navy Amphibious School. Until 1951 or 1952, the underwater demolition teams did all their own training. They trained all the new people. This was not a bad idea, and it was a thing that they were forced to do. There was no training unit or activity that could give them the training. The fact that the UDT personnel were all trained for World War II left them a cadre that could train the new ones. So for a number of years after World War II--until about 1952, I'll say--we did our own training of UDT.

In 1952, I think, they came up with an idea, and the amphibious schools were formed that would do all the school training for anybody in the amphibious force. With that concept, the underwater demolition teams set up billets at the amphibious school, and we filled those billets with people from the teams, and they became the amphibious school's training group. They would train all the neophytes in the UDT, and then they would turn them over to

F. R. Kaine #2 - 168

the teams after their basic training. We would take them once a year to St. Thomas in the Virgin Islands and put them through what we called the scuba training, underwater training.

Q: You are saying "we." Did you go personally?

Captain Kaine: I would go or Saunders would go; one of the teams' COs always went.

Q: How large were the teams at this stage of the game?

Captain Kaine: At this time there were about 13 officers and 80 men. They had all gone to the big-team concept, and superimposed on the two teams was a unit command. It was called Underwater Demolition Unit, and the senior skipper of UDT was the commander of the unit. He usually had a staff of maybe a yeoman, a storekeeper, something like that, and he would deploy them down with the training unit when they went south, and either he or I would go, as well as a cadre from what we had when we went to the big-team concept.

We also went to a platoon concept within the teams. We had so many operating platoons. Then we also had administrative divisions, too, which were your supply, admin section, medical, etc. One of the platoons was

F. R. Kaine #2 - 169

subops, submarine operations, because at the time we were also training to operate from submarines as a method of entry into a country or for sneak attacks or whatever. This subops platoon was usually the biggest one of the teams, and they were all qualified divers and instructors and water safety people. They were the basic unit that would deploy to St. Thomas to train the people in diving.

Q: There was an article in Collier's in 1955. A man named Bill Stapleton wrote about your training experiences in St. Croix, St. Thomas.*

Captain Kaine: I remember the incident. Somebody thought they found the Monitor of Monitor-Merrimack fame down somewhere off the coast of North Carolina. Bill Stapleton, I think, was then a reporter for Life magazine.

Q: In 1955 he was with Collier's.

Captain Kaine: Okay, and before that he was with Life, and he was a photographer. He was a famous photographer at the time. To show you how we had to operate--he had this story he was dying to do, and he wanted some UDT people to go with him. ell, the Navy wouldn't let us go. We couldn't just up and go off with a Life magazine photographer

---
*Bill Stapleton, "Navy Frogmen--Top Skin-Divers of Them All," Collier's, 27 May 1955, pages 84-89.

anywhere. So we put our fiendish minds to work and said, "Well, how the hell can we do this?" And finally we decided that if we could get Life magazine to sponsor the expenses, maybe they'd let us go.

And Stapleton was no dummy. He said, "Well, if Life's going to underwrite this, how about teaching me how to use an aqualung so I can take some pictures?" So we trained him as a diver, and he underwrote the experiment, and we sent a bunch of divers to go down there and look for the Monitor, which we didn't find, incidentally. I understand that since then they have found it.* The upshot of that was that we became very good friends. Stapleton has always been a good friend of UDT, and we've gotten a lot of publicity out of it. We've met an awful lot of nice people over the years doing things like this.

Q: He quotes you in the article. I'll read the quotes, and you can tell me if it's good or not. Because he had observed all the training and how actually rugged it was, and he quoted you as saying, "When a man is ordered to cover three or four miles underwater, packing heavy equipment, to handle a very technical job at the other end, he's got to like his work or he won't be able to do it.

---

*On 7 March 1974, an oceanographic researcher at Duke University reported the discovery of the wreckage of the Monitor on the floor of the Atlantic off Cape Hatteras, North Carolina. The Union ironclad warship of Civil War vintage sank in a gale on 31 December 1862.

Working underwater is tough. But the real UDT men love the work, and you couldn't pry them loose from it."

Captain Kaine: That's true; that's true. And that's one thing that to me is evident. Nobody would do this work if they didn't love it. It's hard, and it's dirty, and you're cold all the time when you're working in the water.

Q: Why would you love it?

Captain Kaine: Well, it's exciting, and it's different, and it's challenging all the time. You're running into something all the time you're underwater. To give you an example, the fleet developed a counter-swimmer attack doctrine, and we used to train the fleet by running sneak attacks. For years we'd send detachments, and this is the sort of deployment I keep telling you about that we did to survive, really. We'd send detachments to Newport, Rhode Island, where they had ships anchored in Narragansett Bay. We'd send them to Boston and a lot of them to Norfolk, of course. We'd send them wherever the Navy anchored a few ships and wanted to practice counter-swimmer attacks. And we would try to have the swimmers sneak up on the ships and try to get aboard. It was just super, because we got aboard almost every ship we went after.

Q: Sounds like playing pirates.

Captain Kaine: It was. And these challenges kept these guys excited. Admiral Fahrion was a great booster of UDT.* He used to run this sneak attack training on his ships as often as he could. I remember one year in the early 1950s when he had a big operation. They gave us a safe haven to operate with the beach jumpers out in the roads off Virginia Beach or off Norfolk. Now the beach jumpers were an electronic deception unit, and they could manipulate. They'd put up chaff and stuff like that to distract your radar. They could put out false messages, and they were pretty handy with electronics.

They allowed the beach jumpers and the UDTs to operate together against the amphibious force on this operation. This is a little bit ahead of my sequence maybe, but we were using midget submarines, trying to develop some of the techniques that the Italians and British had. Using the beach jumpers for tactical deception, and using the midget submarines and using swimmers and the fastest boats we could find, we potentially sank so many of the amphibious force that they called off the exercise.

Q: That should have proved something to someone, I would

---
*Vice Admiral Frank G. Fahrion, USN, Commander Amphibious Force Atlantic Fleet, 1952-56.

think.

Captain Kaine: Oh, yes. Admiral Fahrion took that and used that as an example for his readiness report and told them what a terrible state of readiness they were in. And we operated at that time around the clock. Oh, I forget the numbers, but it was fantastic. It even got to be a little bit of fun and games, because we'd go aboard the ship and watch the security guy coming around the deck. We'd wait until he went by and then write in the log that UDT had been there--just to add a little fun to it.

Q: Now did you personally go on any of these?

Captain Kaine: Oh, yes, I used to go on a lot of them.

Q: The look on your face now suggests that you enjoyed it.

Captain Kaine: Yes, it was a lot of fun, a lot of fun. We used to run those operations night and day, week after week, there at Norfolk. It became part of, I think, refresher training for the ships. I remember that we got aboard one ship and asked the messenger to go get the skipper and tell him that his ship was sunk. He said, "My God, I just got it this morning." He had just taken command that day.

Q: A not very long command.

Captain Kaine: No, but he had the right attitude; it was a training thing, really.

Q: How would they board these ships, climb up the side?

Captain Kaine: Oh, amphibious ships were great. On LSTs we used to go right over the stern anchor. It had a protective barring that came right down to the water, and we'd just climb right up the back of it. On others they'd go up the anchor chain. A lot of them had their gangways out. And all we had to do was to get to the side of the ship and call up. If it was a big ship, you'd just call up to somebody on deck and tell them that the swimmer had attached a limpet mine to the side or something.

Q: Because you could have destroyed it.

Captain Kaine: Sure. But you were interested in the midget submarine business.

We had one of the Italian midgets; we called them pigs. They were an open-cockpit-type submarine; they call them wet submarines. It was probably 25 feet long, I guess, and the whole nose of it was a demolition charge. There was a three-and-a-half or four-foot-long charge that probably weighed in the vicinity of a couple hundred pounds. This was one of the Italian midget submarines that they used during the war. I don't really remember where we got it, but we must have got it through the naval research units that picked it up from the Italians. It had two seats that you could ride two people in, and you kind of sat almost astride the thing like a big cigar, and it had a little windshield or hydro-shield in front of it. We also had a British Wellman, which was a little closed submarine. It looked like a little cigar with a hat right in the middle of it, and I forget the propulsion in that, but it was battery powered. The open Italian submarine was electrical--battery powered.

Q: Pardon me, but how can a submarine be open?

Captain Kaine: Well, the battery compartments and the proper things were closed in within the submarine shell itself, but where the people rode was open.

Q: Was it a suicide mission if they were on it?

Captain Kaine: Not necessarily, but in the Italian Navy they pretty much were, because they could never get any cooperation with the Air Force to help them out with diversions or anything. A lot of them weren't, though, and we had a good friend named Roberto Frasseto who became one of our advisers in UDT; he was one of these Italian "midget chariot drivers," as they called them. They called them chariots, and if I may divert a minute, the Italians had this organization that was really made up of some of the aristocracy in Italy during the war; it was a volunteer thing. They were within the Navy but used their own money to develop this cadre of midget submarines.

Q: That's interesting.

Captain Kaine: They had this very elite, in quotes, group, and they were set up to sink British ships, to sink any ships they could find. Roberto went on one of these missions and mined one of the British destroyers and sank it. But he was captured, and, really, you're almost always captured in one of these things. The warhead was the front end of the submarine, and it was attached magnetically or with big lanyards. You could strap it to the ship, and the charge was such that it was anywhere from 200 to 500 pounds; it was designed to break the back of the ship, really.

But generally, if these people got in, they quite often didn't get away unless they could get ashore somewhere, because these boats were slow. I think the Italian boat would have made probably maximum five knots and underwater maybe two or three. So it's hard to get away with that type of vehicle. But he was captured, and he was also hurt. If I recall correctly, when he went to get away, he didn't get away far enough. The ship blew up, and the detonation injured him, too. He was taken prisoner anyway and spent a long time in hospitals.

Later, when he got through his internment, he went back to Italy and got what artwork he had in his family and came to New York and became an art dealer. He immediately went broke and got employment with the American government as a tests and evaluation person for the UDT teams. He'd spent a long time in this underwater business, and we put him to work in our subops platoon. He used to do things like test and evaluate all the new equipment we got, such things as the various fins and rubber suits. He was with us for years and a very, very delightful guy.

Q: You were saying the British also had a midget submarine.

Captain Kaine: The British had a two-man midget submarine, and this was one that we also used on these sneak attacks with Admiral Fahrion. This was another way of keeping these people going and developing capabilities. One of the things I'd dearly love to point out is that in training the UDT people, you develop terrific kids. You start from every mother's son, ordinary sailors, or whatever you want to call them when they come in. Then when they go through training, they develop tremendously, physically. They also develop in confidence. And from the 1950s to today, the things that we had those boys doing grew progressively from year to year--different training and different schooling and whatnot--until they're what are called today full-fledged SEALs. It's just unbelievable.

Q: When we get into the SEALs, I'd like to have you go back and tell all those facets, because it's intriguing.

Captain Kaine: In something like this tape you can probably see it better than people realize it in life, because the training cycle from a neophyte frogman to an accomplished SEAL is a period of years, and it's not really obvious. Whereas in a compression like this is, you can point it out.

Q: I'm thinking of SEAL as being initially with the Vietnam experience. Is that correct?

Captain Kaine: This was another facet--that we used to give more and deeper capability to the UDTs and make them more essential. Another thing was that, with the beginning of the training by the amphibious school, the training side of the UDT business became more defined, became more definite. It was no longer suffering with the whims of whoever was CO. There were some indications that if you had a good CO, you had a good training class; if you didn't have a good CO, you didn't have a good training class. So the advent of the amphibious schools and the formalizing of the training staff for UDT ended all that, whether there was good or not in it. We standardized the curriculum, and we standardized the tour of duty for the instructors. Everything was a BuPers control.

One of the first people I recall who really worked hard at that was a guy named Al Hodge who happened to go through training when I came back on active duty.* I believe I was then running the underwater phase of his training in St. Thomas, and later he was one of the men that really helped set up this training business over at the school. And it's been there ever since the early 1950s and done a good job. Hodge now lives in Coronado and is a retired captain, as a matter of fact.

So our training became formalized at this period in history. We had a standard program at the school, and then we polished them off in St. Thomas in the underwater phase, which we only ran once a year. They ran maybe three new

---

*Lieutenant Alan G. Hodge, USNR.

F. R. Kaine #2 - 180

UDT classes a year. So we'd hold two classes, and we'd look for other training for them to get into. That's when we started with the parachuting. We did and didn't see a potential in the parachute business. We got so we could argue either way--depending on whom we were talking to--good, bad, or indifferent.

Q: Whether it was to your benefit or not.

Captain Kaine: That's right. However, we did sell it to the Bureau of Personnel as another mode of entry for UDT. It was strange, because, looking back, we saw that as a mode of entry which we knew they'd never use. With the amount of equipment that they had to handle, there was just absolutely no reason for them to jump a UDT. But when we kind of glamorized it to sell it, we were really describing a SEAL operation, and we didn't know it, because, hell, this was 12-15 years ahead of time. So we actually borrowed, unknowingly, from the SEAL bag of tricks to sell them on the use of parachuting school for UDT. I think it was 1954 that they really gave us permission to keep sending people through the parachute school. So we'd send as many a quota as we could.

Q: Was that parachute training voluntary?

Captain Kaine: When we started it was. Now it's part of the training program. After that, we got into a kind of reciprocal agreement with the Green Berets. The Green Berets were forming up then. They were the Army's super elite force then; they were classified as such and thought they were. It was a good outfit, but they decided about that time that they needed to be trained in underwater stuff. I forget how they managed it, but they got quotas, and we started training them in underwater demolition work.

As an aside to that, we got a standard quota at jump school so that we could get everybody to go through. Up until that, it was hit or miss; if they had a vacancy, you could put one or two guys in. But from then on, they maintained a quota for the UDT, so we ultimately got almost everybody in UDT trained in parachuting. This is what I was telling you--you're building quite a man now over the remaining years. You take a young sailor, and you make him a diver and a demolition expert, and now we're throwing in parachuting. And as we go along, you'll see that we add a lot of capabilities to these young people.

The parachuting was another capability, and it gave us another school to send the kids to. At the time, the Bureau of Personnel thought it would be good to publicize the fact that they were parachutists, so we got a lot of mileage, publicity-wise, out of that. A few years before that, we had sent a young officer down there to try it out and see what it was like, and the bureau gave us hell for sending him down there. So it flipflops on you all the time.

Just about this time, too, we were fighting like mad to get some representation in Washington, a billet somewhere. While we didn't get a billet, we got next to some of the people in the Bureau of Ships, in particular a civilian in the bureau who thought we were great people. His name was Hiram Draper, and he kept us abreast of all the goings on in Washington from his desk. He was in procurement and design and had a very active desk. We needed a lot of things that we didn't have. We were poor, and we didn't have an allowance list, per se, and we didn't have a budget, per se. We were really scroungers or scavengers, and we were good scroungers.

Q: I bet.

Captain Kaine: He helped us develop an allowance list and told us how to go about getting on the budget and really educated us in things we just up to that time pooh-poohed and said, "Let somebody else worry about it." But nobody else worried about it. He really kind of brought us up in the world and got us a little representation in Washington. He'd look out for us equipment-wise, and before you know it, we had an officer in his shop that was a UDT training person who could look out for us.

By this time, we had established a good rapport with the amphibious forces on both coasts, and they were all for us, because we were doing a lot of work with them and doing all their landings and reconnaissances and putting on demonstrations for visiting foreign dignitaries and all this stuff.

There were a lot of incidents that occurred that kept us in a rather dull time. Right after Korea, when they were cutting down and everything, they cut off one team on the West Coast, and they cut them back two teams. They were threatening to cut us back to one team, and they did cut us back to one team. But because of this little guy in Washington and the man we put up there, we were allowed to keep the same number of men but go to one team. So we had this one whopping big team, and it was just an exercise in paper all the time. We weren't cut out for that, but we were learning fast. By that time we had our allowance list for equipment, so we kept all the equipment, and we were in pretty good shape.

So we went along like that, and we had good relations with Admiral Fahrion and Admiral Sabin and Admiral Rivero in that same era.* We kept the thing going and developed these various capabilities and operations. By diversifying

---

*Vice Admiral Lorenzo S. Sabin, Jr., USN, whose oral history is in the Naval Institute collection; Rear Admiral Horacio Rivero, Jr., USN, whose oral history is in the Naval Institute collection.

so much and covering all these operations, it seemed like we were always getting inquiries from Washington about some one of these operations: the Antarctic, the Arctic, the Caribbean, the Mediterranean, the midget submarines, or something like that. So we kept involved.

Then they decided along in there to redo the diving tables, which were a big thing. It was smart, because while we were diving, we really didn't know a lot about diving. I had gone to diving school in 1951 or 1952 and had taken a short course in hard-hat diving to learn the physiology of diving. Of course, I had been qualified in oxygen diving by my own standards for years, since World War II, and on the aqualung since it came out in 1949, but really without knowing a lot.

So we started working with the experimental diving unit, which was the authority then for diving in the Navy. We got a lot of good training from them, and they taught us all we should have known for the last ten years--things that we had been getting away with because we were ignorant--and brought us up to speed in the diving area. They taught us all the physiology we should know.

One thing they taught us was that we really should have a doctor in the team. We had corpsmen, but we went to work then, and I forget exactly how we did it, but we got a doctor assigned to the unit. We rarely had anything that

F. R. Kaine #2 - 185

resembled a diving accident in all that time. Then after we got the doctor, it seemed like we had a rash of them, but none serious. The doctors were a godsend. They took care of all our medical problems, and they did all our physical exams. They really made us a good operating outfit, because with the coming of the doctor, he looked at our hospital corpsmen allowance and found out that we should have about ten more than we had because of the deployments. So he upped that, and everything was building all the time.

Q: But wasn't that due to you and your evaluation of what was needed?

Captain Kaine: Oh, yes, well, we were figuring all this out, things that we didn't have that the guy across the street had. It was like keeping up with the Joneses, only we were primarily an operating thing. We operated all the time, and we didn't know the finer things of administration, and we weren't interested in personnel.

Q: You probably wished you didn't have to be.

Captain Kaine: That's right, and we'd just try to keep away from it. But we also realized that we had to grow up.

F. R. Kaine #2 - 186

Captain Kaine: You're always saying "we" again. You were the CO, so you were the man who did it.

Captain Kaine: Yes, but I did it with the other COs, see. We had to grow up and get respectability in order to survive in this elite organization called the Navy. So that was the start of our climb back. As we progressed over those years, we developed a couple of billets in the detailer section of BuPers, smart youngsters who could look out for developments and what we needed. We needed money-- old money that wasn't used up that we could put our hands on. Where else did we have billets? I don't think we had one in CNO yet, but, anyway, it was a time to become respectable, post-World War II, post-Korea, and try and build up what we had.

As we worked at it up through 1958, we were preoccupied with this stuff, as well as committed to all the operations in the various theaters to build this up. We got a lot of help from the amphibious force. They didn't want to lose us, and they didn't want us to dwindle down any more. As a result, whenever we had a problem, we'd go to them, and they'd try to help.

I'll give you one specific. You know Admiral Sabin.* We had a deployment going to the Arctic, and it was going to work for a rear admiral up there on the DEW

---

*Vice Admiral Sabin was Commander Amphibious Force Atlantic Fleet from May 1956 to November 1957.

Line project. I'll leave his name out of it, because I think he's still around. But we used to figure out exactly what our people could do when we'd have so many deployed. We'd deploy a unit that could do the specific job as best described by whoever wanted them. So we sat down and figured out what this guy needed and told him exactly what we were sending and how to use them. We deployed them, and I got a message from this Admiral So-and-so: "Unless otherwise advised, I'm cutting your units in half, deploying this here and that there."

And I went back with a message: "Recommend you do not deplete the units any further. These units were specifically designed to accomplish the task that was outlined in your so-and-so."

He came back with a message: "Dear So-and-so. Appreciate it and dividing units anyway. Signed Admiral Whoopdedoo."

I thought, "Well, there's one I lost."

With that I got a call from a major. He said, "Admiral Sabin would like to see you in his office immediately."

I thought, "Oh, God. What did I do?"

Q: Had you known him up until then?

Captain Kaine: Oh, yes, I had known him, but I had known a lot of individual problems with UDT too. So I thought, "What the hell did we do now?"

So I went over, and he said, "Well, Kaine, I see you're having a little conversation with Admiral Whoopdedoo up there."

And I said, "Yes, sir."

He said, "What's the problem?"

So I said, "Well, we designed these particular units to do exactly what he said, and now he's splitting them. And my worry is that when he splits up personnel, he limits the capability of the equipment that goes with them. If you've got five men that can operate so much equipment and you take two of them, they don't necessarily have the capability of operating with split equipment."

And he says, "Well, I've always wanted to try this. You see those three stars up there? Let's see what three stars can do?"

So I said, "Fine."

And he said, "You're sure you're ready?"

And I said, "Yes, I'm ready, all right."

He said okay, and so he sent a message to this admiral: "You will comply with this operational commitment as designed." And that was the end of it. But that's the kind of guy he was. He was very interested in us, very alert to make us respond properly to protocol and Navy regs and all that stuff. He made you spit and polish, whereas we had a tendency to be in shorts and bare feet or something. He always was right on the ball.

Q: I thought he was a great man. He is a great man. I'm glad to say he still is.

Captain Kaine: Oh, I think he is, too. He was one of our big benefactors. Fahrion and he, and there have been a few real good ones in line.

Q: You remember we hadn't finished, I don't believe, with what you had the miniature submarines for. What did your group do, develop them to be used?

Captain Kaine: Yes, we developed them to be used.

Q: Does the U.S. have any?

Captain Kaine: Oh, yes.

Q: Due to your development?

Captain Kaine: Yes. We had them there, and we, in our ignorance, thought they were great. In reality, they were far ahead of their time in a lot of ways. It's comparable

F. R. Kaine #2 - 190

to what I told you about ordnance in the start of the bombs and the fuzes and how at one time they were so unsafe and they made them over-safe. With this submarine thing, you'll see a likeness.

We had a hell of a time with these Italian submarines, because they were wired like spaghetti; it was just something else. The English boat was good, but it was a three-knot boat, and it was just an awkward thing. We studied these things, and we operated with them over a period of two or three years and learned all we could learn about them. Then we went to the Navy and said, "Well, why don't we design or get somebody smarter than us to design a good one?" We sold this deal. We sold the idea of them designing a midget submarine for UDT, and the premise was that the Italians--with as little cooperation as they had and as little Navy as they had--sunk over 500,000 tons of shipping or some ridiculous number with these little pig boats. And when you start flashing these numbers around, it gives you a really added capability. So the Navy bought it.

In 1954 they laid the keel for a midget U.S. submarine.* I have a report on it right here. My exec went to the keel-laying, because I was down in St. Thomas at the time, and then we followed it up. We stayed with

---

*This was the X-1, the U.S. Navy's only midget submarine. The keel was laid 8 June 1954. The craft was launched 7 September 1955 and went into service on 7 October 1955.

it, as a matter of fact. The outfit that designed and built it was Fairchild Aviation, an aircraft company. This thing was developed and built, and it was a beauty. It was just a great thing.

Q: Does that document you have show dimensions and capabilities?

Captain Kaine: Yes, it was a seven-foot beam; 49 feet, seven inches in length; and it displaced 30 tons, 35 tons submerged. It was designed to have a surface speed of six knots and eight knots underwater. It would run on snorkel 1,300 miles and submerged another 250 on batteries. So it gave it a real good range.

Q: How many personnel operated it?

Captain Kaine: I think it could carry six passengers and it was operated by two men. But now let me tell you the irony of this. It was such a good submarine that the submarine force grabbed it and wouldn't give it to us.

Q: Oh, no.

Captain Kaine: Yes. It was designed to carry UDT swimmers as a method of entry. But we never, never got to use it.

F. R. Kaine #2 - 192

Q: Would they just use their own submarine people to run it?

Captain Kaine: Yes, they said it was a submarine and not a submersible, and nobody but the submarine force could operate a submarine, so they took over.

Q: They didn't even get UDT people to . . .

Captain Kaine: Oh, we operated from it a couple of times, but to all intents and purposes they took it. I think they used it as a target or an exercise submarine to chase and hunt.

Q: And what's the status of this midget submarine as of today?

Captain Kaine: Well, I'll tell you. They used it for a little while, and they put it up on a pier. There was a CO_2 engine in this thing, a carbon dioxide engine, and the system had to be purged. Somebody took it out on a pier and laid it up and didn't purge the engine, and it blew up. They took it out, and I think they put a conventional engine in it, and they used it as an operational target submarine.

Q: But have there been any more developed?

Captain Kaine: Yes, we went on it later, and Convair developed a bunch of two-man wet submersibles--not submarines--for UDT. It's called the SDV, swimmer delivery vehicle, and is a spin-off from the midget submarine. It's operationally approved; it's been used all over the place for delivery of explosives or equipment. It's battery operated. I think we got the first delivery of those in 1968, and they still have them.

Q: And they're functional?

Captain Kaine: They're functional, yes. They have an SDV platoon in each of the teams now, and they operate with them and use them as a training device. Operationally they are doing surveys and doing surreptitious entries to various areas.

Q: On both coasts?

Captain Kaine: On both coasts, yes.

Q: So you were again responsible for the development of that?

Captain Kaine: Well, in a way. There were a lot of us responsible.

Q: Well, what about using helicopters? Was that part of parachuting?

Captain Kaine: No, no. We developed the helicopter's use about this time as an aid to doing hydrographic surveys, for quick insertion of people under the water. You could bring a helicopter in low, and we just dropped out of the helicopters.

Q: Oh, and not use a parachute.

Captain Kaine: No, they'd bring them in real low, about 30 feet. And with as little forward momentum as possible, you'd just drop out of them. It's quite a ride, but it was a quick method for doing hydrographic surveys. And it was a quick method of pulling people out of the water, a good method of rescue. We used them for rescue and for surveys and whatnot.

Rather unwittingly, as it turned out, they developed into the missile recovery program and the recovery of astronauts. I should probably mention that. Along in this time, too, another thing we got a lot of mileage out of was the original astronauts, Glenn and Carpenter.* All these people were beginning their training to prepare for space. They allowed that working underwater was probably good training for them. It gave them the feeling of weightlessness.

Q: Oh, I see.

Captain Kaine: So we got the very enjoyable job of teaching all these people to be divers, aqualung people, and trained them underwater. We had them there for, oh, I guess, over a period of a few months, and they loved it.

Q: Not with the idea that when they came down they might not be picked up, but the idea of the weightlessness, as compared to the space.

Captain Kaine: Just to get a familiarity with weightlessness. Also, I think their training program was so long and drawn-out, with so many fill-in areas, it was a good stopgap, too. You know, it kept them in good physical condition, and we kept them running and whatnot when they weren't diving. It was just a really good program for them at the time, plus it gave them the weightless experience.

---
*John Glenn and Scott Carpenter were two of the nation's original seven astronauts. Carpenter later became involved in Project Sealab, spending extended periods underwater.

So it worked out all the way around. So that was another thing that we did.

And we did a lot of good work at this time with the Red Cross. The Red Cross had no capabilities in aqualung or diving or underwater things. They were big in swimming, as you well know. They were the U.S. expertise in swimming and control of swimming and lifesaving and that stuff. They wanted to develop the same expertise and authoritativeness in the underwater phase. So we in Norfolk--and I know they did it out here on the West Coast--went to work training the Red Cross instructors in all phases of underwater work and diving and whatnot so that then they could go on and become the civilian experts in the field.

At the same time, we had a good adviser in Washington. We got mixed up with the National Safety Council, and we sat in on meetings of those every few months; we were on the underwater side of it. Through that we met Dr. Edgerton, who's one of the foremost lighting authorities in the States.* He is an expert in the field of cameras and underwater photography, Schleringflov photography and stroboscopic lights and all this high-speed, super-duper stuff.

I remember one time later we worked with him when he

---

*Harold E. Edgerton was the inventor of stroboscopic high-speed motion and still photography apparatus and designer of underwater cameras and high-resolution sonar equipment.

was working with Dr. Cousteau, maybe in San Juan.* We were working off the Calypso; he was trying to develop a method of running a light system at a depth and being able to vary the depth as he ran along with, say, a ship. He wanted to take pictures while progressing along the bottom at various depths; it was a matter of having the light and camera on a sled that would follow the contours of the bottom. I mention him only because he or his office and the various scientists in there had something to do with the safety meetings once. Again, we got a lot of spinoff knowledge from these people, because they were very advanced in their techniques and their knowledge.

About the time we got interested in working with the midget submarine, we got interested in working with sonar and underwater television.

Q: Communications generally, weren't you?

Captain Kaine: Right, and underwater, including communications from man to man and man to base. We were working heavily with USNUSL, which is U.S. Navy Underwater Sound Lab. The people at the lab more or less adopted us in this field, and a man named Walt Wainwright was one of their scientists up there. He took a liking to us, and his

---

*Jacques Y. Cousteau is a noted marine explorer, film producer, and writer. His research vessel is named the Calypso.

projects coincided with the fields we were getting into. He was way ahead of us, science-wise, from this stuff. So he would come to St. Thomas with us every winter, and this was probably from 1950 through when I left there in 1958. He'd come down, and he'd work on other things, too. But from the time he left us, say, in March through the next January, he would work part-time on our projects. Some of the projects he worked on were underwater TV so that we could help the swimmer to see underwater.

Through Wainwright we got mixed up with Dr. Edgerton. They also had a system of phones. When we were doing a survey, for instance, and had ten swimmers strung out, we used to communicate by hand signals. And these people were working on developing what they called a buddy phone, and each one wore a little packet, and they could talk to each other and could talk back to the boat. It was really a great system, and it was a big morale factor. You know, you get lonesome in the water, and all these little aids were a big, big factor.

Q: I read in a scientific magazine about a technique called snatch and run, where there would be a boat running at great speed, and it would pick up a great number of UDT men all at one time.

Captain Kaine: That is a system that UDT has used since

World War II. You take whatever your craft is, whether it's an LCPR or any type of boat. You lash a rubber boat beside it, and a man lies in the rubber boat. As you come along to a line of swimmers, he will stick out a snare, a big cable loop, and the swimmer will put his arm through it and be pulled right in the back of the boat. You can pick up a whole line of swimmers very readily with one man.

Q: Is that an improvement over World War II techniques?

Captain Kaine: It's the same technique. Now there was another thing, a system that was developed in the 1950s. They attached an arm to the boat, and they had a bungee cord that had a loop in it, and a swimmer would bend his arm through the loop. But with that system, the bungee would expand so far that it would bring them back like a rocket. A couple of them got badly hurt, so they've done away with that. It got to be too hazardous.

I've found here an old All Hands magazine that is a special underseas issue. I was looking for a picture of them picking up, as you were saying.

Q: Captain Kaine is showing me an interesting publication, All Hands, from March 1959. It is a good reference if anyone should want to pursue that particular issue.*

Captain Kaine: They had a lot of equipment that came out as a result of asking designers and builders to come by and show us equipment. We had one I'll never forget; it was called the Scippolini "skim boat." It was made by an Italian gent named Scippolini, and he worked out of, I think, Florida. The man had a tremendous idea, which was really the advanced concept of today's hydrofoil boats. This man had a little light boat; it would remind you of the old Manila cigar wrappers in shape, and it was big enough. The maximum weight he wanted to carry in it was a man of 200 pounds. It had little outriggers on it and had a funny-looking nose on it; it was a sensor that looked like a praying mantis. If I'm not mistaken, it was powered by something like a 15- or 20-horsepower outboard motor.

You put anything in it that weighed no more than 200 pounds and revved this motor up, and this whole system went to work. The boat raised up on these foils. That nose sensed the waves ahead of you and would raise or lower the angle of the foils so you could tack the waves at the proper angle, and you could get speeds of up to 40 miles an hour out of this thing. It just flew, and our problem was we had hardly anybody that weighed 188 pounds, and we

---

*In addition to covering underwater demolition teams, the issue contains features on submarines and explosive ordnance disposal.

operated in twos, so there was just no practical use for it.

Another development at the time was a machine called the aqua ho motor, and it looked very much like the old three-bottle aqualung, only the middle bottle, instead of being an air bottle, was like a power pack of batteries, and it had a shrouded propeller on the back end of it. You'd strap this on your chest, and you could move underwater at three or four knots. And it was a great idea, just a great idea. It had power enough to last for 30 or 40 minutes, but we couldn't sell the Navy on buying any of these things. We got one for tests, and we had it for six or eight months.

Q: Seems to me that's an absolute natural.

Captain Kaine: Oh, it was a beauty. It was just a great, great thing. But whoever was in the power seat for buying equipment at UDT just didn't want it. But it would have reduced the time it takes to do a hydrographic survey or a reconnaissance by hours.

Q: Of course. Is it still not being used?

Captain Kaine: No, I don't know where it went to. I haven't any idea what happened to the thing.

F. R. Kaine #2 - 202

Q: That's just terrible.

Captain Kaine: The sea sled was a similar thing.

Q: My understanding was that the equipment became so much more complicated and so much larger in volume that a man couldn't possibly carry it himself, and this sea sled somehow went with him to carry his equipment.

Captain Kaine: Yes, the sea sled was another one of these developments that was designed as a come-along-behind-you-type of thing; it would carry explosives or whatever you'd need to do an operation. I don't know what happened to that concept. I vaguely remember it being developed, but I don't know that it ever lasted. Most of the equipment that was developed in those times was pretty good, but you have a hard time when you're an operator selling to non-operators. It was very hard to convince them that a thing was a necessity, especially if it looked like a toy. And most of the things you operate with underwater look like toys; they look like fun. The aqua ho motor looked like fun. They don't see the practicality in things.

Our problem many times is that people cannot understand the incompressibility of water. Oftentimes you look for speed, but you don't really need a lot of speed to improve yourself thousands of percent underwater. A good, strong swimmer maybe can swim one knot for a limited time. A piece of equipment that can move three knots for 40 minutes is a tremendous improvement underwater. If you get up over speeds of three, four, five, six knots without protective hooding, you lose your equipment. Your face mask will come off and stuff like that, so you just can't go really fast. But any improvement, even half a knot, is a jump underwater because some of the limiting factors you forget if you're not dealing with underwater are tides.

Q: Underwater?

Captain Kaine: Yes, or on the surface of water. For instance, you could be in an area with a 15-foot falling tide, and you could develop currents up to eight or ten knots. A ten-knot boat would just stand still as that thing is going out. Flowing waters, such as in rivers, will have a three- or four-knot speed, so if you've got a three- or four-knot piece of equipment, you stand still. So there are a lot of factors that enter into developing equipment underwater.

Q: Now the training of your people at this time included, I'm sure, all of the things that we talked about for World War II, plus all of this new equipment.

F. R. Kaine #2 - 204

Captain Kaine: That's right.

Q: And were the requirements for the people just as tough? How were the people selected now?

Captain Kaine: Obviously, there were so many we couldn't do it personally anymore. So we trained teams. Each coast had a team. We pre-selected the officer and usually one or two enlisted men, and they would go on recruiting trips to places like OCS and other schools.*

Q: Reserve schools where they trained ROTC people?**

Captain Kaine: That's right. They'd talk to ROTC, and that was another thing. I'm glad you mention it, because we were able to get this through BuPers to keep a team on the road, and they did. They went around recruiting various places.

Q: But, of course I'm guessing--they weren't the same caliber people as in World War II?

Captain Kaine: They were when we got through with them.

Q: Did you still have hell week?

---
*OCS--Officer Candidate School, Newport, Rhode Island.
**ROTC--Reserve Officer Training Corps.

F. R. Kaine #2 - 205

Captain Kaine: Oh, yes. The training was probably better, and it was a little longer. I think training about this time was about 13 weeks, where ours was eight to ten weeks. I think today, in 1981, it's something like 18 or 19 weeks.

Q: Did you have the same attrition?

Captain Kaine: Same attrition.

Q: What week did you put hell week in during this time?

Captain Kaine: It varied with whoever was in BuPers and whatever the scream was about personnel.

Q: I see, I see. You described that once before, but I thought you might have been able to control it.

Captain Kaine: We fought to have it in the first or second week. We thought ideally, after going back into the Navy and watching training again, that the second week was probably a little better. Because a lot of these people, with a little bit of encouragement and maybe a week of loosening up and everything, were in better shape to face hell week than they were right cold out of a desk or something.

F. R. Kaine #2 - 206

Q: In my world of no knowledge it would seem they needed a little orientation.

Captain Kaine: Well, it's common sense, if you stop and look at it. We had a little more time, you know. We didn't have any war going on right at the moment. But as pressure came down the hill from the top of the Bureau of Personnel, at one point I remember they made them move it back to the fourth week. The ultimate result was no different.

Q: You mentioned that, which I think is interesting.

Captain Kaine: Well, I might mention, too, that we had during this period, due to pressure from BuPers, a couple of universities do studies on both coasts on the people in UDT, with the idea being what type of person could you put into training to get the maximum number out at the other end. I think the University of Indiana did the most complete study. After really weeks and weeks of study and boiling it all down, they came out with a three-page final paper that ultimately said that if you put some people in, you'll get some people out. We had psychiatrists, psychologists, doctors, trainers--we had everything down there doing these studies, and the key was motivation. It was nothing else but motivation.

Q: I am sure of that in all phases of life, of leadership, motivation.

Captain Kaine: We had some people that were fat, basically fat people that made it through training. We had little people that made it through training. We had big people that made it through training. By the same token, we had the same kinds of people who didn't make it through training. It was a very interesting thing, some of these studies.

Q: I'm curious to know if the attrition was different with no war on than it was during the pressure of war.

Captain Kaine: I don't think it was; I don't think things were that different. Primarily, the attrition comes when your motivation wears out. If a person is really motivated and wants something, he'll get it, he'll do it. But there are people--and I think it's true of everybody to a certain extent--that things gang up and build up and build up, and finally that's it. One second later, they regret it, many times. But, even so, there have been some times in the training when a person has quit, we've let them come back in, and they've not made it again.

There may have been one or two people who have quit, maybe due to circumstances we didn't know about, that have come back and made it, but they're very few and far between. God, there are hardly any. I can't recall any offhand. But it seems to me I remember one guy that quit because he was hurt physically rather than overburdened. I think he made it the second time. I know another kid that broke his leg in training, but he came back and he did fine. But where it's been a buildup psychologically, I don't think any of them have ever made it. There are a lot of psychological barriers in this type of work that I probably should mention.

People have a hard time adjusting to working underwater.

Q: That's the claustrophobic end of it.

Captain Kaine: I think everybody, when they first work underwater, is a little nervous about the other people, the other things that are down there, but most people adjust to that. Some people can never adjust to it. There's a major adjustment in working at night underwater. There are a lot of people who have a reluctance to lock themselves into, say, a little SDV or a little submarine underwater. I'm just trying to think of some of the things where people have problems: swimming into a wreck underwater or swimming into a tight space underwater, swimming under the hull of a ship underwater to examine things. There are a lot of phenomena that become involved. For instance, when you swim under the hull of a ship when it's in shallow water, you get an increase in current. You swim under a ship where the tide is running in, and you can get slapped up against the side and held there by the pressure of the tide sometimes.

Q: Have you experienced any of these things?

Captain Kaine: Oh, yes, a lot of them.

Q: You haven't told me about those.

Captain Kaine: You can come up under a pier when you're doing a survey on a beach or a waterfront or something and be out of air and come up and there's no air space. You have to stop and move one way or another and stay with the move until something happens, until you make it or don't make it. These are all things that are brought out to you in training, and these are the things that I think prey on a trainee as he's going through training that maybe make him become overburdened and want to quit.

F. R. Kaine #2 - 210

Q: As you describe some of these things, we haven't touched on those in your experiences out in World War II. Are you sure you've told me everything that you wanted to?

Captain Kaine: You forget a lot of those things, but when I was thinking of some of the things that could make people quit, I remembered things that happened to me.

Q: And you've experienced all of these?

Captain Kaine: Well, yes, almost anybody does that works in it for any length of time. Now I may have experienced more than others, because I worked in the field for such a long time. And we didn't know what we were doing when we started out, which is another reason that you get into a lot of trouble sometimes. Maybe some of the people nowadays are better trained and they know these things. But, for instance, we used to get a lot of requests to go looking for things in an amphibious operation or after an operation. People would lose anchors, or they'd drop equipment over the side, or somebody would drown, or they'd drop rifles. And when there are a lot of ships anchored around, you don't immediately think, "Well, geez, I'd better stay out from underneath that ship, because it's close to the shore, and if the tide's coming in, it might push me up against it." So that's how you experience these things--through ignorance, really.

Q: Then would you bring all this information back and remember it and put it into your training?

Captain Kaine: You'd crank it into the training; that's right. It's an empirical thing, all the time. On currents, for instance, I can remember the first time in training, like in Florida, where you'd swim in to the beach for recon, and nobody told you about the littoral currents that ran along the shore. We knew of tides going in and out, and we never thought that, as well as that, there were currents parallel to the beach, too. So we'd swim toward one place on the beach, and, God, we'd end up somewhere else.

Another big thing that creates hazards for people working underwater is they become engrossed in their work and forget they're underwater. If you're just skin diving, you get down and get so involved you forget that you don't have any air source. You work and you work and work, and then all of a sudden, you say, "God, I've got to breathe," and you've still got 30 feet to go, maybe, or 35 feet. Or you can be working with a lung or some scuba gear down there and run out of air.

Q: You've got the time limitation of whatever . . .

Captain Kaine: That's right, and you say, "Well, I can hack it," but maybe you're 80 feet down instead of 20 feet down, and it takes a few kicks to get up there. So all those things enter into it. I think sometimes if a kid gets badly scared in training, that preys on him.

Q: I can understand that. Do you think we have covered most of the phases of this period, 1951 through 1958?

Captain Kaine: I think so. There is possibly one statement--this 1951 through 1958 was a period when UDT per se solidified its stand so that it would become a permanent entity in the Navy. I think there were questions all through this period about whether it should be financed, should be continued. Depending on who was the head of what, they'd say, "Well, this should be cut; that should be cut." And there were a lot of units that fell by the wayside or were cut way, way back, as was UDT at times. But I think they established their permanency during this period.

Q: In the 1950s and 1960s, how much interaction was there between the UDTs on the East Coast and West Coast as far as updating doctrine and procedures in uniform fashion?

Captain Kaine: There was not a lot of interaction between the two coasts until about 1966. Then, with the help of BuPers and the Vietnam War, we were able to merge missions, units, personnel, and, finally, training by moving all training to Coronado.

Q: Off the tape you had mentioned one topic you said you should describe, and that was concerning the use of submarines with UDT.

Captain Kaine: That's right. We operated extensively in training with the submarines of the Atlantic Fleet and not just necessarily in St. Thomas, but we did this on a quarterly basis. It was to keep our ability to lock in and lock out of submarines and make surreptitious entry into any area where it might be required. The Submarine Force Atlantic Fleet was very generous in working with us, and most years we would have a submarine committed to us in St. Thomas for a week or so, plus we'd be able to operate on a quarterly basis throughout the year. The idea of this was that the submarines could carry a number of UDT operators and lock them out at depths of down to 100 feet, so that there would be no issue over a compromise of their position, and let them come up. The submarines would even lock out their equipment or release their equipment from the deck and go on in and perform an operation. The teams became very adept at this.

Q: Would they wait and pick them up also?

Captain Kaine: Yes, submerged. And you'd go out, and any equipment that you needed to bring back, you'd have to take down to the submarine. Otherwise, you'd just jettison or bury it if you didn't need it, the idea being that the submarine could lie off there undetected, and you could swim out and go back down to it. It was invaluable training for underwater work, too.

Q: And you're describing this as a technique, but you're not saying whether or not you were included.

Captain Kaine: We were always included. This was one of my favorite occupations, as a matter of fact.

Q: I wish you'd just describe doing it. Describe yourself and how it felt and what you did.

Captain Kaine: You're riding in this submarine, and when the submarine bottoms out in an area where you're going to do your lock-outs, you climb up into the lock-out chamber. The idea is to flood that to a height where there's an escape door in the side of the chamber that you're in. You bring the water level up above that door, and then put enough air pressure on it so that you equalize the pressure inside to the air pressure outside the submarine. Then you can unlock the door and just go right out; there was a little ladder in the old-type submarines, so you'd swim right up the ladder and go on your way. You learn this in the chamber at New London, which is essential training you have to go through before you do submarine lock-out. I should touch on that for a moment.

In New London, Connecticut, or in Pearl Harbor, Hawaii, they have the submarine training facility, and they have this 100-foot tower. The purpose of this tower is to teach you how to escape from the submarine. I don't know whether you're aware or not, but during World War II many of the submarines that were sunk, the people that were in them--rather than go up and face the unknown of the water--just laid down and died in the submarines. A few of them were in such ridiculously shallow water that anybody could escape with a modicum of training. The result was a terrible loss of life, because either they wouldn't try it, or they were in despair and said, "To hell with it." They didn't want to go out in the ocean.

Anyway, the towers are designed so you can make lock-outs from 25 feet, 50 feet, or 100 feet. All they are is tall cylinders, and you have instructors with you all the time, and they teach you how to lock out. The idea in locking out--you come out from a depth, and you ascend freely, exhaling all the time so you have air coming out. Ideally, the way I was taught, you rise with the bubble. You exhale no faster than normal, and you just go right to the surface. The reason for that is that in changing pressures from a depth of, say, 100 feet, your lungs will expand four times their normal size. They're compressed, so that if you hold your breath, you will rupture your lungs. You can never rupture your lungs as long as you're exhaling. So the idea is to exhale slowly as you come up.

Now they have changed it, and they give you a blow-and-go method. You blow everything and you go, you blow and go, you blow and go until you're up to the top. I may be prejudiced, but because I've worked around so many waterfronts where there's jagged metal and ship bottoms and everything else when you're coming up from a depth, I think blowing and going can be dangerous, too, because you blow and then you go up as fast as you can. If someone is escaping, they're usually not in a position to look around and see what's going on above. So if they blow and go, they come up and knock themselves cold on a ship bottom or piece of steel or anything. Whereas, the other way, you're coming up so slowly, you can look up and see what's above you and kind of enjoy the tour on the way up.

So, with that digression, escape from a submarine is the same thing. You flood the chamber and put a cap of air on top of it so it equalizes, and you swim out and you just go up. When you get to the surface, you wait for your buddy, and you spread out and do your reconnaissance. Then, when you come back, you do the reverse.

Q: Are you tied together with your buddy?

Captain Kaine: No, you don't usually tie them together, but you maintain a distance of X number of feet, whatever it is.

Q: What were you wearing?

Captain Kaine: In the latter days, you'd maybe wear a rubber suit or swim trunks. In the Caribbean, where we did most of our training, we just wore a pair of swim trunks, and you'd have fins and a face mask. Now, if this was a totally surreptitious reconnaissance, you wouldn't go up to the surface. You'd just bring your lung out with you, out of the thing, and put your lung on underwater and just go from there. You could go in to the land and back out and into the submarine, and nobody would ever know you were there.

Q: And this is still daytime, of course.

Captain Kaine: You could do it in daytime. You could do it at night if you wanted to take the risk of the inaccuracies of the dark.

Q: I would think that would be the most scary part, that you'd get lost.

Captain Kaine: Well, you know, you can get lost in the daytime, too, because not all water is clear, and you can swim through murky water.

Q: How do you keep contact?

Captain Kaine: A compass.

Q: Your compass tells you . . .

Captain Kaine: You swim with a wrist compass. I should probably tell you that the basic equipment of a swimmer in UDT is a compass, a depth gauge, face mask, fins, either a lung or no lung, and if they're doing a reconnaissance, they'd have a lead line and slate, or some method of recording.

Q: To write underwater?

Captain Kaine: Yes, wax and that sort of thing.

Q: How far apart would you be from your next buddy?

Captain Kaine: Depending on how accurate a chart you had, it would be something like 50 feet.

Q: You lose sight of them, I presume.

Captain Kaine: Yes, oh, yes. You lose them, but you try to keep visual contact with them.

Q: Now with this communication between people, I would think that would be an enormous psychological lift.

Captain Kaine: Personal communication underwater is a psychological lift, because you have a tendency when you're underwater to be alone, and any communication you have is nice, because it gets quiet. So the submarine work was a big part of training during this period. It led to the later development of the submarine, of course. All along during the UDT phase after World War II and the Korean thing, we had a couple of the older submarines. On the East Coast it was the _Sealion_, and on the West Coast, the _Perch_. They were troop-carrying submarines designed for carrying either a Marine reconnaissance outfit or the UDT people specifically for this purpose, to do training.

As these submarines got older, maintaining this close contact with the submarine force and the state of training and the ability to do a reconnaissance submerged led to the conversion of another submarine called the Grayback into one really designed for this purpose. The Grayback was commissioned much after this time. I'm getting ahead of this, but it was designed and commissioned in time for Vietnam.* But it was a direct result of this time period now where we maintained this capability.

Q: Well, I think it's fair to say that your designs, your techniques, your training were responsible for keeping UDT alive.

Captain Kaine: I think so. I had a lot of help on the West Coast, too, from the contemporaries over here. Because while we were doing this, they were doing that. We swapped information a lot, but still maintained our separate entities, too. We always thought that we had a better capability personnel-wise, because we used to have a lot of arguments between the East and West coasts over personnel and performance and everything. Quite often, we

---

*The USS Grayback (SSG-574) was originally commissioned as a Regulus guided missile submarine on 7 March 1958 and operated in that role until decommissioned on 25 May 1964. She was then converted to the transport role and recommissioned as LPSS-574 on 9 May 1969.

would get people from the West Coast transferring to the East Coast. I remember a few incidents where Fane, who was the commander out here and my counterpart, would call up and say, "I've got a guy I'm sending over to you. He's no good. See what you can do with him."* And we'd get him, and he'd be great. I think we just had maybe a little different theory of operation.

Q: Better that, though, than to lose the man.

Captain Kaine: Absolutely. People were too hard to get. We had some philosophic differences in the operations in that the West Coast teams at the time wouldn't touch oxygen; they just didn't want any part of oxygen swimming at all. We were doing a lot of oxygen swimming, and we were looking for better oxygen equipment for mixed-gas equipment or whatnot. They were doing a lot of air equipment, primarily aqualung. I don't know of any real reason for this other than I had great faith in oxygen after I learned something about diving as a surreptitious method, because it leaves no bubbles. You could get in and out, and they'd never know you were there.

I didn't know that much about mixed gases, but I had the same hope for mixed-gas diving at that time, whereas on the West Coast they just didn't have the interest in

---
*Commander Francis Douglas Fane, USNR, commanding officer, Underwater Demolition Team 11.

oxygen. I think they maybe had no vision of sneak attacks or anything like that, whereas we, because of our admirals, were deep into sneak attacks, and we were using the methods all the time. They weren't doing that out here, so I think maybe that accounted for the difference in philosophies.

At any rate, during these periods we were also training a lot of foreign people from various navies--the Turks, Swedes, Norwegians, French, Italians, Greeks.

Q: Any English?

Captain Kaine: As a matter of fact, one of the British Navy people that was responsible for the Wellman submarine, the little midget submarine, used to be a commander that came over and gave us a lot of his experience. But we did train a lot of people. As a matter of fact, one of the people that we trained was a member of the Norwegian royal family. We trained almost every nationality--Israelis, Pakistanis.

Q: I'm digressing, but did any of these nations have occasion to use UDT?

Captain Kaine: Oh, yes, they've all developed their UDT. The Swedes, the Norwegians.

Q: I mean, to use it?

Captain Kaine: Israel has a great team. I don't know about the Pakistanis. The Vietnamese used it; they had them later on. Turks.

Q: I was wondering if the Swedes had used it when just recently the Russian submarine . . .*

Captain Kaine: I'm sure they did. The Swedes had a great fellow who was later killed, Uwe Lund. When he came over here, he brought with him a German-made lung called the Dräger. It was probably one of the greatest pieces of equipment that we've ever used. We tried to procure them; I think we got eight or ten of them at one time, but the Navy wouldn't let us buy them, because we had a buy-America-first rule for the military. Later on, we kept pressuring them and pressuring them, so they redesigned the Dräger lung, and it was a mess. But back in the 1950s the Dräger was just a beautiful, beautiful oxygen lung.

I think that was another thing that kept me interested in the oxygen side of it, because up until that time we had one oxygen rig that we could use. It was called the LARU,

---

*A Soviet "Whiskey"-class diesel submarine ran aground near Sweden's Karlskrona naval base on 27 October 1981 and was discovered the following day by a fishing boat.

Lambertson rebreathing unit or something. It was developed by Dr. Chris Lambertson, who was a doctor and physiologist and a great underwater enthusiast. He probably did more for UDT on the science side than anybody else. He had been with the University of Pennsylvania for years. We had his equipment, developed years and years ago, in the 1940s, and it was adequate. It was not nearly as sophisticated as the Dräger lung, but we did use it. You have a lot of trouble swimming on oxygen, and if a swimmer exerts himself a lot, it's like a Catch-22.

You either over-oxygenate yourself, in which case you go into a fit, or you create anoxia, in which case you go into a fit. So it's a very narrow line, and it can only be used to depths of no more than 30 feet, or else you go into another kind of conniption. So it just has to be used with care. Its advantage is that you get complete secrecy in oxygen, because there's no trace of a swimmer at all.

Q: Did your students hesitate in its use?

Captain Kaine: Yes, yes, we had a lot of problems with it. We had a number of people who couldn't use it. They were allergic to the use of oxygen; they became violently ill. We had a lot of people who would use it if they had to but were afraid of it. And we had a group that could use it just fine.

Q: I know it's foolish of me to ask you if you liked it.

Captain Kaine: I liked it. I loved the way it operated.

Q: You used it?

Captain Kaine: I used it, yes, and I passed out in it once. I'll never forget it. We were swimming in, I believe, St. Thomas. I was swimming with this buddy of mine, and usually when you swim with buddies, you're staggered, kind of like half an echelon. I was swimming along behind him. Sometimes you use a line; otherwise, you try to stay about even with his feet. I was swimming along, and they teach you all sorts of things--you know, that sometimes you can hallucinate in oxygen. If you have the presence of mind to think you are, put your hand out and see if you can feel his feet.

So I was cruising along there, and all of a sudden I saw him very vividly disappear around the corner of a brick building. I put my hand up, and his feet were there. So I stopped. You never really know if you get too little oxygen or too much oxygen, so the first thing I did was blow out and cut down on the oxygen, and I was fine. So I was steaming along, and--all of a sudden--I was up in the boat.

Q: Oh, you had passed out.

Captain Kaine: I had passed out.

Q: How did he know it?

Captain Kaine: Well, I guess somebody was watching us or something. But, anyway, I ended up in the boat. But those things happen, and usually on any swims like that, you're usually utterly careful, and you have people watching.

We used to do a lot of stuff at night, and when you're running things at night, you worry far more than when you're swimming the things at night. If you're responsible for 20 swimmers in the water, you're far more worried than if you're in there swimming and somebody else is worrying about it. So oftentimes when you're CO, you don't get to swim as much as you'd like because of other things. You can't participate all the time.

Q: I understand. I understand. Just knowing you, I figured you would.

Captain Kaine: We got a lot of it. I'm saying "we" again. I used to love to operate, and I was fairly good at it and natural with it, so I enjoyed it very much.

F. R. Kaine #2 - 227

Q: Well, perhaps now we have covered most of the items on the 1951 to 1958 period. You think so?

Captain Kaine: I think so.

Q: Because now we're going on to another phase, 1958 to 1962, when you were chief of staff down at . . .

Captain Kaine: Yes. For years we had been going down to St. Thomas for training purposes, and it was so beautiful down there that I often told my wife, "If there was some way we could only get stationed in St. Thomas or Puerto Rico or someplace." Of course, being in UDT I knew there was no way that I could really get stationed down there. But what I didn't really think about was that from the time I was an ensign, I had always been either an OinC or a CO, with the exception of four months as an XO.* And this didn't ring a bell; I never thought of this.

Q: What was your grade at this point?

Captain Kaine: I had just been selected for commander. The reason I was leaving UDT was that I had been there nearly eight years in more or less the same billet. Well, I had three billets. I was XO for four months and then CO

---
*OinC--officer in charge.

of UDT Two, and then ComUDU 2 for seven or eight years.*
And I said, "Hey, man, nobody stays in a billet for seven
years. I'd been in the three billets for seven years.

Seven years as CO of one unit--God, it was heresy, so
they said, "Do you have any preference?"

And I said, "There's only one place I want to go; that
would be to go overseas and take my family." And then you
mention you've got five kids, and they say that will never
happen. We had an awfully good detailer there. I said,
"Well, how about Puerto Rico? Now I realize I'm not
qualified. I don't know any staff work. I don't know
this."

And he said, "My God, who's better qualified? You've
been a CO for almost 10 or 12 years, and who's better
qualified?"

So then I let him push me into the billet, and, sure
enough, he got the billet for me as assistant chief of
staff for personnel and CO of enlisted people. We had
about ten jobs down there. There was director of
transportation, director of civilian personnel, and on and
on and on and on. When I looked at the set of orders I had
to this job, I thought, "Golly, God, what a mess I've got
myself into now." As it turned out, I was also penal
officer. So we got orders down there and went.

---

*ComUDU 2--Commander Underwater Demolition Unit Two. When
he became the senior UDT skipper, Kaine also became unit
commander.

Q: Now you're saying, "down there," but you're not saying . . .

Captain Kaine: San Juan, Puerto Rico, to the staff of Admiral Dan Gallery.* It was a triple-headed staff. It was Commander of the Tenth Naval District, Commander Caribbean Sea Frontier, and Commander Antilles Defense Command. He had a very far-reaching command that included Panama, Trinidad, Gitmo, so that we had varied duty.**

Well, this was a whole new ball game for me, because I'd never really been exposed to a lot of staff work or personnel work, and it was just fascinating. Admiral Gallery was a great old admiral, and he was the type of person who wasn't really interested in any further promotion. He couldn't care less; he had a nice billet there, and he had beautiful quarters, and he loved it. He loved kids, and he organized the Little League in Puerto Rico; it was a tremendous thing then.

He also started a thing down there called a steel band. His command had a musical group of, I think, 20-some people. The Trinidad steel bands were famous down there, and he kind of kidnapped the guy that made the steel drums, got him up from Trinidad, and kept him in Puerto Rico for a

---
*Rear Admiral Daniel V. Gallery, USN. Admiral Gallery's oral history is in the Naval Institute collection.
**Gitmo--Guantánamo Bay, Cuba.

while. Admiral Gallery had him design the steel drums for his band and train the musicians, and the steel band became world famous and still is. They travel all over, putting on entertainment parties. We had them here, as a matter of fact, this year.

Q: What's their name? What are they called?

Captain Kaine: The U.S. Navy Steel Band, and they're now out of New Orleans.

We were into various things down there. I was the transportation officer, and everybody came in via ship or air into Puerto Rico. The duties involved booking people out of Puerto Rico, Trinidad, Panama, and Cuba. At that time we had the MSTS.*

Q: I was going to ask you about that.

Captain Kaine: They were our main transport, so I worked with the MSTS officers, and we did all the booking in and out of the whole area down there. It involved some traveling. You had to go and visit these various people every couple of months, and it was a great opportunity for family, because we were in a little tiny base and weather

---

*MSTS--Military Sea Transportation Service, a shipping organization run by the Navy. It has since been renamed Military Sealift Command.

just like this. It was just beautiful, a beautiful tour.

And it was interesting because we had an opportunity down there to work with a bunch of kids. I had, of course, been swimming all my life, and when we got there, one of the big interests in Puerto Rico was to start swimming teams. The way they did this, the various hotels, like the Condado Beach or the Hilton, would sponsor these various swimming teams.

When I was down there, there was a Colonel Vandam on the staff.* He was a senior Marine in the area, and he said, "Frank, you've been a swimmer, and I've been a swimmer. Why don't we start a Navy swim club?" So we started a Navy swim club, and we started teaching Red Cross swimming, and we started a club with his daughter and my youngsters and a few other families there, maybe 15-20 kids. When we started it, the Army started a team. I was there four years, and before we got through, I guess we had probably 200 kids on the base in the swimming program, and it was big. We had won the Puerto Rican swim championship, and we'd won the Central American swim championships, and it was just a great, great program.

Q: Were you the coach?

Captain Kaine: I was one of them, and Vandam was another.
_____
*Colonel Norman Vandam, USMC.

Oh, we had a great time. But we were able to get in activities like that and great social life. The family was able to visit Panama and Cuba and other islands. It was also a big transition time for Puerto Rico, because the Governor of Puerto Rico at that time was very favorable to the military. He also was in the effort of trying to create a middle class in Puerto Rico, so they had a tremendous development program called Operation Boot Strap.*

Then Admiral Gallery was very, very interested in the Puerto Ricans as a people. So he encouraged us to mix with the populace and mix with the people and not sit on the base. So we got out socially a lot and mixed, got to know them. They had a mayoress in San Juan who was a delightful person, Doña Felicia, and we got to know her very well and would to go various functions in the city and whatnot. Through this swimming team, we got to know all the hotels, and it was just a delightful sojourn.

But at this same time, with this Operation Boot Strap going on, they imported something like 250 industries or branches of industry to Puerto Rico. He literally created a middle class in Puerto Rico, at least financially. There was always an extreme; it was like Mexico. He brought in such things as sewing-type industries and lingerie manufacturers. While we were there, he brought in 11

---

*The progressive governor was Luis Muñoz Marin.

brand-new hotels. The government built them, and then they'd lease them to the management people, like the Hiltons and La Concha. He really just did a tremendous job, but at the same time we had a furor going on over there in Cuba, so this got to be a boiling point. They were always looking to Cuba as a possible evacuation problem, so I used to have to develop plans on evacuating Cuba.

Q: You mean our base?

Captain Kaine: Our base. It never came to that. It did come to an evacuation of the people later on, the dependents and whatnot. But that was much later. Gallery was there, I think, just about a year and a half, and he was relieved by an Admiral Smith.*

Staff work is staff work is staff work for four years, so I'll give you a few high points. One of the high points down there at the time was some guys stole a ship. I don't know if you remember this or not. I don't remember all the incidents in it, but they stole a big passenger liner. They took over this ship that was steaming out there, and

---
*Rear Admiral Allen Smith, Jr., USN.

F. R. Kaine #2 - 234

they were sending threats back and all this stuff.*

Q: Were passengers aboard?

Captain Kaine: Passengers aboard and everything. It was one of the cruise ships.

Q: I don't know if I ever knew about that.

Captain Kaine: It was a big thing in Puerto Rico. I had the duty the night when this thing came up, and Admiral "Rivets" [Horacio, Jr.] Rivero was in CinCLantFlt.** We had an awfully good operations officer named Ed Hunt.*** He sent out planes looking for this thing, and they sent out whatever ships they had in the area where it was supposed to be, and they were really narrowing down the area. This guy was a real nut, I guess, and they were afraid of what he might do to the people in there.

All of a sudden, CinCLantFlt took over the search from

---
*The 20,906-ton Portuguese cruise ship Santa Maria, carrying 607 passengers, was captured at gunpoint in the Caribbean Sea on 22 January 1961. The seizure, accomplished by 24 Portuguese and Spanish exiles and six crew members, was planned as the first step in the intended overthrow of Portugal's dictator Antonio de Oliveria Salazar. After negotiating with British and U.S. officials, including Admiral Smith, Commander Caribbean Sea Frontier, the rebels surrendered the ship at Recife, Brazil, on 3 February. For an account of the incident, see Facts on File Yearbook: 1961 (New York: Facts on File, Inc., 1962), page 42.
**CinCLantFlt--Commander in Chief Atlantic Fleet.
***Captain Edward R. Hunt, USN.

Washington and changed the whole thing, moved it way out, because they had better intelligence, I guess. Anyway, the search was moved, and we discontinued where we were and moved everything up to the other place. This went on for two or three days. Finally, this guy Hunt says, "Look, I think we're all wet. Let's get one of these planes down here that's not used in the search and have him go cruising out." So he went out, and they found the ship.*

Q: It would have seemed the first thing to do anyway.

Captain Kaine: Well, that's what they were doing. You know, when you've got the whole ocean to search, you do legs and you do distances, and you narrow it down. So finally, after a few days of this Mickey Mouse, they found the ship. But that was a big high point down there, because it created a lot of excitement.

Q: To say the least. And was it resolved with no damage to it?

Captain Kaine: No damage. I forget how they got that guy off the ship. I think that maybe somebody parachuted in. I can't really remember now. But, anyway, it was done with

---
*The Santa Maria was sighted in the Atlantic on 25 January 1961, three days after the capture, by a U.S. Navy P2V patrol plane.

very little damage, and the ship continued on its cruise.

Q: I bet a few would have been crazy.

Captain Kaine: Oh, yes, but militarily the main thing was keeping a finger on Cuba and watching out for a lot of refugees coming from Cuba to Puerto Rico at the time. One time while I was down there, people were escaping from Cuba a lot, and somebody gave my name to some organization, and they came to me and wanted me to train them to swim into Cuba. They were going to assassinate Castro.* To show how ridiculous some of these people get, they had no concept of what it was to work underwater at all. They wanted to swim from Point A, across a bay which was probably five or ten miles, and swim down another way two miles or something. When I told them that, they were utterly incredulous; they just wouldn't believe it. Swimming underwater, if you swim a mile in 25 minutes, you're not great, but you're good. And they were talking about swimming nine miles. So it was a big laugh.

Q: Did they accept it finally when you said . . .

Captain Kaine: Sure, they had to, because I could show

---

*Fidel Castro led a revolution that successfully ousted President Fulgencio Batista of Cuba in 1959; Castro has been Premier of the country since that time.

them exactly. But people get all hyped up with radicalism, and they just spout a cause, and away they go. They never think of how to get from A to B.

That was my first really close acquaintance with WAVE officers in my whole career.* I had three nice WAVE officers that were on my staff down there, and we had a lot of fun with them.

Admiral Gallery was a great, great leader of men, and he was just crazy about enlisted sailors. He just thought they were the greatest people in the world. He was a prolific writer; did you know that?

Q: I've seen some of his articles, yes.

Captain Kaine: He's got some great books that he's written--humor, great humor. But, anyway, he did a thing that I thought was marvelous. He converted his barge to a four-place fishing boat. He had two chairs and two outriggers on it. That was made available to the enlisted men of the command whenever they wanted it.

Q: That's super.

Captain Kaine: One of the provisos was that it had to have

---
*Navy women of the period were known as WAVES, an acronym that originated in World War II. The letters stood for Women Accepted for Voluntary Emergency Service.

F. R. Kaine #2 - 238

a line officer in the boat whenever it went out. There was a limited number of line officers down there, and most of them were captains. So all the lieutenant commanders and the commanders used to go out in the boat whenever it went out. One of them had to go, and there were only about four of us. So I spent a lot of time deep-sea fishing down there.

Q: Oh, dear.

Captain Kaine: It was fun up to a point, but it got to be a drag.

Q: I would think it would.

Captain Kaine: But you didn't have any UDT contacts, I take it.

Captain Kaine: Well, yes, that's the one I was thinking of. While I was there, they had a big tragedy in UDT in that two lads were killed in training over in St. Thomas. Because I was there, I was detached and was the investigating officer for the tragedy. One of the fellows I knew, the other one I didn't. It turned out to be an unnecessary accident in that the two lads were swimming different gases. One was on air and one was on oxygen, and that's pretty hard, because you can swim a lot faster and a lot harder and a lot deeper on air than you can on oxygen.

I think that somewhere in between, the guy on oxygen maybe had a fit or something, and the other fellow tried to save him, and they just struggled and both drowned. But I was tied up in that for quite some time. The investigation became a little controversial, because my theories didn't necessarily jibe with the next reviewing authority. However, they were backed up by the next reviewing authority and concurred with by the third, the last one, so it turned out all right, but it was . . .

Q: Sticky?

Captain Kaine: Well, diving accidents can get sticky whenever you mix up two media like that, because there's a lot of theories, and a lot of people want to blame somebody when there's a death. I would say there was probably a little laxness. They could have been more on the ball; it wasn't done the way I would do it. But also, the people that were doing the swimming were very experienced swimmers, and they had a certain responsibility, too. So, all in all, it was just an unfortunate accident. I might say, really, that in all the accidents and casualties and severe injuries that I've had anything to do with over a period of 20-some years in UDT and the other small organization, 90% of them have been due to a deviation from a procedure.

Q: I can understand that.

Captain Kaine: Which, in this case, was true, too. So I don't think that's very profound, but it's true.

Q: So at some time at the end of your four years, you left that isle of beauty.

Captain Kaine: I left that beautiful place. As a matter of fact, after I was there for three years, then I got extended for a year. I love it. So then we went back. I left there in March 1962. I arrived in the States right after a tremendous Nor'easter had just come through around Norfolk, the 17th of March. I was detached on February 19 and reported to BMU 2 on March 19.

Q: And I assume that's where your duty was, in Norfolk?

Captain Kaine: Yes, I reported in to the Naval Beach Group again. I hadn't been with them since 1951. I went in as commanding officer of a beachmaster unit. We had, off and on, worked with beachmasters many times, because many times in the landings in the Pacific we would report to the beachmaster because he was the honcho that manned that beach. He had work or obstacles to remove or channels to blow or sand to blow out or anything; you would report to him, and he would tell you what he wanted done. So I was a little bit familiar with the beachmaster function. I was not totally familiar with the size of the command or the extent of the command, nor its operational chain of command.

For administrative purposes, they were attached to the Naval Beach Group. They were one of three or four groups. There were the Seabees under the beach group; the beachmasters were under the beach group; the boat unit or the assault craft unit was under the beach group. UDT was no longer under the beach group as it was in 1951. I reported in there on, I think, the 20th or 21st, and normally you have about a ten-day relieving period. I relieved two days later because they were deploying. They had a big operation coming up in the Caribbean, and they were deploying down to Vieques.

Q: Where did the Second Marine Division come in?

Captain Kaine: The Second Marine Division was at Camp Lejeune. The way the setup was, the beachmaster reports to the shore party commander of the specific Marine division. The shore party commander is the man that sets up their beach and the periphery and sets up their maintenance sheds and the engineering and the truck pool and the whole bit. The beachmaster becomes the localized central control for all the beaches and for anything that comes in over the beaches. It's a very interesting job once you get into it.

Q: You mean on one deployment or one operation or one time?

Captain Kaine: One time. It is an interesting job, really an interesting job, and it's a very, very busy job. You have a command of, I would guess, 300 people. You have a tremendous number of vehicles: trucks and amphibious vehicles called LARCs.* The LARC is the one that I helped very much to get in the Navy. It was designed for the Army. When I was with the beachmasters, there were still some DUKWs of World War II vintage.** I was there in what years?

Q: 1962 to 1964.

Captain Kaine: Yes, and they had kept these rascals running over that many years. There were only about three

---
*LARC is an acronym that stands for lighter, amphibious, resupply, cargo.
**The DUKW was essentially an amphibious truck; its designation was from the standard army vehicle description: D(1942); U(amphibian); K(all-wheel drive); W(dual rear axles).

or four left, and they were in dry storage in the desert in Utah. We got the last three out of there, and they were so corroded that it was almost impossible to fix them. So I had been to a couple of demonstrations where they were using this LARC-5 at the time. It was just an overgrown DUKW, much bigger, much stronger, a little more versatile. So I thought, "That's for me. That's a hell of a lot better than fixing old DUKWs."

So we started dropping little notes here and there, and--lo and behold--very shortly the Navy made a buy of a bunch of LARCs. We replaced our DUKWs, and they've been working ever since. But it was a lot more versatile machine, and it was more controllable than the DUKW. The DUKW was slow, and it would be flooded in the surf, and you used them a lot on beaches.

The concept of the operation of the beachmaster is that he goes in to the beach in one of the early waves. The waves structure an amphibious landing. They are numbered, planned, and controlled by the shore party commander. The beachmaster goes and takes over the beach, controls all the incoming traffic. He has two landing craft control ships lying off the beach. All your amphibious traffic comes between those ships. They identify themselves to these ships as they come in. The beachmaster is in communication with these ships and tells them where to come, where to go, and deploys them after they come ashore.

More importantly than bringing them in to the beach, he has to keep the beach open; he has to bring them in, get them off-loaded, and get them out of there. If you have storms coming, or if you have a dropping tide or a rising tide or a cross-current, you have to have lifeguards down there. You've got to have people in there to wigwag these guys in to the right spots, and you've got to have equipment there to off-load these items that need to be off-loaded, or you have to have the drivers ready to make sure the vehicles come out of those boats or people come out of the boats or whatever comes out of the boats. In order to do that, you have to work closely with the UDT, and you have to get proper surveys ahead of time and know what the beach gradients are and where the beaches will work and what currents you've got to fight, and all this stuff.

You've got to work with the engineers, the Seabees, because they come in and help you set the causeways where you want them. You have to have gotten some knowledge of the sand, its trafficability, whether it will handle trucks or whether you have to have four-wheel drive, two-wheel drive, whatnot. And you have to know something about the beach exits, where you can get things off of the beachhead, out into wherever the Marine shore party wants it, whether it be an ammo dump, boat pool, car pool, or whatnot. So

F. R. Kaine #2 - 245

you have a busy, busy job.

Q: That's tremendous pre-planning.

Captain Kaine: Yes, it takes planning, and it takes interested people, again. And it takes terrific coordination between the shore party and the beachmaster. It takes a lot of communication, and it takes pretty good people. You have to have pretty good people.

Q: Now where did you go? Did you go with the first deployment? You said they were deploying in two days.

Captain Kaine: Yes. I got there the 23rd, and I think we deployed the 27th, right back to where I came from in the Caribbean, in Vieques.

Q: Was the man that you were relieving with you?

Captain Kaine: He stayed in Norfolk.

Q: How did you know what to do?

Captain Kaine: Well, you kind of do it by the seat of your pants and hope that you've got a pretty good beachmaster group with you, and we did. It went off like a piece of cake.

Q: That was on-the-job training.

Captain Kaine: Yes. The landing was successful, it worked well, the team was well-trained. To me, that's the advantage of training. His people were well-trained, and he assured me that they were. And I was familiar enough with beaches over the last 20 years to know what was going on. The only problem that I would have would be from the beach group commander. If he ever showed up on the beach, then he might come down and ask you something that you didn't know the answer to. Well, as it turned out, the guy that was there never showed up on the beach anyway. He didn't want any part of it.

Q: How could he do that?

Captain Kaine: He just didn't want to know any problems. So that one worked out fine. Then, after that, to a greater or lesser degree, every operation is a kind of a repeat performance.

Q: Are they practice drills?

Captain Kaine: These are training drills.

Now there was one that was not. I should probably talk about that one, because it was a real highlight. I hate to say high point of my career, but it really was. Here I had spent all my life in UDT, and one of the real high points of my career happened in beachmasters. I was there and got established and had a good command, and we did a lot of operating. You do a lot of local operations along the beaches in Little Creek, where you'll send a detachment and they'll handle the beach.

Q: But your command was actually all training.

Captain Kaine: Keeping them trained and operating with the amphibious force. If they had training landings, we would go and help them train. It's like a large filing system, kind of. After you're there for a while, the fuel farm goes here, the dry products store comes here, the oil comes here, the barrels come here, and whatever comes there. You off-load it and get it out in the boonies somewhere.

But along about this time, the Air Force came out with a big, big hurrah about how great they were and how they were the only military unit that could move a division and air arm in such and such a time. Well, by this time Admiral John S. McCain was Commander Amphibious Force Atlantic Fleet.* He was a terrific man, a big devotee of

---
*Vice Admiral John S. McCain, Jr., USN, held the billet from 1963 to 1965.

sea power; if you could get one person in a room somewhere, he could give you a three-hour speech on sea power and loved to do it. He was just a tremendous little man, just a great guy. Well, he evidently got thinking about that baloney and decided, "They're not the only ones; we can do this."

How it evolved, I don't know all the particulars, but it ended up in an operation called Steel Pike, which was in Spain.* And this was the Navy's answer to the Air Force claims that they were the only ones that could do it in X amount of time. They laid this whole operation on, and we sailed for Spain. We went out to this operating area and started the operation. Well, as we were transiting, everything was getting worse, going downhill. The weather didn't look so hot. An amphibious operation should have good weather--not unpredictable weather and not heavy, stormy weather. Because at this point, due to the terrain in Spain, they were going to have to use a lot of causeways.

Q: What part of Spain was it?

Captain Kaine: It was up north of Huelva, Spain, which is an industrial area, and it was up on the . . .

---

*This exercise was conducted in October-November 1964. For details see Lieutenant Colonel James B. Soper, USMC, "Observations: STEEL PIKE and SILVER LANCE," U.S. Naval Institute Proceedings, November 1965, pages 46-58.

Q: On the Mediterranean side or the Atlantic side?

Captain Kaine: Atlantic side. It was up where Franco had a tremendous reforestation program going on the mesa above the beaches.* The beaches were beautiful.

Q: But it needed causeways.

Captain Kaine: It needed many causeways. We thought this when we went out, judging from the things that we had studied on this stuff. So we had plenty of causeway. When we got out in the operating area, we went into a normal routine for an amphibious landing, as though it were an enemy beach, although it was a training beach. They sent in the UDT to do a reconnaissance, and they came back with their reports. The reports were not real good, but from the reports it was decided we should put the causeway in a certain place. This part of the reconnaissance was good, and the bottom was a lot flatter than we ever dreamed it would be. So instead of using many causeways along the beach, we decided that we could use only one causeway and have it extend way out.

---

*Francisco Franco, a Spanish Army officer, was the dictator who ran Spain as chief of state from 1936 until his death in 1975.

They had never put one together over eight or nine sections. So we had a Seabee engineer there, and I said, "Well, can you put it together?"

He said, "I can put it together, but I don't know how long it'll stay together."

I said, "Well, look, all I have to do is get these things off-loaded. I have to do that. The ships and boats cannot reach a causeway in close, because you can't get over the sandbar." I said, "There's no way you can get them in here."

Ultimately, we made a decision to put in an 18-section causeway. But we had to go to the admiral and say, "We've got to put a 18-section causeway in there."

And he said, "Get it in there any way you want. Get these things off-loaded and get them back out here." He said, "We're going to win this thing."

I said, "Okay."

Well, we put this in according to the survey. However, they didn't have the beach exits in the right place. We had put this causeway in the place most suitable, and the exits weren't there. Well, we struggled through the first day and kept the beach fairly reliable, but we could see from what was coming in the next day that we would never make it. So I went up to my boss, Captain Superfine, who was the same one as for the Vieques landing.* I think he came ashore only once in Spain.

---

*Captain Irving J. Superfine, USN.

F. R. Kaine #2 - 251

But he really didn't know the picture, and I got this Seabee engineer with me. I said, "Hey, can we break this thing down and move it?"

He said, "We can, but it'll take nine hours."

I said, "Well, it's going to take 39 hours if we don't."

So he said, "Oh, I agree. We've got to remove it."

So we went and saw my boss and his boss, too; we were both under the beach group commander, and he totally disagreed with us: "You will not do that."

So I said, "Well, I don't know what the hell to do now."

As luck would have it, I ran into a rear admiral; I forget his name now. He was one of the phib group commanders and over all of us. So I told him the problem and said, "I've got one hell of a problem. We've got this causeway in there. I know Admiral McCain is planning on this thing being the best operation ever, and we've got to move the causeway, or it's going to be a terrible disaster."

Then he said, "Oh, God. Whose fault is that?"

I said, "Well, it doesn't matter whose fault it is. Maybe it's nobody's fault, but is there something we can do?"

And he said, "We'll go see the admiral."

So we went to see Admiral McCain who had a long cigar and swore like a trooper. He asked how it happened and on and on. So I told him how it happened, and he said, "What's the solution?"

I said, "The solution is to move the causeway."

He said, "Can you move the causeway?"

And I said, "Yes, we can move the causeway."

"How long will it take you?" So I told him how long it would take us, and he said, "Where's your boss?"

I said, "I'll get him."

So he said, "You go home, and I'll talk to you tomorrow." So I went back to the beach and did what we had to do, and he got my boss out there. My boss was adamant against moving it. So he called me back. This took hours, you know, really, going back and forth.

Q: Of course, of course. Time is wasting.

Captain Kaine: So he's got my boss, and it was like Solomon. He had my boss in a room, and he had me in a room, and we weren't communicating, boss to me or me to boss. McCain was running between us. I wasn't there more than 15 minutes, but he made two or three trips in to me, back and forth, and he said, "Go and move the causeway." So I went and moved the causeway, and I never saw my boss. We moved it in about six or seven hours, as I recall, and

F. R. Kaine #2 - 253

once we moved it to where it should be in relation to the exit, geez, it went boom, boom, boom. Everything went great.

Q: Why was it not put in relation to the exit?

Captain Kaine: These guys just completely mislabeled where the exits were.

Q: Were they UDT people?

Captain Kaine: No, the survey they did was accurate, but from reading the maps the people of the shore party thought the exits were there, and they weren't; they were farther inland. So the thing went off like clockwork. Well, in the meantime the weather had deteriorated, and there was this tremendous storm coming, and we knew it would break up the causeway. A big, long causeway like that is like a toothpick in a storm. We started back loading then, because we had gotten everything in and proved that we could off-load it, and now to see if we could get it back out. Boy, it went just like gangbusters.

They have a law that due to the various diseases and whatnot in these various countries that every vehicle that you off-load and back load, you have to send through a dip tank; it's like a sheep dip tank. We even had that set up on the beach and dipped all the cars and vehicles as they went back. We got them all back loaded. We got the causeway broken down and back on the ships. There was one boat stuck on the beach, and we got that off. Then we got back to our ship, and that storm hit. It was just like that.

Q: It's like the ship coming over the horizon when you blew up the coral.

Captain Kaine: Just in the nick of time.

Q: I told you you were lucky.

Captain Kaine: Yes, I guess I am.

Q: I used to have a boss who would say, "If I have two people for a job, both equally bright, everything equal but one has a reputation for being lucky, I'll take the lucky one."

Captain Kaine: Well, that's true. This operation was a success, and it was really publicized. It beat the hell out of the Air Force, which was really what McCain was interested in.

Q: Thought it was a good lesson, maybe.

Captain Kaine: I had some of the dispatches. I'll give them to you, because I don't need them for anything. They were all congratulating each other after a big operation.

Q: Did you suffer any recriminations from your boss after Admiral McCain made his ruling?

Captain Kaine: Strangely enough, there were no recriminations. Truthfully, I have always felt that he had so little grasp of what actually went on in those exercises that he may have thought the Seabees were the culprits. However, never was it mentioned to me.

Q: Had you met Admiral McCain before this incident?

Captain Kaine: Yes, I had met him before in UDT when he was ComPhibTraLant at Little Creek at the same time.* But I had never met him on a close personal thing like this. He had known me by reputation in UDT, before this confrontation with my boss came up. When you're the beachmaster and you have UDT people working for you on the beach, you're their boss; you're their reporting authority.

---

*As a rear admiral just before commanding the entire Atlantic Fleet Amphibious Force, McCain was Commander Amphibious Training Command Atlantic Fleet.

F. R. Kaine #2 - 256

Well, I had a bunch of UDT kids down there working for me during surveys, constantly during the day to see how the sand shifted all the time. At night these guys were sneaking up under the bluff, and there was a cantina out there. I guess they were getting drunk as skunks and raising hell and scaring all the senoritas and all this stuff.

Admiral McCain had gotten a call from the flagship, and he had contacted the UDT skipper who was out there and told him to get up there and get the kids out of there. Well, the UDT skipper didn't. He was a young lieutenant. I kind of think this might have been his first deployment or something, and he wasn't too familiar with how hard you have to lean on these kids sometimes. So, boy, one night about 3:00 in the morning, a messenger came down there, and he said, "Admiral McCain says for you to get your butt up to the cantina and get those UDT guys out of there."

I said, "Hey, go get the UDT kid."

He said, "No, you. He said you." So I went traipsing up to this cantina and chased all these guys out.

Q: You were on the ship at the time he gave you . . .

Captain Kaine: No, I was on the beach. We lived on the beach when we were doing these operations. So I went up and got them all out of there. The next night they went back there. So the upshot of it was I went back and got them again. I took them all up to the ship, and I turned them over to their own CO. I told him, "Get them off the beach and keep them out here." And they kept them out there.

I put the kid on report, the young lieutenant, because he wasn't doing his job; he was just hiding somewhere and not doing anything. But this was brought up to McCain evidently. He knew about the cantina, but he didn't know about the UDT kid. So everything went on, and the reason I'm making emphasis of this meeting with McCain is that later on, when I was selected for captain, McCain was the head of the board. I knew Kauffman was on the board, but truthfully, at the time, I had lost all interest in being promoted, because I had been passed over five times, I think it was, for captain.

Q: That really kills a fellow, doesn't it?

Captain Kaine: As you know, I was still a reserve and had survived a number of reserve cuts in strength. I had never augmented into the regular Navy, because the only opportunity to do so was years before and involved reverting back one grade, which at the time I thought rather foolish.

Reserves during those times had not a prayer in hell

of promotion to any extent. Their promotion percentage was down around 3%, stuff like that. I'd lie if I said it didn't bother me. But, anyway, in 1966 I came up for, I think, the fifth time for promotion and was selected. I was at the amphibious school, which was a dead-end street type thing.

I always assumed it was Kauffman's effort, not ever thinking of McCain.* It wasn't until a couple of years ago, just before he died, that I said, "Gee, I never talked to you about that promotion."**

He said, "Frankly, I didn't even know that your name was in the zone." So he had nothing to do with it. I later found out it was McCain that argued for me. Admiral Kauffman told me, "I was wondering why McCain was arguing for you. I didn't think you knew him." And it was McCain all the time, so this had a significant impact on my career. Only one other reserve officer was selected that year, a guy that was his musician for something like 20 years, everywhere he went.

Q: I thought that during this period you were detached for duty in special warfare in Cuba.

Captain Kaine: That's right. The Cuban flap flapped. The

---
*Kauffman by 1966 was a rear admiral.
**Admiral Kauffman died 18 August 1979, while on vacation in Budapest, Hungary.

Bay of Pigs had long gone.* This was going to be an invasion of Cuba or something.

Q: By whom?

Captain Kaine: By us. This was a backup in case they didn't take the missiles out or something.** It was a planned operation, contingency-type thing. We did a lot of planning for it, how you'd get in and all this. It was something that never came to fruition.

Also at this time they had the Dominican Republic fiasco.*** What happened was they set up contingency stations and planning boards, what to do, and all this stuff, which I believe are still classified. So I won't get into the details of it. But I was detached from the beachmasters and sent down to Fort Bragg, North Carolina, and was put on what was called a Joint Unconventional Warfare Board. This is a contingency organization that does planning for emergency operations in case something

---

*From 17 to 20 April 1961, the United States had a hand in trying to land Cuban exiles at the Bay of Pigs on the southwestern coast of Cuba. The attempt to overthrow the Communist government of Premier Fidel Castro was a fiasco, in part because of lack of U.S. military support.
**After discovering the deployment of offensive missiles in Cuba in October 1962, the United States established a naval quarantine around Cuba to block the entry of further missiles. The Soviets agreed to discontinue shipments and to remove the missiles already in place.
***U.S. Marines were landed in the Dominican Republic on 28-29 April 1965 to protect American citizens during the course of a revolution that began there on 25 April.

F. R. Kaine #2 - 260

happens; then you're going to do this thing. So that's what those detachments were.

Q: Can you expand on either one of those?

Captain Kaine: Not a heck of a lot, because I know how they're classified, and all we did was develop a contingency plan in case somebody had to do something about it.

Q: And those plans, I'm sure, are classified.

Captain Kaine: Oh, yes, they're probably still top secret.

Q: And you were involved in the Dominican Republic contingency because of your expertise in UDT?

Captain Kaine: Yes, in the planning of UDT operations, or clandestine operations, and whatnot.

Q: That's why you were part of the plan.

Captain Kaine: That's why I was there, yes.

Q: Well, then you were in the beachmaster group for two years, right?

F. R. Kaine #2 - 261

Captain Kaine: That's right.

Q: Any more comments concerning them?

Captain Kaine: No, we did a number of exercises. The Steel Pike was the largest exercise we did while I was there, and I was there for two complete years, working totally within the amphibious force and any of their exercises outside. It was a good tour and very interesting, and it brought me back more into contact with UDT than I had been in, say, Puerto Rico.

Q: That was a lovely break, so let's continue on. I believe we are going to your next duty assignment, 1964 to 1966, as officer in charge of counterinsurgency training.

Captain Kaine: That was performed at the Naval Amphibious School at Little Creek, Virginia.

Q: I have a whole series of things that you did training in and various weapons and devices that were taught. So I'm sure if you just want to proceed, especially emphasizing SEAL training. You've mentioned several times coming up to this point--a man's development by the time he got to SEAL training. I shall just let you go with it.

Captain Kaine: Okay. I reported to the commanding officer of the school, an acquaintance of mine from previous years. His name was Captain deLaureal, a very fine naval officer.* He was very, very interested in me, not as a close personal friend, but he had followed my career, and he knew of me and where I had been. As a matter of fact, in a previous tour while I was with UDT, he had asked for and gotten me on his leadership team. This would have been in late 1956 or 1957. The amphibious force put on, as did the Navy in general, a tremendous leadership drive and leadership program. The admiral in charge of PhibLant at that time was Admiral Sabin.** He appointed Captain deLaureal to his leadership team. DeLaureal picked me, and the reason was that I was in UDT at the time and our discipline record and overall record for administration was so high that he figured that that smacked of good leadership.

So Captain deLaureal and I had been a leadership team for the amphibious force on a previous tour, so I knew him well when I reported in. As a result, he kind of gave me free rein in my department. He also made me commanding officer of the enlisted people under him, also sort of commanding officer of the staff, I guess you'd call it. He let me have a free rein in running the UDT training. At

---
*Captain Henry H. deLaureal, USN.
**PhibLant--Amphibious Force Atlantic Fleet.

this time, you may remember, counterinsurgency got to be a big buzzword in the military. I had in the past been to the Green Beret school in Fort Bragg. I took a special course in 1964 or someplace in there, and I had also been to the Marine Corps pilot school in counterinsurgency training.

DeLaureal wanted to start counterinsurgency training and have the amphibious school teach it. So we set up our course, and we did it jointly with East Coast and West Coast schools and set up a curriculum. The idea was that because of the Vietnamese situation, everybody should be exposed to counterinsurgency training.

Q: Can you give a one-sentence description of what counterinsurgency means?

Captain Kaine: Well, it had been determined by someone in the Navy that everybody going anywhere into the Pacific or Vietnam or around Vietnam would take counterinsurgency training. It was a course in trying to orient the military people into the customs, background, ethnic origins, and whatnot of the various countries that were interested. At this time it was Vietnam.

Our aim was to orient them with the methods of infiltration that the Communists were using and the type of proselytizing that they were doing with the indigenous people in the country and just giving them a background from which they could draw their own opinions and various things. Also to give them a bit of training in the methods those countries used in fighting the war and propagandizing, in their treatment of prisoners, and a general orientation in what to expect if they went into an insurgent country so that everything would not be cold.

Q: If they were captured or just went in?

Captain Kaine: Or if they were captured. What they could expect if they were captured. In this business, it was, I guess, primarily triggered by the horrible results encountered in Korea, prisoner escape attempts and the like of that. There were very few prisoner uprisings or any attempts at escape in Korea. So this was, if you will, a kind of motivational thing. I don't want to confuse this with SERE now, because it was a little different from SERE.*

At any rate, Captain deLaureal was setting up these programs, and in addition to this, we had the underwater demolition team training, which, as you well know, was a set entity now and had a program and a curriculum and special instructors. So this was kind of taking care of

---

*SERE--survival, evasion, resistance, and escape.

itself. This was not a matter of organization or setting up. Along with this, we now had SEAL teams organized in the Navy; they had been started in 1962.*

Q: Now we need to define SEAL.

Captain Kaine: Okay, SEAL is an acronym for sea, air, and land. And I might give you a little pitch here on the background on the SEAL teams and how they came about. Primarily, the motivation was from Vietnam and counterinsurgency training and the general attitude of the world at the time. In President Kennedy's time the Green Berets were highly financed and were looked upon as the leading light in potential counterinsurgency situations.** Some of the terms that we use now were not in use then, but COIN was, and it meant counterinsurgency.

The Air Force had developed its own counterinsurgency capability and aircraft and the like, and the only one with nothing in the field was the Navy. There was a lot of money laid out for this, so some bright person in the Navy decided, "Well, if there's this much money going out to counterinsurgency, then maybe we'd better get some." So,

---
*Two SEAL operating teams were established officially on 1 January 1962 for the purpose of conducting unconventional warfare at sea and in coastal and riverine areas.
**John F. Kennedy was President of the United States from January 1961 to November 1963.

snap, they created a SEAL team. At the time of creation, there were no such things as SEALs. However, within a few days, there was a core established once the okay was given and money allotted; then we had a SEAL team.

Q: I thought it was established by a directive from President Kennedy. Is that right?

Captain Kaine: Yes, it was established from a directive from President Kennedy, and it was the Navy's attempt to get its share of the counterinsurgency money. The SEAL teams were established by pulling a cadre from underwater demolition teams. We established one team on the East Coast and one team on the West Coast. Each one was made up of ten officers and 50 men, originally. There was a lieutenant in charge of each one.

Q: There's your one-to-five ratio again.

Captain Kaine: Right. It's just a magic number somebody pulled out of a hat. It was all seat-of-the-pants stuff now, because we didn't even know what they'd do. We had no idea what they would do. The SEALs were organized. The skipper on the West Coast was a man named Dave DelGuidice, and the skipper on the East Coast was a man named John

Callahan.*

Well, I didn't have anything to do with the operational part of these people. I did have a lot to do with them because of my former association with UDT and because I had become an elder statesman, so to speak, in the field. The prime aim of these now recently formed teams of SEALs--although they actually had a mission on paper, they really were not sure what their mission would be. As a result of this, the skippers of these teams--although they were young--were very smart, and they tried to get all of the training they possibly could for this new organization. As a result, at one point I think we counted up something like 52 or 58 schools that they were deploying these people to on an individual basis, to give them various capabilities. Their capabilities ran from picking locks, say, to transiting across the sky in a free-fall parachute.

Q: Oh, dear.

Captain Kaine: They were furthering an item that Etta-Belle and I discussed previously in this tape--of developing quite a talented and versatile young man, in that every specialty they added to these people just taxed them further but also gave them an extended capability.

---
*Lieutenant David DelGuidice, USNR; Lieutenant John M. Callahan, USNR.

They made use of such things as SERE schools--survival, evasion, resistance, and escape. They did a lot of practicing at the time in transiting, using free-fall capability in parachuting and working on the ability to travel and transit in the sky so it might be developed as a method of entry into a country. You could come in with an extremely high-flying aircraft, exit without parachutes, free-fall in transit, say, over a border or across X number of miles, then pop your chute at a low entry so you couldn't be picked up by sensors. They spent a lot of time training in the use of sensors. Tremendous training in fire fighting and various weapons. They acquainted themselves with all the foreign weapons that they could get access to through the military.

They took training in all the demolition courses that were possible. In each of these, like the special forces team, these SEAL units were broken down into smaller teams, and each team was cross-trained in the various types of expertise. They were highly trained in traumatic medicine and how to handle injuries and casualties and wounds. They were trained in such things as kitchen demolitions and how to manufacture explosives out of . . .

Q: What do you mean, a kitchen demolition?

Captain Kaine: A kind of home-made demolition thing, where you can synthesize explosives from various dusts . . .

Q: Like a Coke bottle or . . .

Captain Kaine: Yes, or anything like that. Molotov cocktails and various mixtures of powders and chemicals that can be made explosive when necessary. They were also extensively trained in survival, escape, resistance, and evasion. And they did a lot of studying of the customs, ethnic backgrounds, and immutable beliefs of the indigenous peoples in the various countries where they had any idea of being sent. So that when they went into a country, they would not be at a complete loss.

Q: This was all stressed toward Vietnam, of course, at this time?

Captain Kaine: Yes, right. See, if I'm not mistaken, we had people in Vietnam in the early 1960s, right after the SEALs were formed. I think they went out there as advisers. These tours were not all that successful, because they didn't know the people. They got some playback from that, and as a result, this is where they're going right now. They're just trying to develop all the things that they found lacking when they were in that country.

Q: Oh, I see.

Captain Kaine: So they learned from that. I'll give you an example of the types of things that they were trying to learn. They were going to language training. They didn't only concentrate on Vietnamese language; they studied Italian; they studied at whatever language schools they could get into.

Q: How did they have this much time to do this much study? How long did the training last?

Captain Kaine: Forever, as far as they were concerned. They would be doing it over the next how many years. As a matter of fact, they are still doing it. Some of these people are still taking various courses and training and everything. So it's never finished.

Q: Did you have attrition in this group such as you had had in other . . .

Captain Kaine: They had an attrition. They didn't have an attrition when they started out. Their attrition per se is not an attrition, because they can put them back in UDT.

If there's something that they can't handle or get into, they keep them in UDT. Sometimes along the line in this development from UDT to SEAL, it kind of helps the picture if you think of UDT as a passive type of weapon and the SEALs as an active type of weapon. The UDT handle everything up to the waterline and maybe through the beach, and the SEALs are beyond that. The SEAL would be classed as a predator rather than just a passive investigator.

Q: I noticed you used the term "immutable beliefs." That was a term that intrigued me.

Captain Kaine: A lot of countries have immutable beliefs. They're like taboos. They believe in, oh, say the old Indian thing of the happy hunting ground. No matter what you would say, he was going to the happy hunting ground. Whether he went there in style or not, it was incidental; he was going there.

I'll give you another example of an immutable belief. Some of the Vietnamese people bury their dead within the town, and they always have the towns around graveyards, because they wanted to be there when the spirits of these people came up. They thought that if their burial ground and their town weren't enough together, that it was just a horrible thing, and they couldn't live without that. Later on in the Vietnamese thing, the Americans moved whole towns of Vietnamese people to protect them from the Viet Cong. The Vietnamese people would eventually move right back to where their ancestors were buried; they just couldn't stand it. They couldn't live without being near their ancestral burial ground.

A lot of these things we didn't know anything about. We have the term nowadays--culture shock. Well, this was a terrible thing. For instance, I think the first people that we had in there to do with were the mountain people in Vietnam. The Americans didn't find out until years later that the mountain people were at war with the people around Saigon, the city people. They actually signed a peace treaty later on. But we went in on the side of the mountain people, not knowing who was right and who was wrong.

So there's a lot of study that should be done before you get involved in a country. We assume that our people in Washington, in the State Department, know all this stuff. I don't doubt that there are individuals who do know all this stuff; however, it's not well known, and it's not down to the level of the people who participate in a pacifying mission or in a war or in any kind of a mission to a country. Those are the people who should know it.

Q: Should this type of information be made general knowledge among people in our country, that this kind of training is needed and is going on?

Captain Kaine: Oh, I think it is, as a general rule. Well, it was at one point anyway.

Let's see, other training that the SEALs went through included extensive swimming, extensive training with all possible types of diving equipment, midget submersibles. Any methods of entry into an area. They trained in kayaks, surfboards, paddle boards, anything that you can think of. And a tremendous list of small arms and various weapons--limpets, any actual positive method. They were trained in all kinds of defense, so-called manly arts, use of all weapons.

Q: It's incredible for a person to sit and hear you describe what training it was.

Captain Kaine: Well, it's very much in-depth training, and it's also a reaction training. When SEALs are trained later on, as they progressed in Vietnam, I remember and I'll point out to you how they really get to the point of reaction, which a lot of people don't understand, and it might be well not to.

In addition to this position at the school, we also taught the SERE program. This was a new item for the school, not that SERE was new. We had SERE programs before, and most aviators go through one. A lot of us in UDT had gone through SERE programs, and all the SEALs were. They used a program in Canada; they used a couple of them in the United States. But we convinced the powers that be that we should run our own SERE program, because at the time we were training all these counterinsurgency numbers, about 150 people a week were coming into the program for the training.

We needed to teach them SERE as well as the counterinsurgency program, because most of the people we were training were going in country in Vietnam and would be in the position of possibly being captured. So we finally got permission and we set up the program. One of them was set up in Virginia, and we had to import instructors who had been through the program and knew it.

One note I'd like to make here--in all these programs, particularly the UDT, one of your prime problem areas is that of instructors, for many reasons. You have to get good-quality instructors. You have to get people that like teaching. The biggest problem with any of these programs that have to do with the physical, like UDT or SERE or SEAL training, is that you have to stay on top of it all the time. Because for some reason in the American--probably in every group--there's a tendency to become cruel. There's a tendency on the part of the instructor to develop likes and dislikes, a tendency of a lot of them to make people prove themselves more than necessary.

Q: Like drill sergeants sometimes?

Captain Kaine: Yes, and there's a terrible tendency to become extremely cruel if you don't watch them. I don't mean watch them every minute, but you have to have screening, and you have to change your instructors often. You can't let them stay there indefinitely and indefinitely, developing bad habits.

I was fortunate in knowing this before I went to this job, because one thing I forgot to mention--when I was in Puerto Rico, I was director of discipline on that staff. That duty involved inspecting all the brigs in the area, which meant about five, as I recall, and checking on the programs within those brigs. In doing one of them, we found out there was a certain amount of cruelty in it, and we created an investigation. It ended up with about five of the brig-keepers being pulled out.

Q: Were they rated enlisted men?

Captain Kaine: Yes, enlisted men. Several were reprimands and one court-martialed. In creating the investigation and paying attention to it as it went along, we found out that people just have a tendency, when they're exposed to the same routine like that every day, to kind of treat down to prisoners or treat down to trainees.

Q: Maybe they're given power they hadn't had before.

Captain Kaine: A lot of it. They can't handle power. An instructor will develop an attitude about the trainees: "Oh, those guys aren't really good, and I'll get rid of them." He'll try to do things and make an individual get out of the program or make him flunk the program. It's a terribly hard thing, because you can't pick the people that are going to go this way. You can't tell beforehand, and it's just--well, recent incidents here on the ships . . .

Q: Yes, I would say that.

Captain Kaine: It's exactly what I'm talking about. You have to have authority on top of this all the time; otherwise, you get a lot of problems. I'll give you an example of an item I found one night. In the UDT training, I had gone home for dinner at 4:30 or something and was back on base. I just happened to ride by my office, and I saw a youngster out there doing push-ups, out in front of the door. So I walked over to him, and there was nobody else there. I asked him what he was doing, and he said, "Well, instructor So-and-so said to do push-ups until he came back."

And I said, "When did he say that?"

And he said, "About 40 minutes ago."

I asked him how many. He was up doing about 700 or 800 push-ups. So I sent him in, and I got rid of the instructor the next day. His instructor told him to do push-ups and went over to have dinner, and he was going to come back afterwards.

Q: That's one way to lose a good man, I suppose.

Captain Kaine: Absolutely. Another thing we found out doing this instructing was that if a person flunked a written exam or didn't do well on it, a lot of instructors would give him physical punishment instead of studying punishment. So there's a lot of little lessons that I was fortunate enough to learn in being exposed to this.

Q: How many instructors were on your staff? Would it vary?

Captain Kaine: Oh, yes. Lord, I think we had 13 in the UDT program, and in counterinsurgency we had probably six or eight. In the SERE program we probably had 15 or 20. So we had a total of maybe 50, something like that.

Q: It's a lot to keep your eye on.

Captain Kaine: Yes, it was a busy job. It was a good job, though, a very good job.

Q: And where did they go from your training?

Captain Kaine: They went right in country. Usually they were on orders into Vietnam, and ours was a stop for training.

Q: And that length of time would vary, depending on what schools were available?

Captain Kaine: That's right. The SERE program was a revelation to me, because we made it as exact as we could, parts of it, to the prison program that they had, say, in Vietnam--as close as we could get it from any intelligence. Now, when you went into the SERE program, everybody knew it was a training program. It was a rugged training program; there's no question about it. We gave them the teaching necessary and the training necessary, but you must remember now that a lot of these people were just coming from off ship, going in country to Vietnam to a job. A lot of them were going into the river forces; a lot of them were really going to be exposed, where they could be captured. We were told that we should make it as realistic as possible, so we did.

Q: What terrain did you use?

Captain Kaine: We used an old abandoned Army camp in Virginia.

Q: I was just curious.

Captain Kaine: Yes, and it was a heavy growth area.

Q: You didn't take them down to the jungles of Panama or anything of that nature?

Captain Kaine: No, no, we didn't. But we did use the swamp. We had one place that was a swamp area there. I'll think about the name.

Q: I was just curious as to how realistic it could be made.

Captain Kaine: We simulated the prison camps just as closely as possible. We used some of the North Vietnamese methods of harassment, but not torture; we used high-class interrogation.

We used all the survival methods that had been learned over the last 15-20 years. On the survival part of the program, we even gave them a chicken or a rabbit and a handful of rice. Then we'd give them a problem along with it. We incorporated the survival and the evasion and escape part of it together. Their problem was to survive for X number of days in a swamp or woods--depending on what we were using. We'd have people looking for them at the same time. It was amazing how many people would come back with a live chicken. They'd starve to death rather than kill a little chicken and eat it.

Q: That's the American ethic, I think.

Captain Kaine: I think so, a lot of them. And we also gave them something like a big safety pin so they could fish in the water and maybe catch something. A lot of them did this very well.

The prison phase was set up just like a prison camp, and you had guards. We had designated guards that were to be mean and designated guards that were to be soft and sweet and nice. We had soft interrogation and hard interrogation. We had little cubicles that we'd close them in, simulating the little cubicles they used in Vietnam. We had no physical beating or anything like that; that was strictly prohibited. But as close as anything possible, we did it.

Even this created a terrible problem, because we got so many breakdowns. People would just blow; they'd just have almost complete nervous breakdowns. They just couldn't control themselves; it was a mess. And these people were already on orders in country to do a job, and it was just beyond them to endure the harassment the instructors were putting them through on this training phase. So then I really got worried, because if they couldn't stand something that they knew was simulated, what the heck were they going to do in Vietnam?

Q: Now these were not people who had come from UDT?

Captain Kaine: No, these weren't. These were just fleet people, officers and enlisted. The first time this happened, I didn't know what in hell to do. My boss was out of his mind. He said, "My God, we've ruined this man. What are we going to do?"

So I called BuPers and said, "Hey, look, we've really got a problem here, because we have a good program going here, but we're breaking down people. I would recommend that they never be sent to Vietnam or never be sent into a country where they could be taken prisoner or where they would have any access to classified material."

I guess this created such a furor in BuPers that they

went round and round, and they didn't know what to do. I said, "I'll hold these people here until you get back to me, because it's silly to send them in. The only place some of them should be is in a hospital." Some of them were pretty bad.

Q: How soon did it take them to respond and snap out of it?

Captain Kaine: Oh, they'd snap out of it almost immediately. But they were weak, emotionally shaken, terribly upset with themselves.

This was such a bomb to BuPers. It was something they had never thought about, and, truthfully, I hadn't either. They said, "Hell, we can't send them. So just hang on to them." Then they reassigned them to places where they'd never be taken prisoner.

Q: What was the percentage of the people . . .

Captain Kaine: I don't have a percentage, but it was only a few.

Q: I imagine when they went through it they thought very well of themselves, didn't they?

Captain Kaine: Absolutely. And what was hard was trying to convince them that they'd think well of themselves afterwards. We didn't hold anything against them. It was the way they were built; it wasn't their fault, and it wasn't our fault. However, you do have a lot of thoughts about this--whether you've got the right to drive people to this point.

Q: Well, you're a compassionate man and a man of common sense and intelligence. Other people might not react the same way you did.

Captain Kaine: But, you know, my father was a doctor. I guess I told you that. I can remember coming home after the war and talking to him and asking him about all this war fatigue stuff. I said, "Why don't I have war fatigue like all these other people?"

And he said, "Well, some people are going to have it whether they go to war or not. A certain amount of people are going to get in a stress situation where they're going to blow it anyhow." So sometimes that happens, and when you think along those lines, then you can, I guess, rationalize the part you play in these people maybe having minor breakdowns.

That just about covers all the things we taught. Did we talk about all the weapons that they could possibly use?

Q: You said of various countries as well as ours.

Captain Kaine: Right. There are various ordnance museums around in the military, and we pulled as many representative weapons as they had in those various ordnance museums to train these people on. Some of them we could get ammunition for, some of them we couldn't. In some cases we could just show them the weapon and tell them how to operate it. With others we got enough so they could fire them and become familiar with them.

The SEALs had quite a repertoire of weapons that our people had picked up in Vietnam, like Russian weapons, Czech weapons, Chinese weapons, the whole gamut. So we used those, and the SEAL teams were starting to create their own museum of materials they had picked up in countries, and we'd use any of that to familiarize people. People do much better if they go into a strange country and they recognize things.

We also tried to get things like hats, shoes, anything that we could just to show them how the people dressed.

Q: Well, you've made it sound very interesting.

Captain Kaine: It was a very interesting billet and one that I really hadn't anticipated being that interesting, but the times made it. I don't think anybody who has been operating mostly in his career looks forward to a staff billet in school. However, this one turned out to be great.

Q: So that was that two years.

Captain Kaine: That was two years. The next trip was 1966, when I went to become Commander Special Warfare Group Pacific, which was a very rewarding job. I'll tell you a little anecdote about this before we get into the job.

I was a commander when they first started this Special Warfare Group, which was really an imposed command over UDT and SEAL. And then they picked up the beach jumper unit and the boat unit. So it was really a takeoff on the Naval Beach Group, if you will. But it was oriented strictly to special warfare or unconventional warfare.

Just before the captain selection board met in 1965, I was offered this billet on the East Coast. But because I wasn't selected that year, I didn't get it. So I never gave it another thought. As a matter of fact, Audrey and I decided that what I would do was retire and work in Norfolk. Lo and behold, I got selected for captain. I was notified at 5:00 o'clock in the morning, and, of course, I couldn't believe it, because I'd spent ten years as a commander. About two hours later, I got a call offering this job again.

Q: Isn't that interesting. I'm curious to know who called you at 5:00 o'clock in the morning.

Captain Kaine: A chaplain.

Q: Oh, really?

Captain Kaine: Yes. I was amazed to see how you can go from an idiot to a big hero overnight by being selected. I thought that was a big change.

Some lesser tasks were included within the new job. I was special warfare adviser to CinCPac. I was also special warfare adviser to ComNavForV, which was Commander Naval Forces Vietnam. I was also special warfare adviser to Commander Amphibious Force Pacific Fleet. And it was in my charter to budget for and fund a SEAL group, the beach jumper unit, a boat unit, and the underwater demolition teams. When we started in 1966, I think we had something like 1,100 people. By 1970 we were up to around 1,600 people.

Q: Where were you physically?

Captain Kaine: This was in Coronado.

We had a conglomerate detachment of beach jumpers, UDT, and SEALs at times in Okinawa. We had UDT, SEALS, and beach jumpers in Vietnam, and we also had the responsibility for running a huge SEAL training program here in California.

Q: In Coronado?

Captain Kaine: No, it was out here in Cuyamaca, the Chocolate Mountain area. And in training the SEALs we used every new weapon we could find. We used every modern training facility we could use. We had confidence courses with pop-up targets. We had various types of armor and protective clothing. We had people working on new weapons. We had people working on things like fleshettes, which are little darts. Depending on the types, they come so many to a shotgun shell, maybe 20 or 30 of these things. We experimented with those; you'd fire the shotgun, and these little darts would fly into somebody. In Vietnam it didn't prove worth a damn.

We tried all kinds of weapons, things such as the AR-15 and AR-16. There were problems with some of them in that the Vietnamese were so small that if you shot them, the bullets went right through them and wouldn't stop them. They'd still keep coming. Some of the weapons would be deflected by heavy foliage. We had to learn from mistakes in country, because we really had overdeveloped the weaponry for the war we were fighting in Vietnam.

Q: How long did it take you to know that?

Captain Kaine: Almost immediately, because you'd go in country, and the kids would complain the enemy was fighting with crossbows. They were fighting with people, and the people would dig big pits and put stakes in them and cover them over; you'd fall in them, and the stakes had poison on them. They had things hanging from trees, such as a big broad platform with stakes pointing out. A man would go by and trip one, and it would come down and kill him on these stakes. One of the big weapons that was used against us in Vietnam was the BAR, the old Browning automatic rifle, our big weapon in World War II. There were a lot of Chinese weapons, Czechoslovak weapons, Russian weapons used by the Vietnamese.

Most of the thing was to go back to primitive-type warfare. It was hunt and hunt. The Marines landed in Vietnam, but there was no big opposed landing. It was a lot of aerial warfare. Our pilots would follow airplanes, and they could only follow them so far and have to turn around and go back. They couldn't fire in certain areas. Oh, God, it was just a mess.

F. R. Kaine #2 - 289

Q: You mean because of restrictions put on them from Washington?

Captain Kaine: Oh, yes, very definitely.

Q: What was your communication so that you knew what was going on thousands of miles away?

Captain Kaine: I used to go out there. And we always had people going and coming, too. We deployed people in units. But when I got out here to Coronado in 1966, a lot of the people in country that the SEALs were working for didn't know how to employ SEALs. No matter how many trips I made out there to explain it to them, they were adamant against employing them in the fashion that they were trained in, the way they would be most effective.

Q: Who would be the people that you would try to . . .

Captain Kaine: ComNavForV. On one occasion it wasn't necessarily him. It was the people that he would assign the SEALs to, like maybe the riverine force or one of the patrol forces down there. They would want to use the SEALs to their advantage and not to the advantage of the United States. SEALs were designed and built as an offensive weapon, and they might want to use them as perimeter

F. R. Kaine #2 - 290

defense or something, to keep them around there. These kids had tremendous firepower at their disposal with their weapons and everything else. They were trained to operate around the clock if necessary. So one of our big problems was to acquaint the in-country staffs on how to use them.

Q: What were the missions of the SEALs in Vietnam?

Captain Kaine: To my knowledge, those operations are still classified, so I can't say much. But in general the ops were to take prisoners, gather intelligence, disrupt enemy ops, and work with local forces and other agencies of the U.S.

Q: Did the Navy SEALs ever report to any Vietnamese?

Captain Kaine: No. They operated heavily with the Vietnamese, but they never reported to them. So we had a big, big job of orienting the people in country.

Q: Why did you have such a difficult time having the commanders utilize the SEALs for the purpose for which they were there?

Captain Kaine: Because they weren't interested in conducting this type of warfare at the time. I don't know, there was a certain amount of reluctance to disturb the status quo. I guess McNamara was running the war by telephone.*

When the first Commander Naval Forces Vietnam that we worked for was replaced, it got a little better.** We could tell them exactly what the SEALs were and how they were supposed to be used. As more of the amphibious people from here got in country and started taking over the various jobs--like Wade Wells and Art Price--they started taking over the rivers.*** Then they started employing these people to advantage and using the SEALs for the purpose they were created.

In spite of these problems, the SEALs were probably the most effective weapon they had in country--on the ground. I won't say anything about the air, because I don't really know anything about the air. They had integrated the use of helicopters. They had integrated with the boat people so they could be inserted by boat; we had some light, fast boats.

---

*Robert S. McNamara was Secretary of Defense, 1961-68.
**In May 1967, Rear Admiral Norvell G. Ward was relieved by Rear Admiral Kenneth L. Veth, USN, whose oral history is in the Naval Institute collection.
***Captain Wade C. Wells, USN, commanded the Riverine Assault Force (Task Force 117) in 1966-67. See his article "The Riverine Force in Action, 1966-67," 1969 Naval Review (Annapolis: U.S. Naval Institute, 1969), pages 46-83. Captain Arthur W. Price, Jr., USN, served as Commander River Patrol Force (Task Force 116) in Vietnam in 1967-68; his oral history is in the Naval Institute collection.

Q: Now is that the river forces that you're . . .

Captain Kaine: River forces, yes. And also there was another one, 115, and 116 with what is the patrol forces, and they operated with them sometimes off Swift boats, which were patrol boats.* We had our own boats, Boston whalers, that we could use for insertion. A little later we developed a SEAL insertion boat, which was a great boat.

Q: I think you described that, didn't you, before?

Captain Kaine: Yes. It was a really good boat, slightly armored, and it was very effective. But in spite of all the problems with coordinating these people and getting our own people used to using the SEALs, that was multiplied when you had to work with the Vietnamese and had to educate them into the method of operations. We had a terribly difficult time with the Vietnamese people in getting clearances to operate in an area, and it was only because you couldn't trust anybody. In order to run SEAL operations and run them effectively, we had to clear many areas and then pick one and operate in it.

---

*Task Force 115 (Market Time) did patrolling off the coast of South Vietnam to interdict infiltration of weapons and supplies from North Vietnam. Task Force 116 (Game Warden) operated fast patrol boats in the rivers and canals of South Vietnam's Mekong Delta area.

Q: Without letting them know . . .

Captain Kaine: Without letting them know where it was. This also led to a lot of problems, because you had to find out if anybody else was operating in the area. I should tell you a little bit, maybe. The SEALs operated primarily at night, and they would go out on a specific mission, whatever it was. Somebody had decided perhaps that there was a meeting of the hierarchy of one of the provinces or something, and they would go out and see if they could get any prisoners. They were primarily interested in getting prisoners and information.

Well, in order to do that--after we got information on this meeting, we'd have to clear it ahead of time. We might want to clear two or three areas around there and then go into that one, but there might be somebody else operating in it. So it was a terrible mishmash of clearances and everything else.

On top of that, when we first went in there, intelligence was lousy, especially local intelligence. They had two or three really good intelligence officers in there, and they were outstanding, but the rest of them were terrible. Through the good graces of one of the senior intelligence officers out there, we got permission to join with their intelligence people and train them and operate with them so that they could develop the kind of intelligence we needed and could use. They were getting a lot of intelligence, but it was nothing you needed. So after working for maybe a year or so, doing all this stuff, then the thing started going.

In the meantime, we were getting terrific results, even operating under these circumstances. I'm just telling you, because it was a terribly hard area to operate. There was very little cooperation many times with other commands or other people. As the SEALs' reputation started spreading--and it spread like wildfire--it created jealousies. A lot of people wanted to operate with them.

Q: They were in their glory.

Captain Kaine: Yes, as it developed, we started training the Vietnamese. We would take Vietnamese on operations with us, and a lot of them turned out to be really good. As a result of that, we started training them, and we also had UDT operations going on at the same time in Vietnam. They were clearing canals and doing all kinds of stuff. As a matter of fact, they blew one whole new canal with explosives to join a couple of different canals to give them a new area to run through with their boats and everything else. So it was a tremendous project.

At the same time we were working with the Vietnamese and developing them, they decided that they wanted their own UDT. So we helped them develop and train the Vietnamese UDT.

It wasn't until Admiral Zumwalt went in country that the whole thing turned around.* It was just tremendous. He was probably the best influence that ever happened when he got to Vietnam. He turned morale around; he turned around the briefings with the Army general; everything took on new life. He brought just a complete change of everything. Something would happen way out in the boondocks, and you'd hear that some kid did a great job. Zumwalt would fly out there in his helicopter and pin a Silver Star on him or a Bronze Star or whatever it merited--instantaneously. God, morale went up just like that.

He got interested in the SEALs and UDT. He'd call down here to the strand and say, "I need 15 more, 20 more, 100 more SEALs."** The SEALS went from maybe 100 to 500 while he was out there.*** We had to cut out a lot of the training and rush them through. I'll give you a little bit of an idea how interested he was in this stuff. One night my wife and I were out, and the phone rang. Somebody said, "Is Captain Kaine there?"

---
*On 30 September 1968, Vice Admiral Elmo R. Zumwalt, Jr., USN, relieved Rear Admiral Kenneth L. Veth, USN, as Commander U.S. Naval Forces Vietnam.
**The strand is a reference to the naval amphibious base on a strand of beach in Coronado, California.
***Admiral Zumwalt remained ComNavForV until May 1970, when he was relieved to become Chief of Naval Operations.

And our daughter, who was then in high school, said, "No, but this is his daughter Carol."

And the voice said, "Well, this is Admiral Zumwalt."

And she said, "Well, Admiral Zumwalt, I'll tell him you called. Can I have him call you?"

I forget how it ended, but he wound up getting me later. But he was interested in getting more SEALs, and that's an indication of how involved he was personally. He was just all over the place.

Q: I understood initially that there was an attempt to keep the SEALs secret. Only after a cartoonist, Roy Crane, used Buz Sawyer as a SEAL was the Navy willing to admit that it had such a service. One of the people in your staff by the name of Lieutenant Commander Anderson was permitted to issue a statement that, "We operate in Vietcong-controlled areas of South Vietnam, including the Rung Sat--the words mean Killer Jungle--between Saigon and the sea. We have been extremely successful." Is that true.

Captain Kaine: That's true. Right as rain. Frank Anderson was the skipper of the SEAL team at the time.*

Q: I wonder if it was true that somewhere I read that the

_____
*Lieutenant Commander Franklin Anderson, USN, commanding officer of SEAL Team One.

F. R. Kaine #2 - 297

Navy did feed this man Crane some information so that in his cartoons he would have it. Do you know anything about that?

Captain Kaine: I don't know as to the authenticity of that. I did hear that, though.

Q: That was in _Time_ magazine.*

Captain Kaine: One of the so-called restrictions placed on SEALs when they were originally formed was that they had to operate from the water. Otherwise, I guess they would infringe on the territorial rights of special forces, the Green Berets. To keep it legal, so to speak, you had to operate from the water. Well, the Rung Sat Zone was the area between Saigon and the sea, and it was a maze of canals and everything. So the first place they put them to work was right down there. Later, as their successes mounted, it was just unbelievable. They operated all over Vietnam, with the blessings of Admiral Zumwalt.

    He did such things as call Admiral Kauffman, who was then Commander U.S. Naval Forces Philippines, into Vietnam to get his advice on how to speed up the manufacture of SEALs. Of course, Kauffman hadn't anything to do with

---

*"Unconventional Commandos," _Time_, 12 January 1968, pages 18-19.

SEALs; he didn't know a SEAL from a bow-wow. At any rate, he gave him his suggestions, and Admiral Zumwalt sent me a message telling me what Admiral Kauffman said.

So I sent back a message that said, "I couldn't disagree more. It's just a whole new ball game. This would have been fine with UDT. You could have done exactly what he said with UDT, but with the SEALs you can't do it."

So he sent me another one: "Get out here." So I went out there. I don't know whether you're aware of it or not, but Admiral Zumwalt lived in a compound. They had a nice house, and he had a couple of trailers in there for visiting firemen; there was always somebody coming. So I got out there.

Q: In Saigon?

Captain Kaine: Yes. Kauffman was ensconced in this trailer, so Zumwalt put me in the trailer with Kauffman, and he said, "Admiral Kauffman, Kaine here doesn't agree with you."

And Kauffman said, "Well, it wouldn't be the first time, Admiral."

So Admiral Zumwalt said, "All right, you two settle your differences." So we chit-chatted for a while. Then Kauffman said to Admiral Zumwalt, "Well, he's right. I had no idea of the extensive training that these people were doing." So we got into a compromise with Admiral Zumwalt, because he had such a demand and had so many places he could use the SEALs. We were already committed to other special programs, too, where we were putting SEALs, and although he would have liked to get those, he couldn't. The classification on that program then was super high, and I imagine it still is, so I can't tell you about it.

So we reached a compromise, and we cut out some of the training that was not essential to their operation in Vietnam. That way we were able to get more SEALs in country quicker for him to use, without any possibility of hurting the SEALs or their training. We just eliminated the training that was not pertinent to that area. He was quite happy about it, and we had a really good relationship. As a matter of fact, he's one of the guardian angels of the SEALs--as far as all SEALs or UDT are concerned--because he did so much, not only for them but for almost everybody that was in country.

He did so much, he was so active, and he was everywhere; yet I could go out there with a problem and ask to see Admiral Zumwalt and get right in to see him. I would sit there for only three minutes or five minutes and feel I had accomplished as much as if I'd been there for an hour. He answered every question that I had, and I was out and on my way before I knew it, but I was satisfied. So he had a pretty good gift for that. I had great admiration for him and the way he conducted his part of the war out there; he did a great job.

Q: Can you describe some of the operations? Because there is much literature in publications, and I'd like to hear a description of one operation, if there's any such thing as a typical one, from you.

Captain Kaine: Well, a typical one would be maybe they had a report that there was a prison camp in a certain area, and they would like the SEALs to go out and see if they could liberate any prisoners from it. I'll take that as an example, because I think the SEALs were the only ones that ever liberated a prison camp out there.

Q: This would be in North Vietnam?

Captain Kaine: No, this was South Vietnam.

Q: Would the Viet Cong have a prison camp in South Vietnam?

Captain Kaine: Yes, yes. The guy that led the raid, I think, was Scott Lyons. And his people went out in the black of night and searched, you know, running across rice paddies and on dikes and this stuff. They found the prison camp, and they liberated something like 18 prisoners that were in the camp--got in, got out, without any casualties on this particular mission.

As for another type of operation, I remember a couple of our planes were down at a place called the Three Sisters. These were three big, big mountains down in South Vietnam, and they were surrounded by Viet Cong. They told one of our SEAL detachments about it, and the SEAL lieutenant, who I think was Peter Dirkx, took his SEALs in.* They infiltrated through the Viet Cong lines, got the people off the airplane, and got them out and back to safety.

Q: What about some of the operations in the Rung Sat, down in the jungle and swamp areas?

Captain Kaine: Those were sweep-and-kill things; they got out on patrol.

Q: Tell me.

Captain Kaine: The SEALs would look for Viet Cong and find them--or get found and get into a real pitched battle. Sometimes they would go up the river. The original boats we had down there didn't have any armor over the top of

---
*Lieutenant Peter C. Dirkx, USN.

them. They were just regular landing craft.

I remember one incident, one of the first bad things that happened to a whole group. We had an M boat going up the river, and they were going up to a position to insert a SEAL team.* They would then come down the river, and the boat would drift down also--not with them but kind of on call. They always used to test-fire their weapons well before they were inserted in a place so that they'd know everything worked.

What they didn't know was that there were a bunch of Viet Cong in on the bank just above where they tested their weapons. The Viet Cong were crafty; they knew the SEALs were going up the river, and so they knew they had to come down the river eventually. So the team went up and was inserted. They looked and looked all over whatever area they were supposed to look in. They came back and got on the boat, and when they came down the river, the Viet Cong just blew the hell out of them with mortar fire and rocket fire and everything. Let's see, we had one boy killed and another boy almost killed; a whole mess of them were just filled with all kinds of shrapnel.

Q: The reputation was, as I read it, that the casualties were remarkably few.

---

*Sometimes known as a mike boat, the LCM was officially called a landing craft mechanized.

Captain Kaine: Oh, they were. They were remarkable.

Q: This had all to do with their training.

Captain Kaine: I'd say yes, a lot of it. I've forgotten the numbers that were killed, but I think the number was around 29 or 30 when I left in 1970. It ran maybe 72 or 73 through 1972. So they may have had a few more casualties. But percentage-wise, for the number of operations conducted, they were negligible. Because, don't forget, these guys operated every single night for five or six years. We had people who were out there seven and eight times for six-month tours.

Q: Was it true, the story I heard of them having to stand in water for hours at a time in water up to their waists and shoulders?

Captain Kaine: Sometimes, yes. One of them was short?

Q: No, no, but he had a python drop next to him, and he stood immobile for four hours as he and the python watched each other; finally, the python went away.

Captain Kaine: I hadn't heard that one.

Q: You didn't read that issue of Reader's Digest?*

Captain Kaine: No. They had a lot of strange things happen to them, you know. They had tremendous tides in Vietnam, in the vicinity of 15 feet. They have all these dikes and rice paddies, and when the river comes flooding up and down, say, on the Rung Sat Zone, you can walk along one of these places, and just all of a sudden the water is quite deep because it comes rushing in there so fast.

Q: And you say there was a short man?

Captain Kaine: I remember there was a story, and I forget the characters involved, but it did happen. Rapid flooding on a high tide, the river flooding and everything else. They were streaming along, and the big, tall guy grabbed a branch. The little short guy had nothing to do and was floating on down the river. He finally found a snag to get ahold of. But there are a lot of things that affect the conduct of war in a place like that. It's just unbelievable.

You know, we had people attacked by tigers. Now, we didn't personally in the SEALs, but we had reports of American military people who were attacked by tigers.

---

*John G. Hubbell, "Supercommandos of the Wetlands," Reader's Digest, June 1967, pages 49-54.

Q: I didn't know that.

Captain Kaine: There's a snake in the country that will go upstairs, that will go into a shelter or a house. They had a lot of pythons and boas. One of the funniest things I watched one day was a bunch of people in UDT who had captured a big boa and dragged it into the compound. It was a huge, huge snake, maybe 12-14 feet long. Somebody said, "Well, maybe he's hungry. Let's get a chicken and see if he'll eat it." So they took a little chicken out there and staked him to the ground and tied his leg to the stake. Then they brought that big old boa over there, and the boa wasn't hungry, but what he did to that chicken's nervous system you just can't believe.

Q: Oh, that's terrible.

Captain Kaine: You get a lot of that sadistic-type stuff out there.

Q: In troops or in people? They were guilty of savagery?

Captain Kaine: Oh, I think everybody in a war does it at some time or another. I don't know. I do know of incidents where it was reported they were using dead Viet

Cong bodies for fenders on boats and stuff like that. You'd get reports on that. I think there's probably nobody as cruel as the oriental. I'm generalizing now.

Q: But I mean the troops of SEAL or UDT.

Captain Kaine: Oh, I don't know of any; I'm trying to think. I think we had one guy that we got rid of. We pulled him out of country because we thought he had been involved in some cruelty or something. I can't remember if that was before I got out of there or just after I got out of there. But I remember it was a question of whether he was doing right or wrong.

Q: But I think the point that I was trying to make is that in spite of the rough, rugged, incredibly dangerous training that they received, it didn't turn them into monsters.

Captain Kaine: No, no, I don't know of any.

That's probably something I should touch on while we're on the subject. You train people, and I'm a great advocate of training. I believe wholeheartedly in training for anything, and I think that if a person is adequately trained for the field, he does not have extraordinary fear. I'm sure he has a few personal things, but he . . .

Q: I understand what you mean.

Captain Kaine: But he feels adequate to the situation. I think that was highly evidenced on the part of the astronauts. I think that along those lines, probably nothing is more scary than a trip to the moon or a trip to outer space. Yet when these people were finally trained, you just couldn't hold them back; they were so anxious to go. In line with that, and apropos of some of the accusations of cruelty and brutality of American soldiers and sailors and whatnot in Vietnam, I think a lot of people--both civilian and military--don't quite understand what combat training is.

In the type of war that people were fighting in Vietnam--and I realize it's questionable if they call it war or not--but the war the SEALs fought in Vietnam involved guerrilla-type warfare. It was a one-on-one, tough fight. In training people for this, you use every method at your disposal. You try to train them to be alert to every possible enemy that they can have. In Vietnam every possible enemy included children and old women and old men and everything else. There are many documented cases where women on bicycles would ride in through a group of military people and drop hand grenades and just keep going and blow all the people up.

F. R. Kaine #2 - 308

In order to combat this kind of warfare, we in the Special Warfare Group saw to it that our people were highly trained to react. We taught them to listen; we taught them to hear. We taught them to recognize sounds and know what sounds were and to be able to associate certain sounds with certain things. So if a youngster was investigating a native hooch somewhere and it was dark and he heard what sounded like the bolt of a rifle being pulled, he turned and fired at that sound. He might flash a light over there and find an 80-year-old woman with a rifle in her hand. The attendant publicity just ruins the kid's life, but it has nothing to do with that boy. It's just what he's been taught and trained to do.

Q: Is that what you meant when you said a point of reaction?

Captain Kaine: Yes. And this happens so many times. I'm not trying to defend anybody; I'm just trying to explain.

Q: You're stating, I think, the situation, the fact.

Captain Kaine: And the degree to which you train people. Gee, I remember some of the courses you take. I remember one program in ranger school or some school. They would teach you that if you hear something at the door, you don't go open the door. You make sure your hand is ahead of you, and you turn that knob and hit the door with your shoulder, going about 50 miles an hour if you can get that fast.

I saw that happen one time after World War II when I was working as a salesman in a laboratory. I was out in the lab, and we had a big truck driver who was a tremendous athlete. He started to go into the lab door, and as he was going in, he heard something on the back side of that door. He figured somebody was going to hold the door on him, because there was a little peephole you could see through from the inside. We had one young man there that always used to play tricks on everybody. When this truck driver heard the noise, he put his hand down and hit that door about 90 miles an hour. That kid went flying across the room, destroyed literally 25 test tubes and beakers and whatnot in the laboratory. But I turned to the guy and asked what school he went to. He had come out of Army Ranger school.

Q: I'll be darned.

Captain Kaine: It's a reaction thing. I felt I was torn. Remember when they had that Army guy on trial for killing the whole town? I could see how he could get into the situation, but I kind of think that before you kill 35 people or whatever, you would stop and make sure of yourself. That was too much reaction.

F. R. Kaine #2 - 310

yourself. That was too much reaction.

Q: I have another quote from you as Commander Naval Operations Support Group Pacific.

Captain Kaine: Oh, good. What did I say?

Q: I will quote you: "The reason for the unit's success is high-quality men, intensive training, and matchless self-discipline and team discipline." That's the end of the quote.

Captain Kaine: I think that is true. I wholeheartedly subscribe to that. I guess I must; I said it.

Q: Then did you know a Boatswain's Mate First Class Rauch?*

Captain Kaine: Yes, oh, yes.

Q: He says, "Just give us a mission. If it can be done, we'll do it; if it can't be done, we'll try, and nine times out of ten we'll do it anyway."

 I thought this remark was good, that the mission of the SEALs was to ". . . drain the enemy of his war-making

---
*Boatswain's Mate First Class Leon Rauch, USN.

capacity. It is a small elite unit of the U.S. Navy whose exploits were secret until recently, but it has proved in the jungles of Vietnam to be perhaps the most deadly combat unit in military history."

Captain Kaine: I think that's true. Also probably the most highly decorated.

Q: Is that so?

Captain Kaine: Individual unit, yes.

Q: The man who had the python look at him was a Chief Hospital Corpsman Churchill.*

Captain Kaine: Yes, I know Churchill.

Q: I want to be sure we haven't overlooked any of the things that . . .

Captain Kaine: Well, there's one other thing. In the conduct of special warfare there were some great contributions from other types of units. For instance, the beach jumper units which were used in Vietnam. You might remember, I mentioned the beach jumper units in World War

---
*Chief Hospital Corpsman Joseph Churchill, USN.

II in the very beginning. Well, I hadn't seen them again until special warfare and, again, not until Zumwalt got into Vietnam did anybody use the beach jumpers.

They had a great deception and psychological warfare capability. He used that capability very ably in conducting what they call a Cheu Hoi program in Vietnam. That was to entice the Viet Cong to surrender. They did this through hiding tapes and playing tapes and using psychological doctrine from loudspeakers and hailers. At one point they convinced a whole village to turn and come in. He used that to a pretty good advantage. He also tried to use a lot of tactical deception by broadcasting bad messages to them and making sure that they were intercepted and stuff like that.

So the beach jumpers contributed a lot in the war in Vietnam, as did the boat support unit. We had this unit with us for a long time, and they really didn't operate with the UDT or SEAL to any great extent. They supported them, but they didn't work. While I was down here on the strand, we integrated the boat support unit with the SEAL insertion program, and the boat support unit really became the transportation unit for the SEALs.

Q: I was going to ask you how they got places.

Captain Kaine: Surface transportation. They did just a

tremendous job. I mean, they would take those SEALs anywhere and go in and get them in all kinds of enemy fire, blowing up boats and all kinds of traffic. They were just a great, great organization. I don't think it would be fair to close without citing what a great job they did in helping both the SEALs and the UDT in doing practically 90% of their insertion work. They did most of the insertion work that was not done by helicopter. The UDTs that were in country did a lot of work, and, again, there was a difference. They were not quite as offensively oriented; their work was mostly constructive type, clearance and demolition work in country.

Q: Not necessarily on the beaches?

Captain Kaine: Some on the beaches but a lot of it inland, yes.

Q: The SEALs are still here, thank goodness.

Captain Kaine: The SEALs are here; they're strong and well, and I think you may see an added dimension to them in further training. I've used this barometer for years: as the world changes, UDT changes. We've seen UDT come from a bunch of slobs stumbling around a beach to a bunch of highly trained specialists. And now with this terrorism thing throughout the world, I think you'll see that the SEALs will get a lot of training in the counter-terrorist field.

Q: Has anyone written a really definitive description of the SEALs in Vietnam?

Captain Kaine: No chronicle, because I don't think they've released any of the reports because of the classification.

Q: That was to be my next question.

Captain Kaine: Yes. See, that's one of the things. The SEALs were involved in a few other programs besides the main program that I've told you about. I've been out ten years now, and when I left, most of those were top secret programs. I've never heard that they've been lessened, so I really couldn't say. They were quite interesting and quite successful, as a matter of fact. I can tell you they had to do with taking prisoners, but I can't go into the details.

I think unless you have some questions, that about wraps up the SEAL discussion.

Q: Well, it sounds ridiculous, but they're storybook people, practically.

Captain Kaine: They are. I mean, I think you can take many, many of the individuals and write stories about them. You know, it's a funny thing, and many of us have talked about this before. When a bunch of the people from this community get together and start telling stories to each other and about each other, they just walk away if any people from outside the group are there. I think we theorized as to why, and a lot of us think that they think we're lying. Honest to God, when you get a group of these guys together and they start telling stories, you just can't believe some of them.

Q: That's funny.
Now in the ten years that you've been out of the Navy, you have been in Coronado.

Captain Kaine: Yes, we lived in Coronado. We moved up to Newport Beach for a year while I was working for Atlantic Research, and we came back the next year. Except for that, we've been here ever since.

Q: And you're working now with . . .

Captain Kaine: I'm working now with the Bank of Coronado, down the road about three blocks. I do PR, sales, and a lot of building inspections for renovation loans.

Q: And you just briefly mentioned that there are five children and a lovely wife.

Captain Kaine: And that's it, no cats, no dogs.

Q: Four girls, one boy.

Captain Kaine: The son is now a man of 37, and the youngest daughter is 28.

Q: Carole is the young girl, and she's thinking of going in the Navy.

Captain Kaine: She hopes to.

Q: I hope she will, if that's the thing that would make her happy.

Captain Kaine: Yes, I think she wants to.

Q: It's been delightful talking with you. I've enjoyed it.

Captain Kaine: I've enjoyed it too.

N.B. Since this was taped, and in line with progress, UDT has been absorbed by the SEAL organization. Presently there no longer are underwater demolition teams in the Navy, only SEAL teams!--FRK

Appendix--Naval Combat Demolition Unit Personnel
(Ranks and Rates as of 1944)

Naval Combat Demolition Unit Two

Lieutenant (junior grade) Francis R. Kaine
Gunner's Mate First Class William J. Armstrong
Gunner's Mate Third Class William L. Dawson
Gunner's Mate First Class A. H. Pierce
Gunner's Mate Third Class John N. Wilhide
Gunner's Mate Third Class D. E. Williams

Naval Combat Demolition Unit Three

Lieutenant (junior grade) Lloyd G. Anderson
Aviation Ordnanceman First Class C. C. De Vries
Gunner's Mate Third Class H. Q. Eskridge
Gunner's Mate Third Class E. A. Messall
Gunner's Mate Third Class Sam Pahdopony
Gunner's Mate Third Class J. D. Sandy

Index to
Reminiscences of Captain Francis R. Kaine

Aberdeen (Maryland) Proving Ground
   Army established a bomb disposal school there in World War II, 22

Accidents
   UDT swimmer gored by a purplish-yellow fish with a dorsal fin in Pacific, 134-135; Kaine called on by UDT to investigate two drownings in St. Thomas, Virgin Islands, circa 1960, 238-239; Kaine's comments on nature of accidents in the 20-plus years of his UDT service, 239-240

Acorn Units
   Included bomb disposal people during World War II to recover enemy ordnance, 18

Admiralty Islands
   Landings of a reconnaissance group on Lorengau Beach and Hyane Harbor in February 1944 were supported by UDTs clearing out submerged coral reefs, 80-88; Japanese infiltrated American positions ashore in 1944, 121-122

Alcohol
   Kaine chased drunken UDT men from a cantina in Vieques in 1962, 255-257

All Hands Magazine
   March 1959 issue is a valuable reference on UDT, explosive ordnance disposal, midget submarines, 199-200

American University, Washington, D.C.
   Live ordnance delivered to bomb disposal school held there in 1942-43, 19-21; Kaine housed in Lieutenant Draper Kauffman's Quonset hut on campus in 1942-43, 28; bomb disposal school transferred from university to Indian Head, Maryland, 36

Amphibious School, U.S. Navy
   UDT training program at after 1952, 167-171

Amphibious Warfare
   Recruiting of students at midshipman school in the fall of 1942 for duty in the amphibious force, 30; UDTs blasted out coral to support a U.S. reconnaissance landing in the Admiralty Islands in February 1944, 80-88; allocation of UDTs in Seventh Amphibious Force in World War II, 88-90; role of UDTs in the 1945 invasion of Borneo, 100-101, 116, 130, 139-140, 142; role of

beachmaster in an amphibious landing, 243-247; amphibious exercise Steel Pike held off Spain in late 1964, 247-254

Anderson, Lieutenant Commander Franklin, USN
As commanding officer of SEAL Team One, he released a statement in 1968 about SEAL presence in Viet Cong-controlled areas of South Vietnam, 296-297

Anderson, Ensign Lloyd G., USNR
Kaine's roommate at bomb disposal school in 1943, 28; co-captain with Jackie Robinson of UCLA basketball in early 1940s, 29; selected for service in underwater demolition in World War II, 31, 39, service in the Seventh Amphibious Force, 1943-45, 66-67, 69, 71, 73 129, 135, 144-146; anecdotes from time in the Philippines in 1945, 102-106, 123-126

Antarctic
U.S. Navy UDTs conducted experiments at in the early 1950s, 161-162

APD
See High-Speed Transports

Aqua Ho Motor
Innovative motorized aqualung that was developed in the 1950s never purchased for Navy UDT use, 201-202

Arctic
Navy UDTs tested equipment in during the 1950s, 161-162; Kaine's dispute in 1958 with an admiral regarding a UDT deployment to, 186-189

Argentia, Newfoundland
Subpar Navymen stationed at prior to joining Navy combat demolition training at Fort Pierce, Florida, in 1943, 52-53

Army, U.S.
Got involved in bomb disposal early in World War II at Navy school, then set up own school at Aberdeen, Maryland, 22; Army rangers helped teach in naval combat demolition units at Fort Pierce, Florida, in 1943, 44-45; used Bangalore torpedoes for battlefield clearance in World War II, 60; Kaine lectured elements of the 32nd Division in New Guinea late in 1944, 79-80; bomb disposal units attached to 32nd and 41st divisions, 89-90

Astronauts
   Underwater demolition team personnel were involved in training U.S. astronauts in the early 1960s, 194-196

Atrabine
   Quinine derivative taken to prevent malaria during World War II, 144

Australia
   Kaine's underwater demolition unit went through on the way to doing beach clearance work for the Seventh Fleet in 1943-44, 73-74; encounters with great white sharks off Australia, New Guinea, and the Great Barrier Reef during World War II, 135-137

Bands
   U.S. Navy steel band started by Rear Admiral Daniel V. Gallery in the late 1950s in San Juan, Puerto Rico, 229-230; based out of New Orleans in the late 1970s-early 1980s, 230

Bangalore Torpedo
   Italian-developed weapon used by UDTs in World War II, 60, 66, 83-84

Barbey, Rear Admiral Daniel E., USN (USNA, 1912)
   Commander of the Seventh Amphibious Force with whom Kaine worked in 1944, 77

Beach Group, Naval
   Korean War composite of UDT, beachmaster, Seabees, and boat units, 151; Kaine CO of beachmaster unit 2 (NBG) in Norfolk in March 1962, 240; consisted of Seabees, beachmaster, boat or assault craft unit, 241

Beach Jumper Units
   Unit located in Dowa Dowa, New Guinea, late in 1944, 77; involved with UDT in early 1950s in sneak attacks against amphibious force in Virginia Beach/Norfolk area, 172-173; supported UDT and SEAL units in Vietnam in the late 1960s, 287, 311-313

Beachmasters
   Operated in the Admiralty Islands in 1944, 82; one component of naval beach groups in Korean War, 151; Kaine reported to the Naval Beach Group in Norfolk in March 1962 as CO of a beachmaster unit, 240; beachmaster's function described, 241; relationship to shore party commander of any Marine division, 241-242, 245; role defined and knowledge required, 243-244

Boardman, Ensign Thomas L., USNR
    Sent to Casablanca, Morocco, to examine unexploded American projectiles fired at the French battleship Jean Bart in November 1942, 15-16

Boat Units
    Member of naval beach group during the Korean War, 151; tremendous transportation aid to SEAL teams in Vietnam, 312-313

Boise, USS (CL-47)
    Light cruiser that had live ordnance removed at the Philadelphia Navy Yard in late 1942, 21

Bomb Disposal
    Procedures taught at Navy school at Stump Neck, Maryland, 1942-43, 9-11, 21-27, 32-33; procedures used by the British early in World War II, 11-14

Bomb Disposal School
    Lieutenant Draper Kauffman recruited trainees for in the fall of 1942, 4-5; description of in its formative stage in 1942-43, 8-9; practical work at naval reservation in Stump Neck, Maryland, 9-11, 21-27, 32-33

Boot Strap, Operation
    Puerto Rican development program in late 1950s led by progressive governor Luis Muñoz Marin, 232-233

Borneo
    Army's 32nd Division operated there following the U.S. invasion in 1945, 79; LSTs were stranded on mudflats during a landing in the spring of 1945, 100-101; landings at Sarawak and Brunei Bay in June 1945, 116, 130; Balkipapan perfect example of use of UDT, 130; Kaine's evaluation of landings there in 1945, 139-140, 142

Boston Whaler
    Boat used by Navy SEAL teams for insertion into Vietnam in the late 1960s, 292

Britain
    See Great Britain

Brown, Colonel M. G., USMC
    Stationed in Dowa Dowa, New Guinea, in early 1944, he seemed a caricature similar to British officers, 77-78

Bulkeley, Lieutenant Commander John D., USN (USNA, 1933)
    Recruited midshipmen for PT boats from the V-7 program at
    Columbia University in the fall of 1942, 4-5

Bureau of Naval Personnel (BuPers)
    Involved in regulating training of UDTs in the 1950s,
    206-207; had to reassign individuals who couldn't stand
    up to survival training during the Vietnam War, 281-282

Callahan, Lieutenant John M., USNR
    East Coast skipper of SEALS in late 1960s, 266-267

Carpenter, Scott
    Astronaut trained underwater around 1960 by Kaine and UDT
    for the feeling of weightlessness, 194-196

Casablanca, Morocco
    American bomb disposal teams visited in late 1942 to
    ascertain why projectiles fired at the French battleship
    Jean Bart did not explode, 15-16

Castro, Fidel
    Cuban refugees' plan to assassinate revealed to Kaine in
    San Juan circa 1959-60, 236-237

Casualties of War
    UDT swimmer gored by a purplish-yellow fish with a dorsal
    fin in Pacific, 134-135; few UDT casualties, 134-135;
    Kaine's comments on nature of accidents in the 20-plus
    years of his UDT service, 239-240; few SEAL casualties in
    Vietnam, 302-303

Causeways
    Used to move cargo and vehicles ashore during amphibious
    Exercise Steel Pike in Spain in late 1964, 249-254

Cebu, Philippines
    American UDTs had a variety of roles during the landing
    at Cebu in late March 1945, 102-106

Chaplains
    Scarcity of among Pacific Fleet Amphibious Force during
    World War II, 106-107; Lieutenant John Pyle was a
    Presbyterian chaplain whom Kaine encountered during the
    U.S. landing at Cebu in the Philippines in the spring of
    1945, 107

Cheu Hoi
　　Psychological warfare program introduced by Vice Admiral Elmo Zumwalt to entice the Viet Cong to surrender during the late 1960s, 312

Churchill, Chief Hospital Corpsman Joseph, USN
　　Had a close encounter with a python during SEAL operations in Vietnam in the late 1960s, 303, 311

Church Services
　　See Religion

Classified Information
　　Fort Pierce, Florida, site of classified combat demolition unit training program in 1943, 38; SEAL classified operations in Vietnam, 290, 314

Cold-Water Operations
　　Experiments conducted in the early 1950s on divers' ability to operate in cold water, 162-164

Collins, Lieutenant William, USNR
　　Demolition expert who taught at bomb disposal school in Fort Pierce, Florida, in 1943, 43

Collisions
　　A U.S. attack transport collided with a landing craft while supporting the American invasion of Mindoro in the Philippines in December 1944, 117

Columbia University, New York City
　　Site of V-7 training for Naval Reserve officers in 1942, 3-4

Combat Demolition Units
　　See Underwater Demolition Teams (UDT)

Commandos
　　Lieutenant Draper Kauffman recruited British commandos and Army rangers for Fort Pierce, Florida, combat demolition school in 1943, 40, 44-45; designed hell week as part of training program in UDT, 45, 51-52; Kaine's admiration of, 69, 133

Communications
　　UDTs' interest in underwater communications during the 1950s, 197-198

Coral
    Training in blowing channels through at Fort Pierce, Florida, in 1943, 57; coral poisoning and abrasions, 58, 62; UDT work in coral and sand in the Pacific during World War II, 65-66; UDTs cleared out coral reefs in the Admiralty Islands in early 1944, 80-88; comprises the majority of Pacific island beaches, 93; soft sand coral beaches on Leyte Gulf, Philippines, 97; coral reef beaches in the Dutch Schouten Islands during landings in mid-1944, 97-98; caused temporary blindness for one UDT member late in World War II, 135; types and colors of live coral in Pacific waters, 138

Coronado, California
    Site of a naval beach group in 1951, 152; Kaine assigned to in 1966 as Commander Special Warfare Group Pacific, 286

Counterinsurgency Training
    Kaine assigned as officer in charge, 1964-66, at Naval Amphibious School, Little Creek, Virginia, 261-271

Counter-Swimmer Attack Doctrine
    Introduced into UDT training in early 1950s, 171-174; sneak attacks in Newport, Boston, and Norfolk, 171, 173

Cousteau, Dr. Jacques Yves
    Kaine's work with on _Calypso_ in the 1960s, 197

Crane, Roy
    Cartoonist whose character Buz Sawyer was a SEAL, which triggered the 1968 announcement about SEAL presence in Vietnam, 296

Cuba
    Considered a possible evacuation problem by Navy in the late 1950s and early 1960s, 233, 236; Cuban refugees came to Puerto Rico in late 1950s-early 1960s, 236; refugees' plan to assassinate Castro, 236; contingency planning for U.S. attack against in the early 1960s, 258-259

Cultural Beliefs
    The beliefs of the South Vietnamese people governed some of their behavior during the Vietnam War, 271-272

Culver, Ensign William, USNR
    Recommended by Lieutenant Odale Waters for UDT in 1943, 31

Declassification
    See Classified Information

Defusing of Bombs
    See Explosive Ordnance Disposal

deLaureal, Captain Henry H., USN
    Commanding officer of Naval Amphibious School in Little Creek, Virginia, when Kaine arrived in 1964, 262; Kaine in his leadership team in 1956-57, 262

DelGuidice, Lieutenant David, USNR
    West Coast skipper of SEALS, 266-267

DEW
    See Distant Early Warning

DeWindt, Ensign Adrian (Adie) L., USNR
    Worked together with Lieutenant Draper Kauffman on unexploded bombs at Pearl Harbor following the Japanese attack in December 1941, 5

Dirkx, Lieutenant Peter C., USN
    Led SEAL unit into the Three Sisters mountains (Vietnam) to liberate downed American planes, 301

Discipline
    Kaine was director of discipline in San Juan, Puerto Rico, 1960-62, 275-277; Kaine had to discipline UDT personnel who were drinking well past midnight at Vieques in 1962, 255-257

Distant Early Warning (DEW)
    Radar sites constructed in the Arctic to which UDTs were assigned in the late 1950s, 161; UDT unit deployed to in the late 1950s, 186-189

Diving
    Use of early self-contained underwater breathing apparatus by combat demolition units in World War II, 63-64; UDT trained Red Cross instructors in underwater work and scuba diving, 155, 196; cold-water diving experiments conducted by the Navy in the early 1950s, 162-164; Kaine attended diving school in 1951-52, 184; Kaine taught photojournalist Bill Stapleton scuba diving for his pursuit of the Monitor in 1955 under Life magazine auspices, 169-171; Kaine took courses in 1951-52 in hard-hat diving and physiology of diving, 184; experimental UDT diving unit, 184-186; factors that make diving difficult for individuals beginning underwater demolition work, 208-212; use of mixed gases for UDT diving in the 1950s, 221-222; Dr. Chris Lambertson designed diving equipment used by UDT in the 1950s, 224; Kaine passed out

while diving in the Virgin Islands in the 1950s, 225-226; two UDT men were killed in a diving accident in the Virgin Islands around 1960, 238-239; SEAL diving equipment training in the late 1960s, 273

Dominican Republic
Contingency planning for American landing there in 1965, 259-260

Dräger
German-made oxygen lung first brought to Kaine and UDT in the 1950s by a Swedish student, 223-224

Draper, Hiram
Civilian in the Bureau of Ships who secured information and goods for UDTs in the 1950s, 182-183

Drinking
See Alcohol

DUKW
World War II vintage amphibious trucks used by beachmasters in early 1960s, 242-243

Dutch Schouten Islands
See Schouten Islands

Edgerton, Dr. Harold E.
Kaine's interaction with this expert in underwater photography, 196-197; association with Walt Wainwright of U.S. Navy Underwater Sound Lab, 198

Education
Kaine's secondary education at Loyola College in Montreal, Canada, 1937-41, 1-2; premed zoology/organic chemistry and graduate English/literature studies at the University of Rochester in New York in 1941-42, 2-3

Eigell, Boatswain's Mate Robert W., USN
Early in World War II, invented an effective wrench that guaranteed safety of men defusing bombs, 23

England
American Draper Kauffman worked with the British early in World War II in defusing unexploded bombs, 11-14

Enlisted Personnel
Kaine was assistant chief of staff for personnel and CO of enlisted people in San Juan, Puerto Rico, 1958-62,

228; Rear Admiral Daniel Gallery rigged his barge so enlisted men could fish, 237-238; Kaine's recommendations regarding certain officers and enlisted men trained in SEAL and SERE during the mid-1960s, 281-282; UDT officers and enlisted men went on recruiting trips to NROTC and OCS chapters in 1950s and 1960s, 204

EOD
  See Explosive Ordnance Disposal

Explosive Ordnance Disposal
  Disposal of Japanese ordnance at Pearl Harbor in early 1942, 5-6; bomb disposal procedures taught at Navy school at Stump Neck, Maryland, 1942-43, 9-11, 21-27, 32-33; procedures used by the British early in World War II, 11-14; examination of the French battleship Jean Bart at Casablanca to determine why American projectiles fired in November 1942 did not explode on impact, 15-16; live ordnance recovered from the cruisers Boise (CL-47) and Marblehead (CL-12) in 1942, 21; a Marine colonel was concerned about getting rid of mines encountered during the invasion of Tarawa in November 1943, 73-74; units assigned to Pacific theater during World War II, 89-90, 109

Explosive Ordnance Disposal School
  Grew out of the bomb disposal school held at American University, Washington, D.C., and Stump Neck, Maryland, in the early 1940s, 36-37

Explosives
  Training of Navy combat demolition units in use of explosives at Fort Pierce, Florida, in 1943, 56-57, 60; various explosives used by U.S. Navy UDTs during World War II, 61, 65-66; Australian nitro starch explosive was used by U.S. UDTs to free LSTs stranded during a landing at Borneo in the spring of 1945, 100-101; types used by SEALs in the 1960s, 268-269; see also Explosive Ordnance Disposal

Fahrion, Vice Admiral Frank G., USN (USNA, 1917)
  As Commander Amphibious Force Atlantic Fleet, 1952-56, an enthusiastic supporter of UDTs running sneak attack training on his ships, 172-173; approved use of British two-man midget submarine in sneak attacks, 177; Kaine's appreciation of as UDT benefactor, 189

Fairchild Aviation
  Aircraft company that designed and built a U.S. midget submarine in the mid-1950s, 191

Families of Servicemen
    Initially Lieutenant Draper Kauffman did not permit the wives of men undergoing Navy combat demolition training at Fort Pierce, Florida, in 1943 to be present, but then he relented, 48-51; Kaine helped establish a swimming team for Navy dependents while stationed at Puerto Rico around 1960, 231-232

Fane, Commander Francis Douglas, USNR
    Commanded one of the last UDTs formed in World War II, 141; Kaine's West Coast counterpart in 1950s-1960s, 221

Fear
    Human reaction to fear in war, 113-114; fear underwater, 208-210

Felicia, Doña
    Delightful mayoress of San Juan, Puerto Rico, in late 1950s, 232

Fish
    A large fish was killed by underwater demolition team explosions in the Admiralty Islands in early 1944, 87; underwater demolition team swimmer gored by a purplish-yellow fish with a dorsal fin in World War II, 134-135; deadly stone fish in the Pacific, 136; giant clams with corrugated mouths in the Pacific, 136; moray eels' defenses, 136-137

Flynn, Lieutenant William, USNR
    Lieutenant Draper Kauffman's administrative aide at naval combat demolition school at Fort Pierce, Florida, in 1943, 43

Foreign Languages
    SEAL language training during the Vietnam War, 270

Fort Pierce, Florida
    Site of classified naval combat demolition unit training program in 1943, 38; description of facilities and training at, 40-68; physical obstacles used in training, 55-56

France
    Planning for demolition of beach obstacles in World War II, 37, 40, 57, 66; Seabee units made copies of French beach obstacles for use in training in 1943, 54-56; UDTs encountered heavy fire when clearing Normandy beaches in June 1944, 75-76

Frasseto, Roberto
   An Italian midget submarine expert who advised U.S. UDTs in early 1950s, 176-178

Frogmen
   Misconception regarding UDT men's apparel and role during World War II, 59; MacArthur's frogmen, 112; after the Korean War, movies (<u>Frogman</u> and <u>Away All Boats</u>) were made involving UDTs, 156-157; animosity toward the word among UDT personnel, 156; no funding for during peacetime, 160

Gallery, Rear Admiral Daniel V., Jr., USN (USNA, 1921)
   His far-reaching command in the late 1950s included Panama, Trinidad, and Guantánamo Bay, Cuba, 229; Kaine's admiration of, 229-230; set up Little League and Trinidad steel bands, 229-230; concern for Puerto Ricans, 232; relieved of Puerto Rican billet by Admiral Allen Smith, Jr., 233; Kaine's regard for as a great leader and prolific writer, 237; rigged his barge so enlisted men could fish, 237-238

GI Bill
   Kaine's use of after release from active duty in December 1945, 148-149

Glenn, John
   Astronaut trained underwater around 1960 by Kaine and UDT for the feeling of weightlessness, 194-196

<u>Grayback</u>, USS (SSG-574)
   Submarine converted for use as a transport during the Vietnam War, 220

Great Britain
   American Draper Kauffman worked with the British early in World War II in defusing unexploded bombs in England, 11-14; British commando units had a part in the early training of U.S. Navy combat demolition teams in 1943, 40, 44-45, 51-52

Green Berets
   Trained under Kaine/UDT in a reciprocal arrangement in mid- to late-1950s, 181; Kaine attended their school in Fort Bragg, North Carolina, in 1964, 263; support from John F. Kennedy's administration, 265; SEALs' potential infringement on in the Vietnam War, 297

Gulbranson, Captain Clarence, USN (USNA, 1912)
   Skipper of the Fort Pierce, Florida, base that became the site of Navy combat demolition training in mid-1943, 41

Guns
    U.S. Navy SEALs used various foreign weapons in their training during the Vietnam War, 284; some American guns weren't considered sufficient for use in Vietnam, 287; foreign weapons used in Vietnam, 288

Hawaii
    Bomb disposal work at in early 1942 after Japanese attack on Pearl Harbor, 5-6; submarine training facility at Pearl Harbor used by UDT personnel in the 1950s, 215-216

Hawks, Ensign Albert, USNR
    Chosen by Lieutenant Draper Kauffman for underwater demolition training in 1943, 31

Hazardous Materials
    See Explosive Ordnance Disposal

Heideman, Ensign Lawrence L. L., USNR
    Chosen by Draper Kauffman for UDT from bomb disposal school in 1943, 31

Helicopters
    UDT's use of in the 1950s as an aid to hydrographic surveys and missile and astronaut recovery, 194-195

Hell Week
    Critical part of underwater demolition team training that weeded out unqualified candidates during World War II, 45-47, 51-52, 67-68; also employed during UDT training in the 1950s, 204-205

High-Speed Transports (APD)
    Old cut-down, four-stack destroyers converted into high-speed transports for use by UDTs in World War II, 89, 91, 109; Kaine aboard one off Lingayen Gulf in January 1945, 117-118; UDT personnel working off of in Korean harbors, 153

Hodge, Lieutenant Alan G., USNR
    Instrumental in standardizing UDT training in the 1950s, 179

Hund, Ensign Frank C., USNR
    Chosen by Lieutenant Draper Kauffman for underwater demolition training in 1943, 31; hid pregnant wife at Fort Pierce, Florida, during training, 50; head of demolition training at Fort Pierce in 1943, 56

Hunt, Captain Edward R., USN

Operations officer at San Juan in 1961 who dispatched planes to locate the hijacked passenger liner, <u>Santa Maria</u>, 234-235

Hydrographic Surveys
UDTs' use of helicopters as aid to in the 1950s, 194

Indian Head, Maryland
Explosive Ordnance Disposal school moved to from American University, 36

Intelligence
Lieutenant Draper Kauffman set up a system early in World War II to have recovered enemy ordnance sent to Washington, D.C., for experiments on defusing, 16-20; value of for Navy SEALs operating in Vietnam in the late 1960s, 293-294

Italian Navy
Developed midget submarines that were used for commando roles during and after World War II, 174-177, 190

Italy
Italians developed the Bangalore torpedo used in combat demolition work in World War II, 60; the Scippolini skim boat, developed in the 1950s, was an advanced concept of modern hydrofoil boats, 200-201

Jack Brown Unit
<u>See</u> Self-Contained Underwater Breathing Apparatus (SCUBA)

Jacobs, Lieutenant Charles, USNR
Chosen by Draper Kauffman for underwater demolition training in 1943, 31

Japanese
Kaine's opinion of their shooting ability in World War II, 71; action against invading American forces at Tarawa in November 1943, 74-75; Imperial Japanese Marines engaged in combat on Admiralty Islands in early 1944, 80-82; counter-swimmers in the Pacific, 96; Japanese used boat mines to try to counter amphibious landings and to detect American presence when mines were detonated, 98-100; killed Catholic priests and kidnapped nuns on Cebu, Philippines, in 1945, 105-106; General Douglas MacArthur's strategy against in the Pacific, 110-111; employed suicide craft against American vessels, 118-120; Kaine's comments on their clever strategies, 120-122; Zeros shot down over the Philippines as Kaine and Anderson watched, 124

Jean Bart
   Examination of by U.S. Navy explosive ordnance personnel to determine why American projectiles fired in November 1942 against this French battleship at Casablanca did not explode on impact, 15-16

Johnston, Lieutenant (junior grade) Means, Jr., USN (USNA, 1939)
   Sole regular officer working with Lieutenant Draper Kauffman in bomb disposal training in 1942-43, 7, 35

Kaine, Captain Francis R., USNR
   Parents of and childhood, 1, 283; education, 1, 2-3; wife and children, 1-2, 48, 50, 148, 316; got into bomb disposal work early in World War II, 27, 30, 115; combat demolition training at Fort Pierce, Florida, in 1943, 41, 44, 56, 59-60, 64-65, 146-147; service in the Seventh Amphibious Force from November 1943 to the spring of 1945, 66-67, 69, 71, 73, 79-80, 81-85, 89-90, 97-98, 102-108, 112, 115-119, 123-129, 139-140; release from active duty on 10 December 1945 following return from the Pacific, 147-148; civilian employment following World War II, 148-150; recalled to active duty in January 1951, 151, 152; executive officer of UDT Four for two months in 1951, 153, 159-160; commanding officer of UDT Two, 153, 166, 227-228; training others in scuba diving and underwater work, 181, 194-196, 222-223; involvement with National Safety Council in 1960s, 196; San Juan, Puerto Rico, billet as assistant chief of staff for personnel and CO of enlisted men from 1958-62, 227-229, 231-236, 238-239, 275-277; CO of a beachmaster unit in Norfolk in March 1962, 240, 242-243, 260-261; involvement in Operation Steel Pike, 247-254; promotions, 258, 285-288; Joint Unconventional Warfare Board member in 1964, 259-260; officer in charge of counterinsurgency training from 1964-66, 261-271; Commander Special Warfare Group Pacific in 1966, 285-288; reflections on Vietnam War, 293-300; retired from the Navy in 1970, 303; post-retirement work in the 1970s, 315-316

Kauffman, Rear Admiral Draper L., USN (USNA, 1933)
   Recruited and trained people in the Navy bomb disposal program in 1942-43, 4-5, 7-11, 17-18, 20, 22, 34, 37-38; work on unexploded bombs at Pearl Harbor in early 1942, 6; training in England early in World War II, 11-14, 34; leadership and management qualities, 13, 17-18, 20, 27, 32-33, 48-51, 72; World War II assignments in the Pacific, including dramatic swimmer rescue off Saipan in 1944, 66-67, 94-96; post-World War II career progression, 160; on Kaine's selection board in 1966, 257-258; as Commander U.S. Naval Forces Philippines, consulted by

    Vice Admiral Elmo Zumwalt in Vietnam in late 1960s, 297-299

Kauffman, Rear Admiral James L., USN (USNA, 1908)
    Visited his son Draper at American University in Washington, D.C., in 1942-43, 29

Kennedy, President John F.
    Highly supportive of Green Berets in the early 1960s, 265; issued directive to create Navy SEAL program, 266

King, Ensign Myles Cornelius, USNR
    Chosen by Draper Kauffman for underwater demolition training in 1943, 31

Korean War
    Recall of reserve officers to active duty in the early 1950s, 151, 153; amphibious landings at Inchon and blasting the harbor at Hungnam, 153; East Coast UDT units not used in the war, 161; reference to few attempted prisoner escapes from camps during, 264

Lambertson, Dr. Chris
    Doctor and physiologist who designed diving equipment used by Navy UDTs in the 1950s, 224

Lambertson Rebreathing Unit
    Oxygen rig designed in 1940s by Dr. Chris Lambertson and used in Navy UDTs in the 1950s, 223-224

Landing Craft
    LCPR (landing craft designed specifically for reconnaissance work), 91; LCM, upon which Kaine slept to avoid Admiralty Islands' foxholes infiltrated by Japanese, 122; LCS (Landing Craft, Support), a miniature gunboat used in New Guinea in mid-1940s, 124-126; Kaine aboard one caught in a typhoon between Leyte and Samar in late 1944, 127-129; LCM, also known as M, or Mike, boat on rivers in Vietnam, 302

Landing Craft Infantry (LCI)
    Used by UDTs assigned to Pacific theater during World War II, 89, 109; Kaine aboard one anchored off Cebu in the Philippines in March 1945, 103-104; Kaine aboard one en route to Borneo threatened by Japanese suicide raft in the spring of 1945, 118-119

LARC
    See Lighter, Amphibious, Resupply, Cargo

LARU
   See Lambertson Rebreathing Unit

LCI
   See Landing Craft Infantry

Leadership
   Kaine in Captain Henry H. deLaureal's leadership team in 1956-57, 262

Leave and Liberty
   Kaine on home leave in May 1945, 144

Leyte, Philippines
   Soft sand coral beaches on the island for landing in October 1944, 97; General Douglas MacArthur's landing on Leyte, 112; role of UDTs in Leyte landing, 116-117

Liberty
   See Leave and Liberty

Lighter, Amphibious, Resupply, Cargo (LARC)
   Kaine's influence in securing these Army amphibious vehicles for naval beach group in 1962, 242-243

Lion Units
   Included bomb disposal people during World War II to recover enemy ordnance, 18

Liquor
   See Alcohol

Little Creek, Virginia
   Site of a beach group in 1951 that Kaine was assigned to, 152; Kaine assigned as officer in charge of counterinsurgency training at Naval Amphibious School, 1964-66, 261-271

LSTs
   See Tank Landing Ships

Lund, Uwe
   Swede who in 1950s brought German-made oxygen lung to America when he came for UDT training, 223

Lyon, Scott
   SEAL who led a raid to liberate a prison camp in Vietnam, 300-301

M Boat
   See Landing Craft

MacArthur, General Douglas, USA (USMA, 1903)
Strategy against the Japanese in the Pacific theater during World War II, 110-111; landing at Leyte in October 1944, 112

<u>Marblehead</u>, USS (CL-12)
Light cruiser that had live ordnance removed in New York Navy Yard in 1942, 21

Malaria
Gunner's Mate John Wilhide contracted malaria in Samar, Philippines, in 1945, 142-144

Marin, Luis Muñoz
Progressive governor of Puerto Rico in late 1950s whom Kaine respected, 232-233

Marine Corps, U.S.
Mixed classes of enlisted men and officers handpicked by Kauffman taken to Stump Neck, Maryland, for bomb disposal training in 1942-43, 21-22; in the wake of the amphibious assault at Tarawa in November 1943, a Marine colonel met Kaine's underwater demolition unit in Australia and sought solutions to problems encountered in the operation, 73-75; Kaine reported to Colonel M. G. Brown in New Guinea prior to beginning Seventh Fleet UDT work early in 1944, 77-79; Kauffman encountering a Marine on Saipan, 95; Kaine led a swim club/team with Marine Colonel Norman Vandam in San Juan, 1958-62, 231-232; beachmaster's relationship to shore party commander of a Marine division, 241-242, 245; clandestine UDT operations planned for Marine landing in Dominican Republic in April 1965, 260; Kaine attended Marine Corps pilot/counterinsurgency school in mid-1960s, 263; aerial warfare in opposing their landing in Vietnam, 288

McCain, Vice Admiral John Sidney, Jr., USN (USNA, 1931)
Commander Amphibious Force Atlantic Fleet who supervised Operation Steel Pike in late 1964, 247-248, 252-254; Kaine's first contact with at Little Creek, Virginia, in 1951, when McCain was Commander Amphibious Training Command Atlantic Fleet, 255-257; voted for Kaine's promotion as head of his selection board in 1966, 257-258

McNamara, Secretary of Defense Robert S.,
Kaine's appraisal of how he ran the Vietnam War, 291

Medical Problems
Lieutenant Lloyd Anderson's temporary blindness due to coral poisoning during World War II, 135; Gunner's Mate

John Wilhide contracted malaria in Samar, Philippines, in 1945, 142-144

Midget Submarines
British and Italian boats used in UDT training after Korean War, 157, 174-177; interest aroused in developing an American model, 157; using British and Italian techniques in UDT in early 1950s, 172, 190; British two-man used in sneak attacks approved by Vice Admiral Frank Fahrion in the mid-1950s, 177; Navy's development of the X-1 for UDT beginning in 1959, 189-193, 197; designed for UDT swimmers, but snatched by submarine force for its use, 191-192; the March 1959 issue of All Hands magazine is valuable reference on midget submarines, 199-200; original sub blew up, 192-193; Convair designed two-man wet submersibles for UDT, 193; British Wellman designer assisted Kaine in 1950s and 1960s, 222

Mindoro, Philippines
Two U.S. ships collided while supporting the landing there in December 1944, 117

Mines
A Marine colonel was concerned about getting rid of mines encountered during the invasion of Tarawa in November 1943, 73-74; Japanese used boat mines in World War II to try to counter amphibious landings and to detect American presence when mines were detonated, 98-100

Monitor, USS
Civil War ship searched for by Bill Stapleton and UDT members in 1955 under Life magazine auspices, 169-171

Movies
Navy UDTs cooperated in the filming of commercial motion pictures--Frogman and Away All Boats--in the mid-1950s, 156-157

Music
Rear Admiral Daniel Gallery started a U.S. Navy Steel Band in the late 1950s in San Juan, Puerto Rico, 229-230; U.S. Navy Steel Band based out of New Orleans in the late 1970s-early 1980s, 230

National Safety Council
Kaine's participation at the organization's meetings in the 1960s, 196-197

Naval Amphibious School
Kaine assigned as officer in charge of counterinsurgency

training at Little Creek, Virginia, from 1964-66, 261-271

Naval Beach Group
See Beach Group, Naval

Naval Combat Demolition Units (NCDU)
Draper Kauffman's original term for UDT in 1943, 37-38; NCDU training area in Fort Pierce, Florida, in 1943, 43-44

Naval Forces Vietnam, U.S.
See Sea-Air-Land (SEAL) Teams; Underwater Demolition Teams (UDT)

Naval Reserve Officer Training Corps
Underwater demolition team officers and enlisted men went on recruiting trips to in 1950s and 1960s, 204

Naval Reserve, U.S.
Original combat demolition units in 1942 were composed of reserve officers, 7, 34-35; influence on pay raises for Navy regulars, 35; under the critical eye of a U.S. Marine colonel in Dowa Dowa, New Guinea, late in 1944, 78; Kaine was recalled to active duty in the Korean War, 151; cuts in strength and discrimination against in promotions, 257-258

Navy Scouts and Raiders
Organization in Florida formed just prior to the bomb disposal school's transfer to Fort Pierce in 1943, 41-42; with U.S. Marine Colonel M.G. Brown in Dowa Dowa, New Guinea, in 1944, 77

NCDU
See Naval Combat Demolition Units

New Guinea
Kaine reported to U.S. Marine Colonel M. G. Brown in Dowa Dowa prior to beginning Seventh Fleet UDT work early in 1944, 77-79; Kaine based in Dowa Dowa in February 1944, 88; amphibious landings at Hollandia, Tanahmerah Bay, and Aitape in spring 1944, 109, 115-119

New London, Connecticut
Submarine training facility used by UDT personnel in the 1950s, 215-216

Newport, Rhode Island
Site where Kaine was processed when he left the Navy in late 1945, 147; sneak attacks conducted there by UDT counter-swimmers in the early 1950s, 171

News Media
    UDT cooperation with photojournalist Bill Stapleton in 1955 for a story in Collier's magazine, 169-171

Night Operations
    Not employed by UDTs during World War II, 130-131; worries of a CO in UDT operations at night, 226; SEAL teams operated primarily at night in Vietnam, 293

NROTC
    See Naval Reserve Officer Training Corps

OCS
    See Officer Candidate School

Officer Candidate School (OCS)
    UDT officers and enlisted men went on recruiting trips to in 1950s and 1960s, 204

Okinawa
    Site for training beach jumpers, UDT, and SEAL units in the late 1960s, 287

Ommaney Bay, USS (CVE-79)
    Escort carrier sunk off of Lingayen Gulf in January 1945, 117-118

Ordnance, American
    Kaine's criticism of during World War II, 15-16; compared to Japanese and German, 16-17

P-38s
    Shot down Jap Zeros over the Philippines while Kaine and Anderson watched, 124

Parachuting
    Introduced into UDT training around 1954, 180-182; free-fall introduced into SEAL training in the 1960s, 268

Pay and Allowances
    Reserves' influence on salary increases for Navy regulars, 35

Pearl Harbor, Hawaii
    Bomb disposal work at in early 1942 after Japanese attack, 5-6; submarine training facility used by UDT personnel in the 1950s, 215-216

Perch, USS (APSS-313)
    Old submarine used on West Coast for post-World War II

UDT training, 219-220

Philippines
Army's 32nd Division working in, in mid-1940s, 79; conditions for amphibious landing at Leyte Gulf in October 1944, 97, 116-119; landing at Cebu on 16 March 1945 described, 102-106; landing on Mindoro on 15 December 1944, 116-117; landing on Lingayen Gulf on 9 January 1945, 116-118; landing on Palawan on 28 February 1945, 116; Kaine beached on Japanese-held Samar in late 1944 as a result of a typhoon, 127-129; Seventh Fleet based out of Leyte in 1945 when they received orders to report for cold-water training, 142; Seventh Fleet's departure from Samar, 142-143

Planning
Planning for demolition of beach obstacles on French beaches in World War II, 37, 40, 57, 66; UDTs played a part in the planning of operations by the Seventh Amphibious Force during World War II, 132; contingency planning for U.S. attack against Cuba in the early 1960s, 258-259; contingency planning for American landing in the Dominican Republic in 1965, 259-260

Plastic Explosives
Use of by Navy UDTs during World War II, 65-66

Prairie State, USS (IX-15)
Formerly USS Illinois (BB-7), used as barracks for V-7 program at New York City in fall 1942, 3-4

Pre-Bombardment Group
Kaine's description of beach approaches used by UDT in the Pacific, 91-92; UDT joined pre-bombardment group on Lingayen Gulf in January 1945, 117-118

Price, Captain Arthur W., Jr., USN
As Commander River Patrol Force in Vietnam in 1967-68, made good use of SEAL teams, 291

Promotion of Officers
Vice Admiral John McCain voted for Kaine's promotion to captain as head of his selection board in 1966, 257-258; discrimination against reservists in promotions, 257-258

Psychological Barriers in UDT
Claustrophobia and fear underwater, 208-210; loss of sense of time, 211-212

PT Boats
Motor torpedo boats used to transport UDT units in the

Pacific during World War II, 89; used to make waves to dislodge LSTs stranded on mudflats in Borneo in the spring of 1945, 101

Public Relations
Navy UDTs became involved in community relations and movie-making efforts in the early 1950s to help preserve the UDT program, 155-158; UDT cooperation with photojournalist Bill Stapleton in 1955 for a story in Collier's magazine, 169-171

Puerto Rico
Rear Admiral Daniel Gallery started a U.S. Navy Steel Band in the late 1950s in San Juan, 229-230; Kaine was involved in setting up a swim club for Navy families in Puerto Rico around 1960, 231-232; progressive governor Luis Muñoz Marin helped foster economic development in the country in the late 1950s and early 1960s through Operation Boot Strap, 232-233

Pyle, Lieutenant John W., CHC, USNR
Presbyterian chaplain whom Kaine respected, 107

Rangers
Lieutenant Draper Kauffman recruited British commandos and Army rangers for Fort Pierce, Florida, combat demolition school in 1943, 40, 44-45; designed hell week as part of training program in UDT, 45, 51-52; Kaine's admiration of, 69, 133

Rauch, Boatswain's Mate First Class Leon, USN
Comments on SEALs' mission during the Vietnam War, 310

Reconnaissance
Landings of a reconnaissance group on Lorengau Beach and Hyane Harbor in Admiralty Islands late in 1943, early 1944, 80; Kaine met the 40th Seabee Battalion on Admiralty Islands reconnaissance in February 1944, 87; LCPR (landing craft designed specifically for reconnaissance work), 91; USS Grayback (SSG-574) converted for submerged reconnaissance during the Vietnam War, 220; UDTs sent in to do a reconnaissance for Operation Steel Pike in October-November 1964, 249, 253

Recruiting
Lieutenant Commander John Bulkeley recruited among V-7 midshipmen at Columbia University in fall 1942 for the PT program, 4-5; Draper Kauffman's recruiting pitch for UDT at Columbia University in fall 1942, 4-5; Kauffman recruiting Seabees for Fort Pierce, Florida, program, 42; UDT officers and enlisted men went on recruiting trips to

NROTC and OCS chapters in 1950s and 1960s, 204

Red Cross, American
Navy UDTs trained Red Cross instructors in underwater work and scuba diving in the early 1950s, 155, 196

Religion
Kaine landed at Cebu in the Philippines in March 1945 and celebrated Easter with Irish Catholic priest, 104-106; Kaine's Catholicism and the scarcity of chaplains among amphibious forces, 106-107

Rescue at Sea
Lieutenant Commander Draper Kauffman used a motorized raft in a dramatic UDT swimmer rescue off Saipan in 1944, 66-67, 94-96

Research
The Navy conducted cold-water diving experiments in the early 1950s, 162-164

Reserve Officers
See Naval Reserve, U.S.

Rest and Recreation
Rear Admiral Daniel Gallery rigged his barge circa 1960 so enlisted men could fish, 237-238

Riverine Warfare
Captain Wade Wells, as Riverine Assault Force commander in Vietnam in 1966-67, made good use of SEAL teams, 291; Captain Arthur Price, as Commander River Patrol Force in Vietnam in 1967-68, made good use of SEAL teams, 291; LCM, also known as M, or Mike, boat on rivers in Vietnam, 302; tragedy on an M, or Mike, boat up river in Vietnam, 302

Rivero, Rear Admiral Horacio (Rivets), Jr., USN (USNA, 1931)
UDT's good relations with in 1950s, 183-184; while on the staff of Commander in Chief Atlantic Fleet in 1961, involved in tracking the hijacked passenger liner, Santa Maria, 234

Rung Sat
Area between Saigon, Vietnam, and the sea where SEAL teams were present, 296-297; operations in the jungle and swamp areas described, 301-302; dangers of flooding in, 304

Sabin, Vice Admiral Lorenzo S., Jr., USN (USNA, 1921)
UDT's good relations with in the 1950s, 183-184; Kaine's

ally in dispute with another admiral regarding a UDT arctic deployment in the mid-1950s, 186-189; Kaine's respect for and appreciation of, 188-189; appointed Captain Henry deLaurel to Amphibious Force Atlantic Fleet leadership team in the mid-1950s, 262

Safety
  Boatswain's Mate Robert Eigell invented an effective wrench that guaranteed safety of men defusing bombs, 23

Saipan
  Lieutenant Commander Draper Kauffman used a motorized raft in a dramatic UDT swimmer rescue off Saipan in 1944, 66-67, 94-96; Kauffman encountered a Marine on Saipan, 95

Samar, Philippines
  A landing craft carrying UDT personnel was forced to beach on Samar in late 1944 as a result of a typhoon, 127-129

Santa Maria, SS
  Rear Admiral Allen Smith, Jr., Commandant of the Tenth Naval District, was involved in negotiating with hijackers when this Portuguese passenger liner was seized in 1961, 233-236

Saunders, Lieutenant Commander David G., USNR
  Commanding officer of UDT Four when Kaine was executive officer during the Korean War, 159-160; one of the COs who led UDT scuba training at St. Thomas, Virgin Islands, in the early 1950s, 168

Schouten Islands
  Amphibious landings on Biak and Noemfoor in May and July 1944, 97-98, 115-116; landing at Morotai, Halmaheras, in September 1944, 116

Scippolini Skim Boat
  Italian-designed advanced concept of modern hydrofoil boats, developed in the 1950s, 200-201

SCUBA
  See Self-contained Underwater Breathing Apparatus

SDV
  See Swimmer Delivery Vehicle

Sea-Air-Land (SEAL) Teams
  Connections with UDT, 178, 180, 266, 270-271, 274-275, 298-299, 317; use in Vietnam War, 178, 269-270, 278-279, 287, 289-291, 292-295, 299-300, 301-302, 307-308, 310-

311, 312-313, 314; trained at various facilities, 261-271, 267-268, 273-274, 284, 287, 299; restrictions in their early phase of development, 292; casualties, 302-303

Seabees
   Lieutenant Draper Kauffman picked Seabees among the first Navy combat demolition unit trainees in 1943 at Fort Pierce, Florida, 31, 40, 42-44, 47, 52; units assigned to build training obstacles similar to those on French beaches, 54-56; Seabee handbook used in NCDU, 57; the 40th Seabee Battalion operated in the Admiralty Islands in early 1944, 87; one of several components of naval beach groups in 1950s and 1960s, 151, 241; engineers coordinating efforts with UDT, 244; used in Operation Steel Pike, October-November 1964, 250, 255

SEAL Teams. See Sea-Air-Land (SEAL) Teams

Sealion, USS (APSS-315)
   Old submarine used on East Coast for post-World War II UDT training, 219-220

Sea Sled
   Innovative equipment developed in the 1950s but never purchased by the Navy for UDT use, 202-203

Second Marine Division
   Relationship to the naval beach group Kaine was assigned to in March 1962, 241-242

Selection Boards
   Vice Admiral John McCain and Rear Admiral Draper Kauffman were on the board that selected Kaine for captain in 1966, 257-258

Self-Contained Underwater Breathing Apparatus (SCUBA)
   Jack Brown-type unit used by UDTs in World War II, 63-64, 72-73; Navy provided SCUBA training to Red Cross instructors following the Korean War, 155; adopted as a piece of Navy equipment in 1949, 162; Kaine qualified on since 1949, 184; innovations in motorized aqualung called aqua ho motor in the 1950s, 201; West Coast UDT's primary use of aqualung, 221; the Dräger was a German-made oxygen lung first brought to Kaine and UDT in the 1950s by a Swedish student, 223-224

SERE
   See Survival, Evasion, Resistance, and Escape

Service Rivalry

Operation Steel Pike was an amphibious operation in October-November 1964 in Spain to challenge Air Force claim of superiority, 247-254

Seventh Amphibious Force
Acquired first UDTs in late 1943, 77; involved in reconnaissance operation in the Admiralty Islands in early 1944, 80-88; allocation of UDTs within, during World War II, 88-90; procedures used by UDTs for pre-bombardment beach reconnaissance, 90-94; developed great capability by the latter part of World War II, 110

Sharks
Kaine's encounters with great whites off Australia, New Guinea, and the Great Barrier Reef, 135-137

Smith, Rear Admiral Allen, Jr., USN (USNA, 1927)
Relieved Rear Admiral Daniel Gallery of Puerto Rican billet in 1959, 233; negotiated with hijackers of the passenger liner Santa Maria in 1961, 234

Snakes
Encountered by Navy SEALs in Vietnam in the late 1960s, 304-305

Spain
Site of Exercise Steel Pike, conducted by the Atlantic Fleet Amphibious Force in late 1964, 247-254

Special Warfare Group Pacific
A takeoff on the Naval Beach Group oriented to special, or unconventional, warfare, 285; leaders' goal was to train men "to react," 308

Stapleton, Bill
Photojournalist trained by Kaine in scuba diving for his pursuit of the Monitor in 1955 under the auspices of Life magazine, 169-171

Steel Band
Started by Rear Admiral Daniel Gallery in the late 1950s in San Juan, Puerto Rico, 229-230; based out of New Orleans in the late 1970s-early 1980s, 230

Steel Pike, Exercise
U.S. amphibious exercise in October-November 1964 in Spain to challenge Air Force claims of superiority, 247-254

Stump Neck, Maryland
Practical work for bomb disposal school took place at a

naval reservation there in 1942-43, 9-11, 21-27, 32-33; work on disposal problems to find more effective methods, 16-17; fuses, detonators, etc., shipped from bomb disposal school to, 19-23

Submarines
Used by UDTs for training in the late 1950s, 213-220; use of troop-carrying submarines for UDT training in the late 1950s, 219-220; see also Midget Submarines

Submarine Training Facilities
New London and Pearl Harbor facilities used by UDTs in late 1960s, 215-216

Superfine, Captain Irving Joseph, USN (USNA, 1938)
Kaine's boss for Exercise Steel Pike (October-November 1964) and for Vieques landing in 1962, 250-251; dispute with Kaine over moving causeway for Exercise Steel Pike, 251-253, 255

Surveying
UDTs' use of helicopters as aid to hydrographic work in the 1950s, 194

Survival, Evasion, Resistance, and Escape (SERE)
Differentiated from counterinsurgency, 264; used by SEAL teams in their training during the Vietnam War, 268, 273-274; need for supervision within training program, 274-275; number of instructors in, 277; men deployed directly in Vietnam upon completion of training, 278-279; training paralleled North Vietnamese interrogation and harassment methods, 279-281; weapons training, 284

Survival Training
See Survival, Evasion, Resistance, and Escape (SERE); Sea-Air-Land (SEAL) Teams; Underwater Demolition Teams (UDT)

Swimmer Delivery Vehicle (SDV)
Spin-off of midget submarines developed by Convair for UDT in 1968, 193

Swimming
As part of naval combat demolition unit training at Fort Pierce, Florida, in 1943, 44, 59; Kaine helped establish a Navy swim team while stationed at Puerto Rico around 1960, 231-232

Tank Landing Ships (LSTs)
LST loaded with explosives as part of coral-clearing operation in the Admiralty Islands in early 1944, 81, 84;

LSTs sometimes had UDTs on board in World War II, 89, 109; directly off-loaded onto beaches of Dutch Schouten Islands in mid-1944, 97-98; stranded on mudflats on Borneo, 100-101, 130; targets of swimmer sneak attacks in the 1950s, 174

Tarawa
In the wake of the Marines' amphibious assault in November 1943, a Marine colonel met Kaine's underwater demolition unit in Australia and sought solutions to problems encountered in the operation, 73-75

Tetratol
Explosives pack used in U.S. Navy UDTs in World War II, 61, 66

Three Sisters
South Vietnamese mountains surrounded by Viet Cong in which American planes were downed and personnel rescued by a SEAL team, 301

Tokyo Rose
Predicted during World War II that General Douglas MacArthur would never return to the Philippines, 112-113

Training
Kaine received commission through the V-7 program in October 1942, 3-4; bomb disposal procedures taught at Navy school at Stump Neck, Maryland, 1942-43, 9-11, 21-27, 32-33; procedures used by the British early in World War II, 11-14; combat demolition training in Fort Pierce, Florida, in 1943, 41-68; in the early 1950s, naval amphibious schools took over the training of UDTs and standardized curriculum, 167-168, 179; the SEAL and UDT training programs wrought substantial changes in young men in the 1950s and 1960s, 178; diving school in 1951-52, 184; underwater demolition team personnel were involved in training U.S. astronauts in the early 1960s, 194-196; the Bureau of Naval Personnel was involved in regulating training of UDTs in the 1950s, 206-207; factors involved in the success of individuals in UDT training in the 1950s, 206-208; Exercise Steel Pike was conducted near Spain by the Atlantic Fleet Amphibious Force in late 1964, 247-254; from 1964-66, Kaine was officer in charge of counterinsurgency training at Naval Amphibious School, Little Creek, Virginia, 261-271; Green Beret school in Fort Bragg, North Carolina, in 1964, 263; training of SEALs during the Vietnam War, 267-273, 307-309; survival, evasion, resistance, and evasion (SERE) training in the 1960s, 273-276, 279-281

Typhoons
   Kaine on board a landing craft when caught in a storm between Leyte and Samar in late 1944, 127-129

UDT
   See Underwater Demolition Teams

Underwater Demolition Teams (UDT)
   Kaine's participation in and evaluation of, 27, 30, 139-140, 153, 154, 161, 166, 170-172, 177, 220-221, 239-240, 261, 262-263, 305-306; recruitment for, 31, 39, 47, 204; compared and contrasted with other naval specialty programs, 33, 88, 181, 297-298; how training and programs evolved and were standardized, 33, 69, 107-108, 109, 140-141, 156, 167, 168-169, 179, 180-182; term popularized around mid-World War II, 37; designed to get onto French beaches in World War II, 40; hell week and attrition during, 45-47, 68; equipment used in, 63-64, 184-186, 191-193, 194-195, 201-202, 203, 218; units blown up by German 88s in Europe, 76; coral-clearing during reconnaissance operation in the Admiralty Islands in February 1944, 80-88; procedures used by UDTs for pre-bombardment beach reconnaissance in the Seventh Amphibious Force, 90-94; Pacific operations, 100-101, 115-119, 130; night operations, 130-132; accidents and casualties, 134-135, 238-240; participation in Korean War, 151, 153-154, 160-161; administrative organization of in the early 1950s, 151-155, 166, 168-169, 183; reputation of, 155, 183-184, 186; status suffered in the period between World War II and Korea, 159-160; Arctic and Antarctic assignments in the early 1950s, 161-164; simultaneous commitments in early 1950s to Arctic, Antarctic, Mediterranean, and Caribbean, 161-164, 166-167, 184; counter-swimmer sneak attacks introduced in 1950s, 171-174; employing Italian Roberto Frasseto as a tests and evaluation person in early 1950s, 176-178; UDT training person assigned to Bureau of Ships in mid-1950s due to Hiram Draper's influence, 183; Kaine's mention of problems within, 188; training others in scuba diving and underwater work, 194-196; involvement with National Safety Council, 196; involvement with Dr. Harold Edgerton and Jacques Cousteau in underwater photography, 196-197; studies conducted as to what personality types do best in, 206-208; integrated into Navy (1951-58) as permanent entity, 212; interaction in 1950s and 1960s of East and West coast teams, 212-213; use of Submarine Force Atlantic Fleet off St. Thomas in late 1950s, 213-220; submarine training facilities in New London and Pearl Harbor used in late 1960s, 215-216; involvement in Vietnam War, 287, 294-295, 299-300, 305-306, 312-313;

changing roles in naval groups, 241, 244, 249, 253, 313-314, 317; clandestine operations planned for Marine landing in Dominican Republic in April 1965, 260; need for supervision within training program, 274-275, 276-277; number of instructors in, 277

Underwater Sound Lab, U.S. Navy
Cooperation with UDT in underwater communications research in 1960s, 197-198

Uniforms--Naval
Green coveralls worn by UDT men during training in 1943 to avoid abrasions and poisoning from coral, 58, 62, 83; equipment carried (e.g., fins, face masks), 59-60, 137; wearing swim trunks, fins, and face mask in the Caribbean, 217; standard equipment in 1950s and 1960s, 218

V-7 Program
Kaine received his training as a Naval Reserve officer at Columbia University in New York City in the autumn of 1942, 3-4

Vandam, Colonel Norman, USMC
Senior Marine on staff in San Juan, Puerto Rico, who co-led a swim club/team with Kaine around 1960, 231-232

Vetter, Ensign Alvin E., USNR
Recommended by Lieutenant Odale Waters for UDT in 1943, 31

Vieques
Naval Beach Group deployed to this island off the east coast of Puerto Rico in March 1962, 241; Captain Superfine was Kaine's boss during the landing there in 1962, 250; Kaine chased drunken UDT men from a cantina in Vieques in 1962, 255-257

Viet Cong
Americans moving Vietnamese villagers to protect them from, 271-272; North Vietnamese methods of interrogation and harassment simulated in SERE training, 279-281; prison camps in South Vietnam, 300-302; surrounding the Three Sisters where American planes were downed, 301; sought out by SEAL teams, 301-302; crafty strategy, 302; their dead bodies used as boat fenders, 306; Cheu Hoi program of psychological warfare used to entice them to surrender, 312

Vietnam War
SEAL teams deployed in, 178, 269-270, 278-279, 307-308;

submarine <u>Grayback</u> (SSG-574) converted for submerged reconnaissance in, 220; Captain Henry deLaureal's insistence on all personnel having counterinsurgency training in light of Vietnamese tensions, 263, 265; traditions and immutable beliefs of the indigenous peoples, 271-272; North Vietnamese methods of interrogation and harassment simulated in SERE training, 279-281; weapons used in, 287-288; Marines landed in, 288; improper and proper use of SEAL teams in country, 289-291; difficulties, due to mistrust, in securing clearances to operate in given areas, 292; training a Vietnamese UDT, 294-295; beach jumper units employed in, 312

Virgin Islands
   Positive image of UDT established through lifesaving efforts in St. Thomas in early 1950s, 158; UDT scuba and underwater training was conducted at St. Thomas in the 1950s, 168; Kaine passed out while diving in the Virgin Islands in the 1950s, 225-226; two UDT men were killed in a diving accident near St. Thomas around 1960, 238-239

Wainwright, Walt
   Scientist with U.S. Navy Underwater Sound Lab who cooperated with Kaine and UDT at St. Thomas from 1950-58, 197-198

Washington, D.C.
   Live ordnance delivered to bomb disposal school held at American University in the mid-1940s, 18-20

Waters, Lieutenant Odale D., Jr., USN (USNA, 1932)
   Worked in mine disposal early in World War II, 14; recommended ensigns for UDT training in 1943, 31

WAVES (Women Accepted for Voluntary Emergency Service)
   Kaine's first interaction with their officers was in San Juan, Puerto Rico, 1958-62, 237

Weather
   Kaine on board a landing craft when caught in a typhoon between Leyte and Samar in late 1944, 127-129

Wellman
   British midget submarine used in UDT training in early 1950s, 175, 190

Wells, Captain Wade C., USN
   As Riverine Assault Force commander in Vietnam in 1966-67, made good use of SEAL teams, 291

Wilhide, Gunner's Mate Second Class John N., USNR
    Seaman who contracted malaria in Samar, Philippines, but sneaked aboard UDT's departure vessel in the spring of 1945, 142-144

X-1
    U.S. midget submarine built in the 1950s for use by UDTs but taken over by the submarine force, 190-193

YMS
    Motor minesweeper used to transport UDT units in the Pacific during World War II, 89; UDT units careful not to interfere with their sweeping capability, 108

Zumwalt, Vice Admiral Elmo R., Jr., USN (USNA, 1943)
    Kaine's appraisal of his tremendous benefit to morale as Commander U.S. Naval Forces Vietnam in the late 1960s, 295-296; consulted with Rear Admiral Draper Kauffman, then-Commander U.S. Naval Forces Philippines, 297-299; pro-SEAL and UDT units, 295, 299-300; employed beach jumpers in Vietnam, 312; introduced Cheu Hoi program of psychological warfare in Vietnam, 312